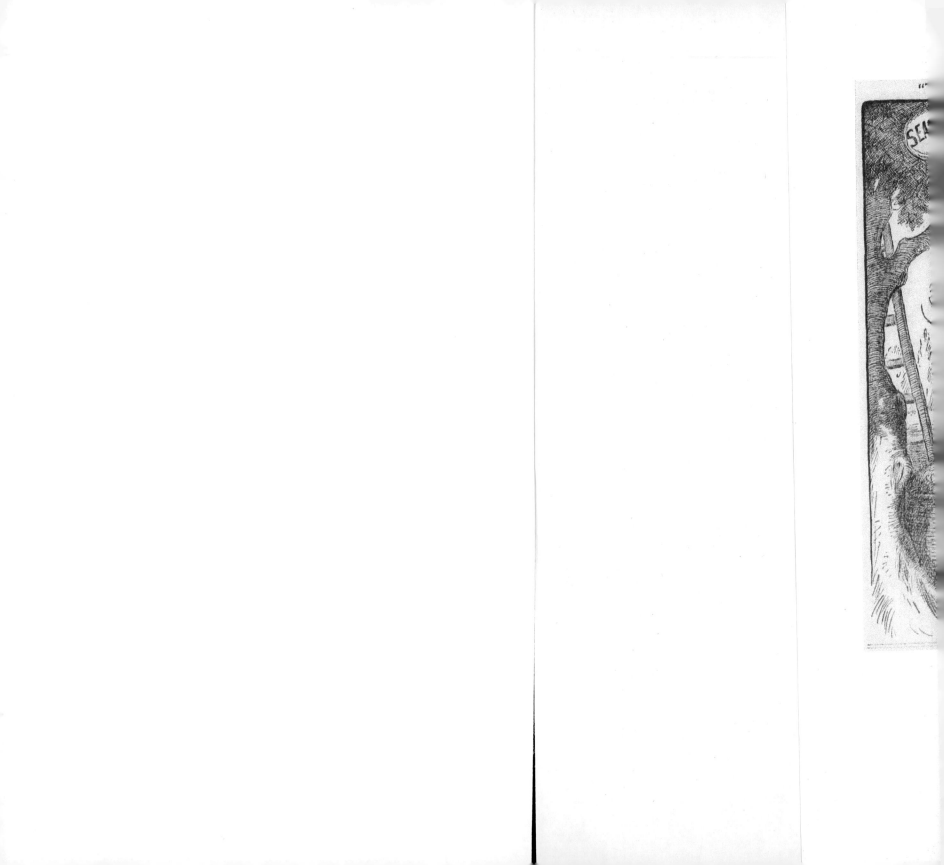

THE RISE AND FALL OF PROTESTANT BROOKLYN

AN AMERICAN STORY

**STUART M. BLUMIN
AND GLENN C. ALTSCHULER**

THREE HILLS
AN IMPRINT OF CORNELL UNIVERSITY PRESS
Ithaca and London

Frontispiece. "They Don't Grow in Manhattan" (cartoon by Nelson Harding, *Brooklyn Daily Eagle*, March 29, 1908).

First published 2022 by Cornell University Press

Printed in the United States of America

Library of Congress Cataloging-in-Publication Data

Names: Blumin, Stuart M., author. | Altschuler, Glenn C., author.
Title: The rise and fall of Protestant Brooklyn : an American story / Stuart M. Blumin, Glenn C. Altschuler.
Description: Ithaca [New York] : Three Hills, an imprint of Cornell University Press, 2022. | Includes bibliographical references and index.
Identifiers: LCCN 2021052025 (print) | LCCN 2021052026 (ebook) | ISBN 9781501765513 (hardcover) | ISBN 9781501765520 (pdf) | ISBN 9781501765537 (epub)
Subjects: LCSH: Protestantism—New York (State)—New York—History—19th century. | Protestantism—New York (State)—New York—History—20th century. | Brooklyn (New York, N.Y.)—History—19th century. | Brooklyn (New York, N.Y.)—History—20th century. | Brooklyn (New York, N.Y.)—Emigration and immigration—Social aspects.
Classification: LCC F129.B7 A48 2022 (print) | LCC F129.B7 (ebook) | DDC 974.7/23—dc23/eng/20211026
LC record available at https://lccn.loc.gov/2021052025
LC ebook record available at https://lccn.loc.gov/2021052026

In memory of
Faye and Harry Blumin
and
May and Herbert Altschuler
First- and second-generation Americans

"... a gathering into one place of multiple dissimilarity, each culture to its own cloth and style and tongue and gait, each culture and the earth itself with commonlode center and variable surface."

—A. R. Ammons, *Sphere: The Form of a Motion*

CONTENTS

ILLUSTRATIONS

ACKNOWLEDGMENTS

This book originated in discussions with our colleague Ralph Janis, a native of Brooklyn and the long-time director of the Cornell Adult University. Trained as an urban historian at the University of Michigan, Ralph has a special interest—and expertise—in architecture, the character of residential and commercial neighborhoods, and the impact of transportation on migration and urban population growth. *The Rise and Fall of Protestant Brooklyn* ventures into other areas of Brooklyn's history, but it was Ralph who came up with the topic and gave us this title. We are grateful for this and his many other suggestions.

Several friends contributed as readers and discussants. Carol Berkin and Margery Mandell were ideal readers who helped us shape and sharpen our argument at many turns. Jerry Heinzen, David Glaser, Patrick Burns, Jed Horwitt, Robert Summers, and the late and much-missed Isaac Kramnick offered ideas while expressing (or feigning) interest in our own. Thomas Campanella, a historian of city planning and the urban built environment at Cornell (and another Brooklynite), gave us a preview of his superb book, *Brooklyn: The Once and Future City*, and shared information, insights, and bibliographic suggestions about his project and ours. Two anonymous readers of our draft manuscript for Cornell University Press suggested revisions that have significantly improved the book.

We are grateful to the staffs of the Center for Brooklyn History (formerly the Brooklyn Historical Society), the New-York Historical Society, the Cornell University Library, and in particular the Brooklyn Public Library, which digitized copies of the *Brooklyn Daily Eagle*, the newspaper of record for Brooklyn's history during much of the nineteenth and twentieth centuries, and provided a free database of issues from 1841 to 1955. We are indebted as well to Arianna Gonzalez, a Cornell undergraduate, who translated articles published in *Il Progresso* from Italian into English; and to Beth Beach, one of the world's greatest administrative assistants, who found primary and secondary sources about Brooklyn, picked them up at the Cornell University Library, ordered them on interlibrary loan, and sent us digitized texts. Michael

McGandy, our editor, who knows quite a lot about Brooklyn, never stopped trying to make this book better.

We close with an acknowledgment—and celebration—of a collaboration that has now produced three books. More than collaborators, we are friends. We doubt that we have another book in us, but we intend to spend lots of time together, gossiping about Cornell University, talking about American politics, the Boston Red Sox, and the Buffalo Bills, eating good food, and most of all, sharing the benefits of a long-standing and genuine friendship.

THE RISE AND
FALL OF
PROTESTANT
BROOKLYN

Prologue

America's Brooklyn

Brooklyn, New York, is a place like no other. There is hardly a city in America, or even a large section of a city, that is not, like Brooklyn, ethnically, racially, economically, and culturally diverse. But the mosaic of Brooklyn's sections and neighborhoods—scores of them—many with names and identities known well beyond the borders of this "outer" borough of New York City, seems different from other places. Coney Island, Prospect Park, the long-lost Dodgers ("dem Bums"), the breathtaking views of lower Manhattan—these too lend a distinctive identity to the borough. And a striking stereotype of Brooklyn and its inhabitants endures through many years and changes, including the flood of up-and-coming artists and well-heeled professionals that has gentrified old neighborhoods. The stereotypical Brooklynite would not be from any other place. If challenged about the prospect of Brooklyn's becoming something unrecognizably new—perhaps even ordinary—this dyed-in-the-wool Brooklynite might well respond in the borough's once-distinctive language: Fuhgeddaboudit!

Brooklyn's uniqueness stems in no small measure from the borough's location just across the East River from Manhattan, New York's only "inner" borough and the center of America's most powerful metropolis. The dominance of Manhattan has been a constant in Brooklyn's history and an ongoing annoyance to boosters who point out that by 1855, when it absorbed neighboring Williamsburgh—which in the process dropped its concluding "h"—Brooklyn had become the nation's third largest city; that by 1930, thirty-two years after Brooklyn joined Greater New York City, its population exceeded Manhattan's; and that Brooklyn's East River piers and basins had long been the real center of the Port of New York. But for all that, Brooklyn grew up as and has remained a satellite of Manhattan—a "town across the river," even to the point where the first bridge that finally spanned that river, though a Brooklyn-based initiative, was ultimately named from the point of view of Manhattan (as was the East River itself). It is the Brooklyn Bridge, the bridge that leads to Brooklyn, not the other way around. True, a Manhattan Bridge was built some years later, but with much less fanfare and no discernible contribution to American urban legend. The Manhattan Bridge awaits its Hart Crane, its Joseph Stella, and its David McCullough. No one will try to sell it to you.

America has many towns across the river—Somerville and Cambridge across the Charles from Boston, Camden across the Delaware from Philadelphia, Covington across the Ohio from Cincinnati, East St. Louis across the Mississippi from, well, St. Louis, to name a few. But none is as large, as complex, and as significant as Brooklyn, and none has so interesting a history. Brooklynites will hate reading this, but the uniqueness of their town across the river does reflect the uniqueness of that place on the other side. Only New York could have created Brooklyn.

The Brooklyn it did create is known for that mosaic of neighborhoods within which ethnicity and race have been the primary modes of local identity. Williamsburg and Brownsville were known for their Jews; Bay Ridge and Bensonhurst for their Italians; Sunset Park for its Norwegians (and then its Chinese); Bedford-Stuyvesant for its African Americans. The boundaries between such places are not always clear, and many ethnic and racial transitions—and conflicts—have occurred within areas once clearly associated with a particular population. The banker Nathan Jonas, who grew up in Williamsburg, recalls that "the Jewish boy in Brooklyn was more than ordinarily likely to get into a fight."[1] In Gravesend, which was predominantly Italian in the 1920s, but with an adjacent Jewish community north of Avenue U, the Protestant memoirist Lionel Lindsay tells us, "there were Italian kids who were willing to accept me for being not Jewish, and Jewish kids who warmed up to me because I was not Italian." For many, the path between ethnic hostilities was not so easy to navigate. Lindsay's father, ironically enough the neighborhood's Dutch Reformed minister, was known as the "false-priest" to his Catholic neighbors, many of whom crossed the street to avoid walking by his "false-church." One can imagine how much more difficult it was for the Jews ("morte-christas") and Italians ("swartzers") of Lindsay's Gravesend to get along with each other.[2]

How—and whether—Brooklyn's ethnic groups got along is an important subject of this book. Here we merely note that the familiar story of massive ethnic migrations from Manhattan's Lower East Side does not capture the whole of the history of this town across the river. Far less well known is another story, of a Brooklyn vast and vanished, yet hidden in plain sight; of a new and rapidly growing city and suburb of busy wharves and waterside factories, wealthy brownstone neighborhoods and middle-class streets of brick and frame single-family homes, boulevards and parks, open spaces and not-yet-leveled hills, and above all proliferating churches, many of them grand, and built of stone in then-fashionable neo-Gothic styles.

Even before it received its city charter in 1834, and throughout the nineteenth century, Brooklyn was "the City of Churches." To Brooklynites, this sobriquet was far more than a booster's slogan and more than a way of contrasting the new city with the Sodom across the river (though it was certainly both of these things). And it was more than a census of steeples. Brooklyn did indeed have more churches in proportion to its population than Manhattan, but that often-repeated boast only began to express the meaning of City of Churches. Above all, it signified the dominance of a New England-style Protestantism, still Calvinist in spirit if not in the letter of old New England ecclesiastical law, that permeated the Presbyterian and Congregational churches formed in Brooklyn Heights and other neighborhoods during the early days of village and city growth, and that deeply affected Episcopal, Methodist, Baptist, Reformed, and other churches rooted in different Protestant traditions. To be sure, there were also Roman Catholic churches from the earliest periods of Brooklyn's growth, and somewhat later a small number of synagogues. But these served far less influential populations. The understood elision from City of Churches—the part written in invisible ink—was "Protestant."

Rooted in social class as well as religious thought and practice, Protestant dominance extended to the politics, economy, society, and culture of the new city to the east of Manhattan. Although the term defies precise measurement and is revealed more in outcomes than in explicit expressions of intent, hegemony, defined as a preponderant influence or authority over others, is not too strong a term for the nature and force of Protestantism—particularly Yankee Protestantism—in nineteenth-century Brooklyn. We use it in this book to refer to the extension and power of certain religious norms beyond the church to the shaping and control of Brooklyn's secular institutions, public space, values, and discourse. This Protestant cultural hegemony was by no means absolute in its reach; it was repeatedly challenged as Brooklyn grew from a small village to one of the nation's largest cities. But it was notable for its endurance in the face of these challenges, especially the growing ethnic and religious diversity that finally overcame its influence. *The Rise and Fall of Protestant Brooklyn* describes a nineteenth-century city that contrasted markedly with the borough that succeeded it and tells the story of the transformation from one to the other.

That transformation was far from complete in 1905, when the Tammany Hall ward boss George Washington Plunkitt, seated comfortably at the bootblack stand of the New York County courthouse, and surrounded by his Manhattan-based cronies, dictated a series of "very plain talks on very practical politics" to the newspaperman William L. Riordon. Riordon's popular volume reporting (and no doubt embellishing) these lectures includes Plunkitt's dismissive account of the "hayseeds" of Brooklyn, who can never become real New Yorkers:

> And why? Because Brooklyn don't seem to be like any other place on earth. Once let a man grow up amidst Brooklyn's cobblestones, with the odor of Newtown Creek and Gowanus Canal ever in his nostrils, and there's no place in the world for him except Brooklyn. And even if he don't grow up there; if he is born there and lives there only in his boyhood and then moves away, he is still beyond redemption.[3]

Plunkitt offers as proof of his contention the story of just such a Brooklyn native, discovered as a young boy, nurtured by Plunkitt in the art of New York City politics, and sent eventually to the State Assembly from a Manhattan district. "You'd think," asks Plunkitt, "he had forgotten all about Brooklyn, wouldn't you? I did, but I was dead wrong." The young assemblyman showed no interest at all in Manhattan's political affairs and was eventually caught by his mentor trying to hide a Brooklyn newspaper. To Plunkitt this was the final indignity:

> "Jimmy, I'm afraid New York ain't fascinatin' enough for you. You had better move back to Brooklyn after your present term." And he did. I met him the other day crossin' the Brooklyn Bridge, carryin' a hobby-horse under one arm, and a doll's carriage under the other, and lookin' perfectly happy.[4]

To Plunkitt, Brooklyn had already developed a special magnetism, at least for the hayseeds who were born there, and we are again invited to believe in the uniqueness of the place, even before the crowding in of ethnic and racial communities in the twentieth century. Not identified with any ethnic group, Jimmy migrated to New York well before the unraveling of the Protestant domination that characterized his native city. Should we be convinced that Brooklyn, even then, "don't seem to be like any other place on earth"? Perhaps, but we would point to something else about Plunkitt's description of the liberated Jimmy: the hobbyhorse and doll's carriage he so happily carried home to his children. The Jimmy we see on the Brooklyn Bridge was a young husband and father, and his traipse across the bridge was most likely that of the metropolitan suburbanite. Rather than some sort of mystical magnetism of place, that little scene evokes one of the most American of experiences, the family lives of the men, women, and children who moved into or were born and raised in the emerging suburban neighborhoods that surrounded every nineteenth-century American city. Brooklyn, more specifically Brooklyn Heights, has been called America's first suburb, a claim not only of its uniqueness, but also of its participation in what would become a far more widely shared phenomenon.[5]

This broader perspective should include "Greater" Brooklyn, for as Manhattan continued to grow, so did its largest town across the river, as a suburb of New York and of its own expanding urban center. Nineteenth-century Brooklyn did become a city, and not just in its form of local governance. As the maritime and canal-borne commerce of New York dramatically increased, so did the demand for new wharves and warehouses, many of which were built on the Brooklyn side of the East River above and below the Brooklyn Navy Yard. The new Atlantic Basin in the South Brooklyn neighborhood of Red Hook became the main destination for upstate and Midwestern grain shipped through the Erie Canal and down the Hudson to the metropolis. The new port facilities also attracted manufacturing firms to the Brooklyn waterfront. This added to the demand for dockside and industrial workers who settled in Williamsburg and parts of South Brooklyn, having neither the need nor the means to ferry across the river to New York. Banks, insurance companies, newspapers, and a downtown to house these and other businesses were the secondary and tertiary effects of industrial and commercial growth. And as urban Brooklyn grew, so did suburban Brooklyn, well beyond the Heights, first to nearby South Brooklyn and toward Fort Greene and Clinton Hill, then, relentlessly into the farmland of Kings County, eventually consuming it all. It may be true that no other American city developed in quite this way and that Brooklyn really was a place like no other. But all the elements of its growth, urban and suburban, were the same as those that drove and defined other American cities and suburbs.

The same developmental pattern applies to Protestant hegemony in the City of Churches. Its various manifestations—rigid Sabbatarian laws, an active temperance movement, resistance to the presence of theaters and other morally threatening amusements, a public discourse that revolved around expressions of Christian piety and moral correctness, proliferating Sunday schools and an annual Sunday school celebration—all but the latter were present in cities and towns all over New England and across a wide swath of the northern United States, especially in upstate New York and the upper Midwest, where New Englanders had migrated in force. Brooklyn's Protestantism may have been peculiarly strong, but it was not peculiar.

Nor, as we have said, was Protestantism's power absolute. Opposition, particularly to its strictures on drinking and Sunday entertainments, came from a variety of sources familiar to readers of nineteenth-century American history: Irish Catholic workers from the docks and dockside factories, Germans (Protestant and Catholic alike) who cherished the conviviality of their beer gardens, restive young bucks from the "best" native Protestant families. Nineteenth-century Brooklyn was not a social or cultural monolith, but a fairly diverse city in which an atypically large middle- and upper-class suburban population gave extra force to that population's Protestant traditions and values.

That force receded during the early decades of the twentieth century with the settlement in Brooklyn of vast numbers of immigrants from Eastern and Southern Europe. Increasingly, elegant suburban neighborhoods were hemmed in by miles of tenements and apartment buildings inhabited by working-class Jews and Catholics. Erasmus Hall, the great high school that once prepared Protestant boys for college, taught a decidedly different clientele. The newcomers expressed their own ideas about the meaning of "Americanization." And many Protestant families decamped for greener, more homogeneous pastures on Long Island and in other distant suburbs. Albeit in different ways, at different times, and with a different scale and scope, these developments occurred in many other places besides Brooklyn. As our subtitle suggests, this book in all its dimensions tells an American story.

Even as we depict Brooklyn as a lively laboratory for changes that swept across much of the United States in the nineteenth and twentieth centuries, we are in no sense surrendering our claim that the County of Kings "don't seem to be like any other place on earth." In this book, we have tried to capture the special character of this special place and the unique as well as representative ways in which Brooklyn experienced the cultural, social, and political power of native-born Protestants and the eventually overwhelming challenge to that power posed by waves of immigrants who claimed no descent from Pilgrim Fathers.

CHAPTER 1

Brooklyn Village

From the beginning, Breuckelen enjoyed the advantage of location over the other five European settlements—four Dutch, one English—on the western end of Long Island. Breuckelen's farmers and husbandmen sent produce, meat, and cattle directly across the tidal strait to New Amsterdam, a trade made more reliable in 1642 by the establishment of a ferry located just south of where the eastern tower of the Brooklyn Bridge stands today. Unlike the great bridge, the ferry was a modest affair, a small skiff whose departures were announced by the blowing of a horn that dangled from a nearby tree. But it helped secure an advantage that strengthened with the years, long after New Amsterdam became New York City and Breuckelen became Brooklyn.[1]

If this was a New World success story, however, it was a long time coming. For nearly a century and a half Breuckelen/Brooklyn remained a small country settlement of scattered farms, centered if at all around the Dutch Reformed Church located a mile inland from the ferry landing. When a new minister arrived in 1660 to take charge of this church, he found only 134 inhabitants.[2] And yet this tiny community of Europeans had already largely replaced the native Lenape, Munsee-speaking members of the Delaware nation, who for countless years had hunted, fished, and farmed from a number of communal sites in what would later become Kings County. Armed conflicts, including the ruinous war against the natives pursued by New Netherland governor Willem Kieft in the early 1640s, along with the spread of smallpox and other European diseases, devastated the Lenape population in Breuck- elen and beyond. Hard-pressed survivors moved away. Daniel Denton, a co- founder of the nearby town of Jamaica, wrote of the Lenape in 1670: "It is to be admired how strangely they have decreast [sic] by the hand of God . . . for since my time, when there were six towns, they are reduced to two small villages."[3] These remaining villages did not survive. By the 1680s all but a handful of natives were gone from the hilly, forested land that had long been their home.

European expansion into former Lenape land was slow, even with the significant assistance of African slaves in the clearing and cultivation of new farms. A full century after the initial Dutch and English Kings County settle- ments, a 1738 English census recorded only 547 free inhabitants in Brooklyn along with 158 slaves.[4] These are hardly impressive numbers, even as they call attention to the role of slave labor in Brooklyn's mostly rural economy. The substantial involvement in the slave trade of Manhattan-based merchants in both the Dutch and English eras made New Amsterdam/New York and its hinterland a major center of African habitation in the northern American colonies. Many slaves who were brought to Manhattan remained in the city to perform diverse tasks essential to an urban economy. But neither were those who were carried across the river to Kings County subjected to the gang labor increasingly characteristic of the rural South; rather, they toiled along with white families and perhaps one or two other slaves on small and medium-sized farms. Partly because of this dispersal their numbers re- mained small, in absolute if not relative terms.[5] Even with the injection of enforced labor into Brooklyn, this largest and most commercially connected of the townships of western Long Island increased at an unremarkable pace during its first century of European (and African) settlement.

A 1767 map of Brooklyn shows an emerging village in the area surround- ing the ferry landing, and in 1785 a number of inhabitants of this village thought their collection of wooden houses, barns, taverns, workshops, and stables large (and vulnerable) enough to warrant the formation of a fire company. Three years later the state legislature recognized the landing area as an official fire district.[6] Nonetheless, only about 350 people lived in the village and some 1,600 in the township as a whole.[7] The village and rural populations, moreover, were by no means distinct. Many of the villagers were butchers and produce dealers who slaughtered cattle and took in farm produce for sale in New York City's markets.[8] In Brooklyn before the last years of the eighteenth century, the more things changed the more they stayed the same.

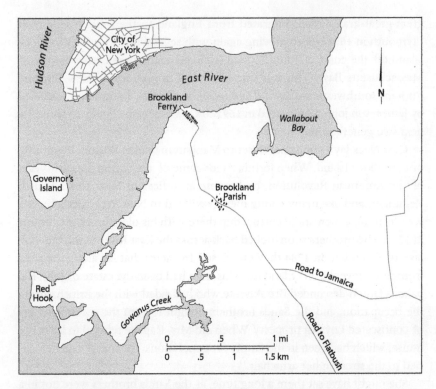

FIGURE 1.1.   New York City and Brooklyn, 1767 (cartography by William L. Nelson).

By the waning of the century, however, men appeared with new ideas for themselves and the town. Two in particular, Joshua Sands and Hezekiah Beers Pierrepont, had important effects on Brooklyn's future; to tell their stories is to gain a glimpse not only of the city and suburb that flourished during the coming years, but also the close connection between the individual entrepreneurship and the communal religiosity of Brooklyn's Yankee leaders. Sands and Pierrepont were the vanguard of a larger cadre of New England-born or New England-descended businessmen and professionals who endeavored to build their own fortunes (material success, according to age-old Puritan doctrine, was an outward if imperfect marker of God's grace) and at the same time shape Brooklyn as a moral community, subject to the will of its Protestant leaders.[9] In ways they themselves may not have fully realized, they were builders of Brooklyn's Protestant hegemony.

Joshua Sands was born in Cow Neck, now in the village of Sands Point, on the North Shore of Long Island, in 1757. Though a New Yorker by birth, Sands came from a family with New England roots. James Sands, his great-great-grandfather, migrated from England to the Pilgrim colony at Plymouth in 1658 before moving again with several other families to Block Island off the coast of Rhode Island (claimed at the time by the colony of Massachusetts Bay). This was one of several migrations of New England Puritans southwestward toward and into Long Island, a migration sustained by James' son John who moved in 1691 to Cow Neck, the family base for the next two generations.[10]

Cow Neck lay a good deal closer to Manhattan than to Boston, Plymouth, or even Block Island. When Joshua Sands came of age during the early years of the American Revolution, he became an officer in New York's Fourth Regiment, and like many young men gravitated to New York City after the war, forming a mercantile partnership there with his older brother Comfort in 1783. The brothers soon looked back across the East River to the little village of Brooklyn. In 1784 they purchased 160 acres that lay along the river from just above the ferry landing. This tract had been the estate of John Rapalje, a Dutch-descended Brooklynite who had sided with the British during the occupation, and the Sands brothers bought it from the commissioners of confiscated Loyalist property. When old Mrs. Rapalje refused to leave her house, which had been in the family for generations, the sheriff had her carried to the street in her armchair.[11]

She might have sat there a long time, as the Sands brothers were not in a great hurry to improve their investment. Comfort did not leave Manhattan for Brooklyn, but in 1786 Joshua moved his family into a new frame house, the largest in the village. And then, in cooperation with his brother, he did two novel things. First, he divided the old Rapalje estate into building lots, gave the area the grand name City of Olympia, and proceeded to sell many of the lots. The City of Olympia was not officially recognized, and its aspirational name seems not to have lasted much past the end of the century. But Sands did introduce the idea of planned urban development to the village emerging along the river and the lower ferry road.[12] He was convinced that with the end of the Revolutionary War, and New York and its East River harbor certain to flourish, Brooklyn would grow rapidly. And grow it did. From the 1,600 or so inhabitants in 1790, the township increased to 4,400 in 1810, and more than 15,000 in 1830. Five years later, the state census tabulated 24,529 residents in the newly incorporated City of Brooklyn, nearly 15,000 of whom lived in the downtown wards where Sands had once promoted the City of Olympia.[13]

The second initiative was even more closely tied to New York's (and the Sands brothers') commercial prospects. Soon after moving to Brooklyn Joshua built a rope factory (in the language of the day a "ropewalk") to supply rigging and cordage for the ships owned by the brothers' mercantile firm.[14] The first of many such projects, it proved a stimulus to the development of other manufacturing enterprises along the Brooklyn waterfront.

Among the people who purchased lots from Sands were maritime tradesmen who in 1798 fled a yellow fever epidemic in the coastal town of New London, Connecticut. Their arrival helped fulfill Sands' idea of Olympia as a center of trades and industries supporting maritime commerce. Around the same time John Jackson gave this idea a further boost by building a shipyard and more ropewalks on land he had bought where Sands' land ran eastward toward Wallabout Bay. Jackson named his smaller development Vinegar Hill to honor the latest futile rebellion against English rule in Ireland. This helped him attract Irish workers, and Vinegar Hill soon became Brooklyn's first Irish neighborhood. At the turn of the new century Jackson sold land that abutted Wallabout Bay to the US government, giving rise in 1801 to the Brooklyn Navy Yard.[15]

Joshua Sands may have considered these developments the seeds of a real city on the Brooklyn side of the East River. When a City of Brooklyn did emerge, the long-forgotten City of Olympia, along with Vinegar Hill, became its downtown district. But Sands' vision was, in contemporary terms, more suburban than urban. In the late eighteenth century "suburb" did not convey the middle- or upper-class bedroom community of more recent times but described instead an often unattractive and even foul-smelling urban fringe of cattle yards, slaughterhouses, tanneries, and various proto-industrial activities, along with the shanties and other cheap houses of workers who toiled in such places. Hospitals, insane asylums, poorhouses, and prisons were also built on this noxious periphery, where land was cheaper and the places themselves less visible to the urban population. While merchants' docks and warehouses along the waterfronts were located as closely as possible to the banks, exchanges, and merchants' homes of the urban core, shipyards, iron foundries, and ropewalks were built at more distant landings. The City of Olympia and Vinegar Hill might well have formed the emerging core of urban Brooklyn, but they were in a prior sense part of the "suburbs," properly understood, of New York City.

Brooklyn became a suburb in the more modern sense as well, and it is here that we encounter the contributions of Hezekiah Beers Pierrepont.[16] Pierrepont sprang from a New England family with long ties to the civic and religious life of Massachusetts and Connecticut. John Pierrepont arrived in Massachusetts around 1640, purchased land in Roxbury, and served as a town officer and a delegate to the General Court (Massachusetts Bay's colonial legislature). John's son James rose still higher. Ordained as a minister in

1685, he soon moved to New Haven where he helped found and then served as a trustee of what became Yale College. James married three times, all to daughters of New England clergy, the third time to the granddaughter of Thomas Hooker, principal founder of the colony of Connecticut. His daughter by this third marriage married New England's most notable divine, Jonathan Edwards. James was no doubt the most distinguished of the colonial era Pierreponts and the most influential within the church. But the family lost no luster during the next two generations, which produced Hezekiah, an impatient Yale student who promised his father that he would ask for no further financial support if he were allowed to leave the college to seek his fortune. Granted that permission, he trained for a mercantile career in several firms and the New York Custom House, and in 1793 formed a partnership with his cousin William Leffingwell to engage in trade with France. As a young merchant in revolutionary Paris his adventures included watching Robespierre mount the guillotine. Pierrepont was quite successful, but the loss to a French privateer of a ship loaded with goods from the Far East cost him his fortune. He returned to New York in 1800 determined to regain it. Marriage to the daughter of one of New York's wealthiest landowners (who gave him a wedding present of half a million acres of upstate land) enabled him to purchase a distillery on the Brooklyn waterfront.[17] In 1804 the Pierreponts moved to Brooklyn, settling on the long, high bluff south of the village, and into its most elegant home, named Four Chimneys, which they expanded and surrounded with an estate of sixty acres. Pierrepont's distillery was successful for a time, but profits eventually lagged. In 1819 he abandoned it and turned his attention to the land around him on that high bluff.[18]

The Lenape called it Ihpetonga, the English Clover Hill, and it would soon become Brooklyn Heights. It could not have been more unlike Sands' City of Olympia, which rose more gently from the river and was more easily developed as a productive waterfront and densely inhabited village. South of the village, across from the road that leads to the ferry landing, the land rises rapidly into a long ridge overlooking the river, Manhattan, the bay, its islands, and distant New Jersey. It was a grand place to establish a country home. There were old woods of oak, chestnut, sycamore, and cedar, a few substantial eighteenth-century houses surrounded by orchards and vegetable gardens, spectacular views, reliable sea breezes that contemporaries believed essential to good health, and a beach on the narrow strip of land below the bluff. Hezekiah Pierrepont had a small dock down there and a staircase leading down the steep hill. Each day, even as an older man, he rowed across the river to and from his office on Water Street in New York City.[19]

Pierrepont hoped to transform Clover Hill into a nightly retreat for well-to-do New York businessmen, a commuter suburb, although he did not use that term.[20] This idea became more feasible in 1814, when Robert Fulton and his partner William Cutting were granted the right to run a steam ferry from the old landing, supplanting a system that relied on oarsmen and sails with one far less susceptible to the variations of wind and tide, and to some extent the dangers of winter ice.[21] Scheduled to leave hourly from each side of the river, the *Nassau* could carry two hundred passengers and many horse-drawn wagons on each trip. When a second boat was introduced some years later, crossings were made each half-hour. According to Brooklyn's first newspaper, the *Long-Island Star*, the trip could be made in five to twelve minutes. A friend of Fulton's and an early supporter of this enterprise, Pierrepont became a director of the ferry company after Fulton's death from tuberculosis in 1815.[22]

Pierrepont did not rush into selling his land, even after the steam ferry made daily travel between Brooklyn and Manhattan practical for New York businessmen. One reason may have been the unincorporated village's inability to establish adequate policing, street cleaning, lighting, and other municipal services, which, according to some, discouraged Manhattanites from relocating to Brooklyn.[23] A Brooklynite who lived in Gowanus, several miles from the village, wrote to the *Star* that "nothing but the total want of good regulations in Brooklyn (particularly relating to streets and markets) prevents them from giving your village a preference over every other place at the same distance from the centre of business."[24] Another correspondent, under the heading "Brooklyn, to the state's disgrace, / Thou art a horrid dirty place," argued facetiously that the ladies of Brooklyn should be grateful for Brooklyn's filthy streets, which require them to use water-tight footwear, thereby sparing them the illnesses and early death so prevalent among fashionable New York women who wore dainty, thin-soled shoes. They benefited, too, from the absence of street lighting, as their lovers, after having "barked their shins" a few times in the darkened Brooklyn streets, learned to go home sober.[25] Yet another correspondent maintained that even migrants to Clover Hill suffered from these problems: "It is in vain that our heights display their inviting charms to the man of wealth and taste if he finds in the village some disgusting circumstances to counterbalance those charms.—He tries it for a year or two, and returns to town, *as several have done.*"[26]

Determined to establish more effective government services, Hezekiah Pierrepont joined a committee to petition the state, which in 1816 incorporated the Village of Brooklyn. Clover Hill was included within its bounds, and Pierrepont became a village trustee. But the plan for expansion adopted by the new village government presented him with a new problem. A few years earlier, a disputed boundary between the Hicks and Middagh families, land-owners who lived at the northern edge of the heights, resulted in a survey that included the mapping of streets and lots on and around the two proper-ties. When the new village government considered this plan for expansion Pierrepont objected. If this spectacular site were to attract wealthy Manhat-tan families, he argued, it must have wider streets and larger blocks and build-ing lots. Pierrepont hired his own surveyor and submitted just such a plan. The village adopted it for the area south of Clark Street, which included all of Pierrepont's property and about two-thirds of the high land. Unsatisfied with this compromise, Pierrepont extended his holdings further north by buying land between Clark and Cranberry streets from the Hicks brothers.[27] By 1823 he was ready to advertise his larger "Building-Lots on Brooklyn Heights" (the name was now established) "as a place of residence combining all the advantages of the country with most of the conveniences of the city," aiming his appeal to "Gentlemen whose business or professions require their daily attendance in the city."[28] Thus was born "America's first commuter suburb."

As they laid the groundwork for two different types of development in late eighteenth- and early nineteenth-century Brooklyn, Joshua Sands and Hezekiah Pierrepont set the pattern of Brooklyn's growth for decades to come. Sands' commercial and industrial village of wharves, manufactories, slaughterhouses, artisan shops, taverns, groceries, and retail shops was the more populous and economically diverse of the two areas. The numerous smaller shops and taverns of an emerging Brooklyn downtown were housed, as were the people who ran them, in a dense array of modest wooden frame buildings, intermixed with several of greater size and style, and some of brick, that were owned by the village's wealthier families. Brooklyn Heights, on the other hand, retained for a long while—on many streets even to our own day—the elegant and more uniformly residential character Pierrepont had intended. Between the two areas, one prospectively urban, the other sub-urban, lay the Old Ferry Road, renamed Fulton Street within village bounds, and this became a distinct and consequential boundary, an "invisible line of demarcation between the social sheep and goats," according to a long-time Brooklyn Heights resident, and a "veritable Chinese wall of exclusion" that became more pronounced over time.[29]

A large and well-known painting by Francis Guy presents an intriguing snapshot of part of Sands' Brooklyn—where the social goats lived. Trained initially as a tailor, Guy became both a dyer of fabrics and a landscape painter. He migrated to America from England in 1795 in straitened circumstances,

plied his several trades with varying success in New York, Brooklyn, Philadelphia, and Baltimore, and wound up back in Brooklyn in 1817.[30] Guy completed *Winter Scene in Brooklyn* (now in the Brooklyn Museum) shortly before
his death in 1820. The painting was so popular in the village, even before it
was finished, that Guy published a "Card" in the *Long-Island Star* announcing
he would allow only visitors who were represented in the painting to stop by
his studio to watch him work.[31]

To an unknowing viewer, Guy's painting depicts a rustic village that could
have been located nearly anywhere. The buildings are mostly modest, a barn-
yard and village pump occupy the center of the painting, and the scene is
filled with villagers in unhurried social concourse or at a winter day's outdoor work. Brooklynites might well have loved it for that, or for the portraits
of people they recognized, or for the mere fact that their own village was
emerging on the canvas. But they must have known that what Guy left out of
the painting was more important and more indicative of Brooklyn's present
and future than what he included. For whatever reasons—one, surely, was
that it was cold outside—Guy chose as his point of view his own second-story
window on Front Street, a major street that runs parallel to the river. Because
the window faced away from the river the painting does not depict Brooklyn's waterfront, its proximity to New York City, or the ferry that since 1795
ran from Main Street to link the two.[32] And because of the location of Guy's
house, the center of his view across Front Street is of the backs of the houses

FIGURE 1.2.   Francis Guy, *Winter Scene in Brooklyn*, lithograph copy (Wallach Division Picture Collection, New York Public Library).

that lined Fulton Street, the so-called Chinese wall that was also the village's main artery running inland from the old ferry landing. We see neither the street nor the fronts of structures that could have given the viewer a sense of Brooklyn as a rising city. Two of the village's most imposing homes, including that of Joshua Sands, are barely seen at the left edge of the painting.[33]

Winter Scene in Brooklyn does reveal something of the range of village society in the portraits and character types that populate the scene. On the far left, the two men engaged in conversation are the wealthy manufacturer and philanthropist Augustus Graham and his next-door neighbor, Joshua Sands; two men who were decidedly not social goats. They stand in front of Graham's large and elegant brick house, built recently on land purchased from Sands. Other village notables are included—the portly man on the near left is Judge John Garrison—as are several tradesmen. The carpenter Thomas Birdsall stands to the right of the judge, while Abiel Titus, a butcher, feeds his chickens in front of his barn and slaughterhouse. Other personae include a wood sawyer, a shoveler of coal, and at least two wagon drivers. Several characters in the painting represent Brooklyn's African American population, among which were a small number of slaves awaiting the general emancipation mandated by the state for 1827. (In 1820 190 slaves lived in the township along with 676 free Blacks.) It is difficult to say whether anyone in the scene, about half a mile from Vinegar Hill, is Irish.

Francis Guy did not carry his easel or sketchbook up to the Heights, even in warmer weather. Our view of the area comes from descriptive accounts and from trying to place back in time existing homes that were built there in its early suburban days. Many did survive, though some of the grandest of them, including Four Chimneys, were demolished to make way for new streets and structures. Hezekiah Pierrepont's initial vision of a parklike cluster of houses similar to Four Chimneys—free-standing mansions surrounded by large gardens—was not realized. Some houses of this sort were built, and one or two still exist, but most of the homes built by wealthy New Yorkers were attached wooden, brick, or brownstone townhouses that conveyed the urbanity of Manhattan as much as or more than a new suburban aura. To be sure, the streets were lined with trees and below Clark Street the large townhouses had ample room for gardens. Many of these were enhanced by a neighborly gesture from George and Isabella Gibbs, a pair of early Heights settlers who had transplanted a grapevine from North Carolina to their garden on the corner of Willow and Cranberry. The vine flourished and the Gibbs shared cuttings of it with their neighbors. "Isabella" grapevines soon grew nearly everywhere and became a signature of the Heights as a green space, even as trees were felled for new residential construction.[34]

Pierrepont's efforts to promote the Heights were impelled in part by another yellow fever epidemic, this one in the heart of New York City, which
in 1822 had driven some Wall Street merchants and bankers to relocate their
businesses and homes to the then distant village of Greenwich. The fear was
great enough and the exodus large enough that the Fulton Ferry abandoned
its city landing place for a time, skirting lower Manhattan for a Hudson River
landing at Greenwich Village nearly two miles north of Wall Street.[35] Some
of the city refugees relocated their homes and families (but not their businesses) to the still safer high ground across the water in Brooklyn Heights.
Brooklyn was not immune from this epidemic, but it recorded only six
deaths, all of them on Jackson's wharf in Vinegar Hill, far from Brooklyn
Heights.[36] In any case, a number of New Yorkers did buy and build on the
Heights, initiating a construction boom that resulted in some nine hundred
new homes by the end of the decade.[37]

Pierrepont prospered from this boom, but most construction occurred
north of his property, where the Hicks and Middagh estates had been platted

FIGURE 1.3.   Hezekiah Beers Pierrepont (from Henry R. Stiles, *A History of the City of Brooklyn*,
vol. 2, 1869).

Figure 1.4. Nineteenth-century mansions and row houses in Brooklyn Heights (Eugene L. Armbruster Photograph Collection, 1894–1939, New-York Historical Society).

into more modestly sized lots, and homes were more often in wood than in brick or stone. Most of the grander houses of the Heights, south of Clark Street and on Columbia Street running along the brow of the bluff, were built somewhat later, after the severe economic depression of the late 1830s and early 1840s played itself out. In a memoir written many years after her family had moved from Greenwich Village to a large house near the Heights, and then to one of Pierrepont's prime properties on the Heights itself, Elizabeth Leavitt, daughter of Wall Street banker, merchant, and manufacturer David Leavitt, recalled the openness of the land surrounding their Willow Street home. "Possibly there may have been two or three other buildings near, but all about us were open fields, with, of course, an unobstructed view of river and harbor."[38] She also pointed to the continuing presence of wooden houses, as well as the proximity of the Heights to lower Manhattan, in her description of New York's Great Fire of 1835: "Many of the houses on Brooklyn Heights were of wood, and men were on watch all night as sparks and burning pieces came over the river."[39] The brick and brownstone townhouses, as well as most of the grand, free-standing mansions, including one with two-story Corinthian columns built by Elizabeth's father in 1842, lay mostly in the future.[40] Hezekiah Pierrepont, who died in 1838, did not see the completion of his suburban project.

Whether they lived in Olympia or on the Heights, Brooklynites needed public institutions that went beyond their individual businesses, homes, and private lives. With one significant exception, however, the institutions they built were limited in number and scope. The new village government was one such institution, and its trustees quickly set out to clean and light the streets, improve fire protection, and provide more effective policing. They also experimented with a version of a New England town meeting by inviting villagers to convene to approve the board's annual budget. But complaints in the local press and poor turnouts at the budget meetings spoke as much to the limits as the achievements of Brooklyn's local government.[41] Accepting these limits, residents reached beyond village government to address several communal needs. They took steps, for example, toward what would become a highly regarded educational system, supporting the first of their public schools and, more notably, several private schools, particularly those devoted to the education of girls and young women. In a similar spirit they funded an Apprentices' Library, which opened in 1823, first in makeshift quarters, and then two years later in its own building. The laying of the cornerstone of this, Brooklyn's first public building, was attended by no less a figure than the Marquis de Lafayette, who made a quick trip across the river as part of his triumphal tour of the country he had helped bring into existence half a century earlier.[42] The modest two-story structure the great man helped dedicate was enough to induce the village trustees to abandon the back room of a grocery to make it their headquarters.[43] A Hibernian Provident Society and a Brooklyn Savings Bank were founded in 1824 and 1827 to foster thrift among village workingmen.[44] By 1830 there was a Young Men's Literary Association, soon renamed the Hamilton Literary Association of Brooklyn.[45] For purely secular institutions that was about all the Brooklynites accomplished. Their communal energies lay mostly elsewhere, in institutions that bring us closer to understanding the culture of this growing village.

Those institutions were, of course, the churches of Brooklyn and the moral and benevolent societies spawned by them. For more than a century the only place of worship in the town of Brooklyn was, naturally enough, the Dutch Reformed Church. This changed only in the 1780s and 1790s when Episcopal and Methodist (formally, Methodist Episcopal) churches were organized. The Dutch church, as we have seen, was located a mile inland from the ferry landing and remained in this somewhat rustic spot even when a new church structure replaced the old building in 1807. That it was not moved into the growing village almost surely reflects the church's long-standing relationship with the Dutch-descended farmers of Brooklyn's interior. "It is plain that the church derived its real strength from the soil," wrote local historian Ralph Foster Weld, "which had sustained the families of the town of Brooklyn for six generations."[46]

The Episcopal and Methodist churches were, in contrast, very much *of* the village. Episcopal (Anglican) worship began in Brooklyn during the British occupation, but when the redcoats departed they left no physical church behind. In the mid-1780s, under the auspices of the American church, Episcopal worship continued in a private house, a barn, and finally an abandoned British barracks, before settling into a small church on Old Ferry Road (not yet Fulton Street). This church was built in 1785 by newcomers from Connecticut, who preceded the influx from New London, and styled themselves Independents. By 1787 the Independents had merged with and turned over their church to the Episcopalians. In 1795 the church was incorporated as St. Ann's, in honor of Ann Sands, Joshua's wife, and a larger church soon appeared on Sands Street.[47]

As this dedication suggests, St. Ann's attracted support from the better-off inhabitants of the village as well as the wealthy landowners of Clover Hill, including the Pierreponts, Hickses, and Middaghs. This was less true of the Methodist Church. Methodism had emerged earlier in the eighteenth century within the Church of England as a more emotional and immediate style of worship, and as a theological departure stressing the doctrine of "perfect love" and the possible salvation of all souls. Although Methodism originated at Oxford University under the guidance of the brothers John and Charles Wesley, it appealed mainly to the working classes and smaller farmers of England and, after George Whitefield brought a more Calvinistic

FIGURE 1.5. St. Ann's Protestant Episcopal Church, Washington Street (Milstein Division, New York Public Library).

version of it across the Atlantic, the American colonies. Methodism came to Brooklyn during the 1790s, when a group of whites and free Blacks (including former slaves) initiated open air services on land purchased from Sands, and then built the Sands Street Wesleyan Methodist Episcopal Church on the site. A few prominent men joined Brooklyn's Methodist Church—John Garrison, the judge depicted in Guy's village painting, was particularly active—but most adherents were small retailers, artisans, and less-skilled workers. In 1800 about one-third of the church's membership was African American. "The plain white wooden building on Sands Street, without spire or belfry," Weld observed, "was a symbol of the unpretentious character of the sect."[48]

Racial integration at this church was never complete and survived less than a generation. According to one account, whites at Sands Street demanded that the growing number of African American congregants pay ten dollars per quarter to sit in galleries set aside for them. Unwilling to pay this discriminatory fee, the African Americans withdrew from the church and for a time prayed together in private homes. In 1817, each family began to contribute fifty cents per month to a building fund. Two years later they built Brooklyn's first African Wesleyan Methodist Episcopal Church on High Street, just a block from Sands. The church thrived. In 1854 the congregation moved to larger quarters on Bridge Street, and from its new downtown home this Methodist body remained a core institution of Brooklyn's African American community through and beyond the remainder of the nineteenth century.[49]

There was no doubt little if any New England influence on Brooklyn's African Wesleyan Methodist Episcopal Church. But that influence was strong in the three white or mostly white churches present at the incorporation of the village, however much these institutions differed in organization and doctrine from the Congregational and Presbyterian churches that were the most direct descendants of Puritan Massachusetts and Connecticut. These denominations, too, soon came to Brooklyn, as part of a wave of church founding that would justify the title "City of Churches." In the meantime, the three churches on the ground in 1816 anticipated in various ways the role of New Englanders in Brooklyn's religious and secular life. The Dutch Reformed Church was Calvinist in tradition and historically linked in the Old World to England's Puritans. In the New World, the Dutch church often called upon New England Presbyterians for its clerical appointments. In 1816 Brooklyn's Dutch Reformed Church was led by Selah Strong Woodhull, a Yale graduate of New England stock.[50] Seventeen years later we find a more remarkable connection: Pastor Maurice W. Dwight, a native of Northampton, Massachusetts, was the grandson of Jonathan Edwards.[51]

The New England influence on the Episcopal Church of St. Ann's was found mainly in its laity, which included not only Joshua Sands but also leaders such as Rebecca Spooner, who worshiped at St. Ann's in anticipation of the forming of a local Presbyterian Church. Rebecca's husband, the *Long-Island Star* editor and publisher Alden Spooner, a native of Vermont, was a direct descendant of John ("speak for yourself") Alden of Plymouth. And as we have seen, some less easily named congregants were the Independents from Connecticut who provided Brooklyn Episcopalians with their first house of worship. New England Methodists are harder to trace in Brooklyn, but a significant number of worshipers at the modest church on Sands Street were likely drawn from those maritime artisans and workers who came from New London around the same time the church was founded.

The heart of New England influence in Brooklyn was the First Presbyterian Church, formed in 1822 on Brooklyn Heights and installed in a large new church on Cranberry Street the next year. Except for the new African American Methodist Church that had hived off from Sands Street, this was the next Brooklyn church to be formed and the first to be located on the Heights.[52] Its leaders and early communicants were prominent Brooklynites, including several, Rebecca Spooner among them, who transferred their affiliation from St. Ann's. And First Presbyterian soon became the spiritual destination of wealthy newcomers from Manhattan. David Leavitt was a member, as was the young New York merchant Fisher Howe, who bought a building lot from Leavitt, married his daughter Elizabeth, and became the manager and treasurer of his father-in-law's manufacturing firm, the Brooklyn White Lead Company. The Willow Street homes of the Leavitt and Howe families, both of whom had New England roots (the Leavitt's were all from Connecticut; Howe was born in New Hampshire), were two hundred yards from the new church.[53] "Less closely identified with the past of the village community than the three church organizations which preceded it," wrote Weld, the First Presbyterian Church "represented more than any of them the combination of Puritanism with the new spirit of aggressive material progress, a synthesis which was to characterize much of the social activity in Brooklyn for years to come."[54]

This new force—whether more properly called Puritan or post-Puritan—was by no means confined to Presbyterians. Founded a year later, the First Baptist Church gave its support to the various movements emanating from Cranberry Street.[55] Cooperation between Presbyterians and Baptists—so different in doctrine, organization, and the social class identities of many of their adherents—suggests a larger Protestant outlook and agenda, and the point is easily extended to additional churches that proliferated in Brooklyn.

FIGURE 1.6.   First Presbyterian Church, Cranberry Street (Eugene L. Armbruster Photograph Collection, 1894–1939, New-York Historical Society).

Nor should the older churches be excluded. The Calvinistic Dutch Reformed and the socially active Episcopalians and Methodists participated in and even anticipated some of the initiatives that flowed, from the mid-1820s, primarily from the Presbyterian Church on Brooklyn Heights.

In May 1815, seven years before the founding of First Presbyterian, adherents of the three Brooklyn churches (including the then racially united Methodists) formed an Association for the Suppression of Vice. Less than five months later, possibly in response to the large but all male roster of members of this association, "a number of females, of different religious denominations" met to create the Brooklyn Female Religious Tract Society.[56] The following April saw the formation of the Brooklyn Sunday School Union Society, which sponsored a nondenominational Brooklyn Union Sabbath School.[57] And in June 1816, the new village government got in the act, passing a comprehensive Sabbatarian law prohibiting "any work or servile labor on the Lord's day," as well as "shooting, sporting, playing ball, or other unlawful exercises or pastimes on said day" for anyone over fourteen years of age.[58] Children were evidently still allowed to play, but this quite comprehensive measure was enacted very early, when the village trustees were busy setting up mechanisms for cleaning streets and protecting villagers from fire and crime. It must be said that all these initiatives reflected not only the will of local leaders but a more general religious reform movement in the early republic, one that extended well beyond Brooklyn's borders. By far the strongest lines of influence flowed westward (and in Brooklyn's case a bit southward) from New England, across New York State and as far as the Northwest Territory, even to those places that lacked Congregational or Presbyterian worship. Brooklyn's Association for the Suppression of Vice was based on the Connecticut Society for the Reformation of Morals, founded in 1811 by one of New England's most prominent clergymen, Lyman Beecher.[59]

Some resisted these efforts at moral reform, for it was not just the streets that were rough in Brooklyn Village. Brooklyn was not an especially dangerous place, but there was a good deal of drinking, horserace gambling, and general rowdiness in this waterfront community, and no small amount of resentment toward those who made it their business to control such behavior. There was even the occasional genteel objection. Organized temperance had not yet taken hold in Brooklyn, but enough people railed against the frequenting of the village's many taverns and grogshops to elicit the reminder (from a correspondent to the *Star* signing himself PUBLIC DECENCY) that respectable men often "go to quiet and decent porter houses where they can read the newspapers, and enter into conversation," a custom "not to be styled 'vice and debauchery.'" AN EPICURE was less concerned with defending public drinking than in celebrating the "wines, brandies, etc." available to "friends of the Turf" at the Steam Boat Hotel. Alden Spooner published many articles on local horseracing during these years, and only rarely disparaged the gambling that accompanied it. He gave favorable reviews to the occasional local theatrical performance, too, while gently suggesting to his sterner peers that the theater could be "a medium for conveying fine ideas and noble sentiments to many who would not take the trouble to obtain them in any other way." A solid Presbyterian, he defended dancing against the strictures of an upstate Presbytery. And as a New Englander he wrote with sympathetic humor about an eccentric, old-fashioned Dutchman who could not "withstand the force of yankee intrusions."[60]

Those "yankee intrusions" grew stronger as Brooklyn's churches multiplied and the Heights began to fill up with residents who considered themselves guardians of public decorum. In 1826 Reverend Joseph Sanford of the First Presbyterian Church urged parents to enroll their children in his Sunday school to counteract the "overflowing of the lava from the great volcano of vice and immorality in our immediate vicinity."[61] Sanford was succeeded in the Cranberry Street pulpit in 1829 by Daniel L. Carroll, lately of Litchfield, Connecticut, where he had succeeded Lyman Beecher. The Brooklyn Temperance Society was founded in that year and was soon joined by a Young Men's Temperance Society, both organizations headed by men attached to the First Presbyterian Church. The Young Men's Society, whose president was David Leavitt, reached a membership of three hundred within three years. One of its members, George Hall, was elected president of the village board in 1832, with the result that the number of licenses for the sale of liquor in the village was greatly reduced.[62]

Some of the earlier local organizations had faltered and disappeared, but they were revived or replaced in this more vigorous era of Protestant reform. The Apprentice's Library—which was not so secular after all, having been a response to drinking, gambling, and other youthful sins by "those who represented the social conscience of the community"—reappeared as the Brooklyn Institute. The Brooklyn Union Sabbath School, which had also died out, was revived under the auspices of the Methodist Church, with cooperation from the Dutch Reformed and Presbyterians. A Sacred Music Association and a Lyceum, both offered as respectable alternatives to the theater, were founded in 1833. The driving force behind the latter was Alden Spooner. A Brooklyn Theater built in 1828 soon disappeared, having been opposed as an inducement to immorality by local Presbyterians, Methodists, and Baptists.[63]

Brooklyn's surviving institutions expressed the values and aspirations of a New England Protestantism that transplanted as easily as Isabella grapevines to "America's first commuter suburb." It also transferred to at least parts of that industrializing waterfront community—which had its share of Manhattan-bound commuters—once known as the City of Olympia. The effects were real, even on the once-filthy streets. Brooklyn, declared Ralph Foster Weld, "had become the city of homes and churches, a lecture-going, church-going community, a pleasant suburban place, quieter and more sedate than New York. . . . The disheveled, unkempt village of 1816 had undergone a metamorphosis."[64] To Spooner, this metamorphosis would continue until it yielded something more than a suburb. "And what is Brooklyn now?—a pleasant populous village, the vegetating seed of a progressive city, which the future will ripen into greatness, ere many waning moons."[65]

CHAPTER 2

The City of Brooklyn

On Thursday, April 24, 1834, the *Long-Island Star* announced a civic procession and church ceremony in celebration of the incorporation of the City of Brooklyn: Local military and civic organizations will assemble at one o'clock on Friday afternoon in front of the Dutch Reformed Church. Under the auspices of the marshal of the day, Major F. C. Tucker, they will then march through the new city's streets, first in the downtown and then in Brooklyn Heights, ending on Cranberry Street in front of the First Presbyterian Church, in which the ceremony will be held.

The restrained tone of this announcement is somewhat surprising, given the long struggle that preceded the incorporation. The event is neither Grand nor Glorious nor Triumphant, as any political party victory of that era surely would be, just a "City Charter Celebration," headlined in bold print. More noteworthy is the symbolism of the procession itself—leaving from Brooklyn's oldest church and marching toward the city's powerful new center of Yankee Protestantism. Inside this post-Puritan church, the ceremony was to include an unspecified ode, oration, and anthem, and a song in praise of "The Pilgrim Fathers."[1]

Alden Spooner, who bore the name of one of those Fathers, would not have resented this rendition of Brooklyn's past. Neither, apparently, did the author of a long letter published in his newspaper, who focused on the benefits of incorporation. The new city charter, he predicted, would distinguish

FIGURE 2.1. New York City, the City of Brooklyn, and the Village of Williamsburgh, 1834 (Lionel Pincus and Princess Firyal Map Division, New York Public Library).

Brooklyn from the many villages that dot the state; attract the attention of men with capital to invest; and "lead to efforts for the recovery of *other rights* which have long been withheld from us."[2] That last prediction deserves a closer look. Among other things, the concern for those "other rights" helps explain why it took nearly a decade to get the act of incorporation through the state legislature.

In 1825, when local citizens first assembled to petition for a city charter, Brooklyn was already the third largest locality in the state. Of the four cities already incorporated, the second most populous, Albany, was only moderately larger than Brooklyn, while the third and fourth, Troy and Hudson, were smaller.[3] Surely, it was time for Brooklyn to be granted the dignity and enhanced powers of an incorporated city. But when Brooklynites arrived at the district schoolhouse in December for a public meeting called by citizens who favored incorporation, they found that the meeting had been hijacked by their opponents, who unanimously rejected the incorporation proposal and then adjourned for twenty-one years! Although no one took that last gambit seriously, the rejection set back the movement for a charter by half a decade. Spooner attributed the opposition to an unwarranted fear of tax increases and, more crucially, to the concern of real estate speculators that their property lines for lands lying beyond the bounds of the present village would be overridden by a new city plan. He reiterated what was becoming, and would long remain, a common complaint—that Brooklyn suffered from a weak civic culture, born of an excessive preoccupation with individual speculations and many commuters' identification with the big city across the river.[4] That said, when the drive resumed an external foe, the Board of Aldermen of New York City, emerged as the major threat, bringing into prominence those "other rights" a City of Brooklyn might finally claim as its own.

At the end of 1830 a revival of the petition for a city charter was discussed at another public meeting, but the only outcome was a call for the appointment of delegates to a convention charged with repairing defects in the village charter. When the delegates completed their work fully a year later, their only proposal was to petition the state legislature once again for a city charter. This time the public meeting approved the charter proposal unanimously, perhaps because the inclusion of the village's most prominent men on the roster of convention delegates (Hezekiah Pierrepont and David Leavitt represented the Heights) snuffed out any opposition.[5] Spooner, who was a delegate, had little to say on this occasion about the failures of Brooklyn's wealthy men to uphold the common good. Rather, he wrote of the good spirits prevailing at the annual supper celebrating the transition to a new village board, at which, to much applause, a guest offered this impromptu song:

> Heaven send us blessings down,
> Make a city of our Town,
> Daily may honors and benefits flow—
> Bedford and Wallabout,
> Join in united shout,
> City of Brooklyn! Behold how we grow![6]

The drafting in Albany of legislation conferring the city charter took a long time. Presented to the Assembly, New York State's lower house, in 1833, it passed with no difficulty. But then the New York City Board of Aldermen exerted its influence to defeat the bill in the Senate. At issue were those "other rights": control over the East River ferries and even the Brooklyn shoreline, both of which had been granted to New York City by the English colonial government more than a century earlier and confirmed in the postcolonial era by the State of New York.[7]

The ferry rights gave New York City control over nearly every aspect of this vital link between Brooklyn and Manhattan, including the awarding and financial terms of ferry leases, the locations of landings on both sides of the river, and the approval or disapproval of new ferry lines. Passengers often complained about fares, schedules, the quality of service, and the unfairness of New York's collection of annual rent from the ferry company, which resulted in Brooklyn's people paying higher fares to cover the cost.

The 1708 grant to the city from the English governor Cornbury included the unappropriated land between the high and low watermark on the Brooklyn side of the river, from Red Hook to Wallabout Bay.[8] Brooklyn was already expanding its footprint along this shore, filling in land and building wharves into the river. Would a city charter increase Brooklyn's right to build wharves without interference from or ransom to New York City? Even before news of the charter's defeat came down from Albany, Spooner confessed that a better course might well be surrender to New York's superior powers through consolidation with the city—foregoing the City of Brooklyn project to become so many new wards of the metropolis. The most prominent reason for this surrender, he noted, was "the extinction of all controversy relative to jurisdiction on the shores—interest in the ferries—water rights—boundaries, &c."[9] Brooklyn might become a city after all, but the charter debate confirmed it would never be done with New York.

Spooner may have been right about New York's tenacity and power, but the local movement for city incorporation revived almost immediately, with the influential lawyer John Greenwood, who had served as secretary of earlier meetings, taking the lead. The initiative was given a boost by New York mayor Gideon Lee, who urged the city's Board of Aldermen "to see if a mutual and friendly arrangement cannot be had for the benefit of the governments of the two places."[10] Unmoved, the aldermen were joined in their opposition by the other townships in Kings County. And yet, with support from upstate assemblymen and senators, the bill passed both houses in 1834.[11] By this time eight cities in New York State had been incorporated, six of them considerably smaller than Brooklyn. It was clear, too, that Albany, New York's second city, would soon be eclipsed by this upstart on the East River. Perhaps the obvious injustice of denying Brooklyn its due, combined with ongoing upstate resentment toward New York City, carried the day. In any case, the victory was a partial one, for the new city charter did not affect New York's jurisdiction over the ferries and the shorelines of the East River.[12]

Emboldened by their charter, Brooklynites mustered compelling arguments for gaining that jurisdiction: New York City's ancient grant no longer served its original public purpose and functioned mainly as a stifling monopoly; the sovereign state of New York was under no obligation to honor a grant from the defunct government of the colonial era; the true drivers of resistance were Manhattan property owners seeking to minimize competition from Brooklyn's more attractive neighborhoods; even that the East River was not really a river but a salt-water tidal strait running between Long Island Sound and New York Bay—an "arm of the sea" whose banks were part of the Atlantic coastline, held in public trust.[13]

These arguments proved persuasive to most assemblymen and senators when a bill was brought forward early in 1835 to transfer authority over East River ferries to a commission made up of the highest officers of the state government. Unfortunately for Brooklyn, the Senate set the bar for passage at a two-thirds majority, and the bill failed by a single vote.[14] Sensing the danger of so close a vote, the New York City aldermen soon approved a new ferry—South Ferry, with a landing at Atlantic Street (today's Atlantic Avenue) at the southern edge of Brooklyn Heights—which was a widely sought link in Brooklyn's transportation system and a gateway for the city's expansion into what had come to be called South Brooklyn. South Ferry took the steam out of Brooklyn's protest, and it did not build up again for a decade. In 1845, with John Greenwood again in the lead, Brooklyn finally succeeded in getting its ferry jurisdiction bill to pass. The *Star* responded enthusiastically: "FIRST GREAT BLOW FOR BROOKLYN RIGHTS"; "The Ferry Bill Triumphant!!!" "We have hardly language to express our feelings of gratification."[15] As it turned out, Spooner's former restraint would have been more appropriate. New York City successfully challenged the law in court, and Brooklyn eventually gave up its plan to appeal. The aldermen from across the "arm of the sea" approved new ferries, which served Brooklyn well. As early as 1837 there were four ferry landings in Brooklyn, and another two in neighboring Williamsburgh.[16] But New York City continued to collect on the ferry leases, as well as quitrents from waterfront properties. And little would change until the consolidation of the boroughs in 1898, sixty-four years after Brooklyn had gained its city charter.

The expansion of ferry service was itself an important victory, as it made possible the continuing expansion of the new city. In the half-dozen years after incorporation Brooklyn added about twelve thousand inhabitants (an increase of some 50 percent) and surpassed Albany to become the second largest city in the state. By 1845, the year of the ferry law, it was nearly two and a half times as populous as the city of 1835.[17] Brooklyn's newest newspaper, the *Brooklyn Eagle*, commented wryly: "We do not believe there is another city in the State which can exhibit any such gain as this. Brooklyn now contains 60,000 inhabitants, or, '*with its suburbs*,' about *half a million!*"[18]

Brooklyn's growth thickened old neighborhoods, but the city also enlarged its footprint, southward from Brooklyn Heights into areas now known as Cobble Hill, Boerum Hill, and Carroll Gardens (a little later into Red Hook and Gowanus), and southeastward from the heavily settled downtown toward Fort Greene and Clinton Hill. Each of these peripheral areas (the 6th and 7th wards of the new city) increased fivefold between 1835 and 1845, accounting for nearly half of the city's growth. The expansion of the downtown required no new ferry service since many of the people who lived there worked in Brooklyn's own factories and workshops and on its waterfront. But South Brooklyn, which was almost entirely the product of the new ferry, soon became the focus of most discussions of Brooklyn's development. Atlantic Street was emerging as an elegant commercial boulevard, made more attractive by the new Long Island Railroad's decision to run trains down to the ferry landing through a paved-over tunnel. South Brooklyn's answer to Fulton Street, Atlantic also served the rapidly developing southern half of Brooklyn Heights.[19]

A particularly notable development, about a half-mile farther south, was the construction of the Atlantic Basin, a huge harbor enclosing forty-two acres of the passage known as Buttermilk Channel that runs between Governor's Island and Brooklyn's waterfront at Red Hook. This was the project of Daniel Richards, an upstate émigré to New York City and then Brooklyn (and another descendant of early Puritan settlers). Richards was one of several entrepreneurs who tried to get ahead of Brooklyn's expansion by buying land in Red Hook, leveling its hills, and filling in its marshes and ponds in anticipation of yet another ferry and another market for suburban houses. When this project faltered Richards turned to cotton manufacturing and then to improving the South Brooklyn waterfront by incorporating the Atlantic Dock Company in 1840. This enterprise succeeded, although after a few years control passed to James S. T. Stranahan, yet another former upstate New Yorker with New England roots. Richards retained ownership of several warehouses that ringed the basin and in 1846 built a steam-powered grain elevator that drew to the Atlantic Basin nearly all the western grain that came to New York harbor through the Erie Canal and down the Hudson River. By far Brooklyn's largest waterfront project, the basin helped secure another of Richards's ambitions, a Hamilton Avenue ferry that drove Brooklyn's southward expansion well beyond Atlantic Street.[20]

The Atlantic Basin and other new docks, warehouses, and waterfront factories, along with the retail stores, rail tunnel, and terminal on Atlantic Street, added to the commercial and industrial character of the Brooklyn cityscape. Below the Heights, the sandy beach and small wooden dock where

FIGURE 2.2.   Aerial view of the Atlantic Basin, 1846 (from Henry R. Stiles, *A History of the City of Brooklyn*, vol. 3, 1870).

Hezekiah Pierrepont had kept his rowboat were, over time, replaced with docks, warehouses, and a street (Furman) that ran between the Fulton and South ferry landings, linking the South Brooklyn waterfront with the old downtown.[21] By the 1850s, Hezekiah's son Henry and several of his wealthy neighbors had built tall warehouses against the bluff on the east side of Furman Street (and landscaped the roofs of these buildings as extensions of the rear gardens of their Brooklyn Heights mansions).[22] But as South Brooklyn took shape homes and residential streets predominated, amplifying the perception of Brooklyn as a beautiful suburb. The streets immediately below Atlantic were built up with frame, brick, and brownstone row houses intended for South Ferry commuters, and this expansion extended into today's Carroll Gardens and Boerum Hill. Contemporaries who largely ignored the mixed business and residential expansion of Brooklyn's old downtown into the 7th ward were impressed by the suburbanization of the 6th. An 1841 article in *The Ladies' Companion* describes "New, or South Brooklyn," as "crossed by broad airy streets, ornamented with trees, containing large handsome private dwellings, surrounded by gardens glowing with flowers," the residences, mostly, of "merchants engaged in business in New York."[23] "The exertions of many prominent merchants" in building up South Brooklyn, wrote the *Star* a year later, "have rendered it inferior to no other portion of our city in architectural beauty."[24]

Many South Brooklyn streets were lined with elegant townhouses, set well back from the street to provide room for ample front gardens. But the district had a good deal of more modest housing as well, and some of the larger houses were rented to two or more families, answering complaints that too much of the domestic construction in this area and elsewhere ignored the

FIGURE 2.3.   Nineteenth-century townhouses, Kane Street, South Brooklyn (photo by Stuart Blumin).

needs of less affluent commuters.[25] Housing prices and rents remained lower in Brooklyn than in Manhattan, helping to explain Brooklyn's rapid growth during the severe economic depression that began in 1837. "The pressure of late circumstances have driven many people from the city," wrote the *Star* in 1838, "and induced others to quit larger dwellings for smaller." New Yorkers who had been paying $1,000 and upward in yearly rent could now find "quite as handsome houses" in Brooklyn for $500 or $600.[26]

Brooklyn did suffer during the depression. If bold business plans such as the Atlantic Basin were realized, others were not.[27] Banks, manufacturing firms, stores, and other businesses contracted and failed, driving up unemployment and crippling the nascent union movement. And hard times hobbled local government. When the City of Brooklyn received its charter officials planned to construct a city hall adequate to both the day-to-day conduct of public business and its newly exalted status. The city purchased a triangular plot of land east of Brooklyn Heights, bounded by Fulton, Joralemon, and Court streets, near the old Dutch Reformed Church, a location that expressed not only a connection to Brooklyn's long history but also the city government's neutrality toward its old and new neighborhoods. Calvin Pollard, a New York builder, won the design competition and construction began in 1836, only to be halted a year later. The building had barely cleared ground level and there it lay, a low stone wall surrounding a large, triangular hole in the ground. When the depression ended in the mid-1840s, construction resumed on a somewhat more modest Greek Revival design of Gamaliel King. Brooklyn's City Hall was completed in 1848, fourteen years after the conferral of the city charter.[28]

With the return of good times Brooklyn's robust growth continued, as it did in neighboring Williamsburgh, a village of fewer than three thousand souls in 1835, that nearly quadrupled over the next decade, and then jumped to thirty-one thousand by 1850.[29] As it grew it began to take on the suburban character we have observed well below Wallabout Bay. "South Williamsburgh is destined to rival South Brooklyn in the regularity of its streets and good taste displayed in erecting houses," wrote the *Eagle* in 1849. "Many of the New York merchants and lawyers reside here, and a few editors."[30] In 1852 Williamsburgh was incorporated as a city, even as proposals were made to unite it and more distant sections of the Town of Bushwick with Brooklyn. The two riverfront settlements, Brooklyn and Williamsburgh, had long been separated by the Navy Yard, Wallabout Bay, and the marshy lands around the bay, but growth brought them closer together, giving force to the idea of merging them into a single city. New Yorkers looked across the East River

FIGURE 2.4. Brooklyn City Hall (Wallach Division Picture Collection, New York Public Library).

with an appetite for still larger consolidation: "Brooklyn is to take Bushwick for its breakfast," wrote the New York *Courier and Enquirer*, "Williamsburgh for its dinner, and when it goes joyously out, rollicking and revelling like a fat alderman . . . it will find itself seized upon and swallowed by New York."[31] That last meal was savored prematurely by nearly half a century, but the table was set for the first two. Bushwick and Williamsburg became the 13th-through-18th wards of the City of Brooklyn on January 1, 1855.[32]

At a stroke, Brooklyn became a city of more than two hundred thousand inhabitants. Five years later the US census confirmed its standing as the third largest city in the nation, trailing only New York and Philadelphia, and surpassing Baltimore, Boston, and New Orleans. The combined 1860 populations of New York and Brooklyn introduced to the United States a new phenomenon, a metropolitan area of more than one million inhabitants—in a country that sixty years earlier had no city larger than sixty thousand.[33]

Even without the annexation of Williamsburg and Bushwick, Brooklyn's growth during these years stretched the city well beyond the old neighborhoods. By 1845 the five wards of the old village housed only 60 percent of the city's total population. That proportion dropped to 30 percent by 1860 (20 percent with Williamsburg and Bushwick included), despite the addition

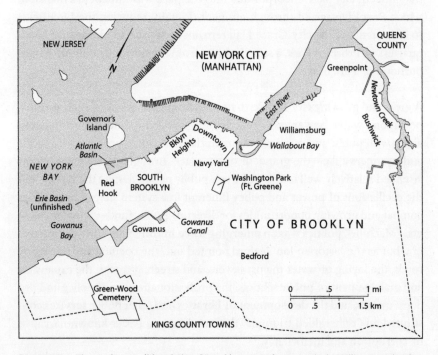

FIGURE 2.5. The newly consolidated City of Brooklyn, 1856 (cartography by William L. Nelson).

of twenty thousand people—equal to a Manchester, New Hampshire; a Dayton, Ohio; or a Paterson, New Jersey—to these wards. Brooklyn Heights and the old downtown were vastly outpaced by the peripheral wards, especially by South Brooklyn, which grew from ten thousand inhabitants in 1845 to nearly seventy thousand by 1860, mostly in areas within easy reach of Atlantic Street, but also further south in parts of Red Hook and Gowanus. Most of the hills and wetlands east of Gowanus Creek, however, and nearly all the land rising toward Prospect Hill—land that would eventually be called Park Slope—were still largely rural.[34] Edwin C. Litchfield, who had made a fortune from Midwestern railroads, purchased a square mile of real estate in this part of the city during the early 1850s, and hired the renowned architect Alexander Jackson Davis to build a majestic mansion at the top of Prospect Hill, an excellent perch for gazing down on the land he expected to become the next Brooklyn Heights. Like Daniel Richards and James S. T. Stranahan, Litchfield was an upstate New Yorker with a New England background—and, like Richards in Red Hook in the 1830s, he was too far ahead of Brooklyn's expansion. The fashionable neighborhood he imagined was only beginning to take shape when he died in 1885.[35] In between were a Civil War, a bridge, and the laying out at the top of Prospect Hill of a magnificent city park. Incorporated into the park was Litchfield's mansion, which Brooklyn seized through eminent domain, reducing the Litchfields to life tenants of the city. Grace Hall remains today the administrative headquarters of Prospect Park, a stone's throw from the now fully built-up neighborhood of Park Slope.

A great and growing city, Brooklyn needed municipal services, such as transportation, water, sewerage, street lighting, policing, and fire protection, along with public and quasi-public amenities that would proclaim—to locals and strangers alike—the grandeur of the place. Brooklyn's city government attended relatively well to most of these public needs, despite the rancor and the oscillations of power and policy inherent in a system shaped by partisan combat and growing opportunities for diverting public funds to private pockets. "Machine" politics was an emerging force in American cities during this era, but as the historian Jon Teaford pointed out, the opening and paving of roads, the laying of water mains, sewers, and streetcar tracks, the expansion and management of public schools, the professionalization of police and fire departments, and the development of libraries and other public services constituted an "unheralded triumph" that moderates a better-known narrative of corruption and inefficiency.[36]

Brooklyn had its share of party politics throughout the nineteenth century, but accusations of public malfeasance never rose to a fever pitch, and once the pigs were cleared from the city's streets most Brooklynites seemed fairly satisfied with the work of their city fathers.[37] As the city implemented a plan for a new water system illicit money may well have been made from this huge project: a reservoir in Ridgewood, just over the Kings County line in Queens, a secondary reservoir on Prospect Hill, and many miles of water mains laid throughout the city. But when the system was completed in 1859 the *Star* did not allege corruption, and Brooklynites were as proud of their city as New Yorkers had been when its Croton system was opened in 1842.[38] The Brooklyn City Rail Road Company franchise to lay tracks and operate horse cars across the city in 1853 was not generally scorned as a lucrative—or undeserved—political reward.[39] Once larger and more comfortable cars began to carry commuters away from ferry landings, and on other routes that stitched together the rapidly spreading city, they were celebrated as a vast improvement over the omnibuses and stages that for decades had bumped along Brooklyn's streets.

One of the most important issues facing Brooklyn's city government was the creation of public parks. Because parks involved the removal of land from the real estate market and the apportionment of payment among the city's inhabitants, their creation was more controversial than any other initiative within Brooklyn's civic culture. The issue first arose during the village era over the preservation of the brow of the Heights as a public promenade. For years locals had strolled along the Heights, on private land, without harassment from landowners. Seeking to convert this trespass into a public right, Hezekiah Pierrepont asked other landowners to cede land to the village along the edge of the Heights. When a close friend did not agree, Pierrepont dropped the idea. But he remained committed to the provision of public space on the Heights, and after his death the executors of his estate made a large square of land available to the city for purchase as a public park. Faced with opposition from those who feared a significant tax assessment, the Common Council turned down the offer.[40] The lost opportunity troubled many Brooklyn boosters. Spooner's *Star* urged the city endlessly but in vain to buy land on the Heights for a "promenade, which for beauty, is unsurpassed in the whole world."[41]

The *Eagle*, which opposed the *Star* on most things political, agreed, lamenting "the shameful loss which has occurred to the city of Brooklyn, and its 'generations yet unborn.'" This 1846 editorial, which may have been penned by the *Eagle*'s new editor, Walt Whitman, looked forward as well as

backward, calling attention to a proposed park on the hill topped by the Rev-
olutionary-era Fort Putnam (renamed Fort Greene during the War of 1812),
around which lay a good deal of vacant land in an area that was clearly in the
path of the city's eastward expansion. The site was close to Brooklyn's only
existing public park, which sat on low land next to the Navy Yard and was dismissed by Whitman as "that miserable piece of a place . . . which will never
amount to anything, whatever amount of money should be expended on it."
Far better to develop the land remaining on the edge of the Heights and the
area around Fort Greene as Brooklyn's first truly usable public parks.[42]

The Heights promenade was a lost cause, but on April 27, 1847, the state
legislature authorized the city to acquire thirty-seven acres of land around
Fort Greene for what was to be called Washington Park, and to levy a tax
on property, according to current valuations, within seven of the nine city
wards (exempting the more distant and entirely rural 8th and 9th wards).
Not surprisingly, the taxing provision caused trouble. On May 4 the *Star*
denounced those who refused to recognize the park, or any other costly
civic improvement, as a shared responsibility.[43] For years Spooner had railed
against wealthy commuters whose interest in Brooklyn extended little beyond their own domestic comfort, a prospering church, and low taxes. Such
a person, it seems, was Lewis Tappan, New York City silk merchant, founder
of the credit-reporting Mercantile Agency (predecessor to Dun and Brad-
street), and leader of the New York-based American and Foreign Anti-Slavery
Society. Tappan, who eventually led and financed several reform organizations in New York, but whose name is not on any of the lists of officers or
benefactors of Brooklyn's cultural or benevolent institutions, was a leader of
the opposition to the taxing scheme for Washington Park. As the principal
speaker at a mass meeting on the subject, Tappan (who lived on Pierrepont
Street in Brooklyn Heights) argued that since the owners of land immediately surrounding the park would benefit more than anyone else from rising
land values, they should bear most of the expense. This argument was based
on language in the city charter. But to Alden Spooner, Walt Whitman, and
many of their correspondents, it demonstrated a limited commitment to
Brooklyn's civic culture—to Brooklyn as a community to which all its inhabitants were required to sacrifice for a larger public good.[44]

Many of Brooklyn's prominent men joined Tappan in this protest. David Leavitt chaired the meeting at which Tappan spoke, and the long list of
attendees included Leavitt's son-in-law Fisher Howe; Henry J. Pierrepont,
representing the estate of his father; Seth Low, grandfather of his namesake,
who would become mayor of Brooklyn and later the consolidated New York
City; and the wealthy entrepreneur James S. T. Stranahan, who would lead

the movement for Prospect Park.[45] But men of equal distinction led a well-attended meeting in support of the tax. It was chaired by the aging Augustus Graham, who was widely venerated as one of Brooklyn's most liberal benefactors, and among its vice-chairs were former mayor Joseph Sprague, the prominent Reverend Evan Johnson, and Alden Spooner. Speeches were delivered by Spooner, his son Alden J., a local attorney, and John Greenwood, the Supreme Court commissioner, soon to be city judge, and surely one of Brooklyn's most dedicated citizens.[46] This second side argued that good citizenship required setting the public good over personal interest. The argument had failed to secure a promenade on the Heights. Would it succeed with Washington Park?

Before the month was out both sides agreed that the city should acquire the land and build a public park. They agreed as well that three disinterested commissioners, appointed by the Superior Court of New York City (not Brooklyn), should assign the burden to each ward in proportion to the benefit its residents would derive from the park—the greater burden falling on the property owners near the park, and lesser amounts, diminishing with distance from the park, borne by owners residing in the other wards. To buy the land the city would issue bonds maturing in twenty years and assess an annual tax on each ward equal to one-twentieth of its apportioned responsibility. Spooner was pleased, as the compromise showed the way to draw on the resources of all the city's residents for other public projects. By April 1848 he was pointing out another excellent spot for a city park on Prospect Hill.[47]

The controversy surrounding the expansion of Brooklyn's public institutions and amenities should not obscure a larger truth: many of the initiatives that gave shape and character to the growing city were private or quasi-public and lay largely or entirely outside the domain of city government. This was even true, in one spectacular instance, with a type of park. By the 1830s the filling up of small churchyards in the city called for new facilities to inter the dead. In this era of Romantic aesthetics the solution seemed almost foreordained: a large "rural cemetery," located on beautiful land that could be made still more beautiful by shaping the natural landscape according to design principles Romantics called the "picturesque." The first application of these principles in the United States appeared in 1831 when Mount Auburn Cemetery opened outside of Boston. A visit to Mount Auburn in 1832 (and some European cemeteries the following year) inspired Henry E. Pierrepont to explore the idea of developing a rural cemetery in Brooklyn. The private project of a joint-stock company, the Green-Wood Cemetery Company was incorporated in 1838 to purchase and develop nearly two hundred acres of hilly and wooded land above Gowanus Bay. The first interments were received by the autumn of 1840. As a cemetery, but just as notably as a quasi-public park, Green-Wood was a spectacular success and would eventually grow to more than four hundred acres. Too far south to receive many pedestrian visitors from the more densely populated parts of the city, Green-Wood became such an immense attraction to carriage-owning residents of Brooklyn and New York City (who took the South Ferry and drove three miles to the cemetery) that separate entrances were created for funerals and more casual visitors. Wags noted that all wealthy New Yorkers made at least one trip to Green-Wood Cemetery—more than one if they intended to enjoy the view.[48]

Most of the large new rural cemeteries, including Green-Wood, belonged to no church or denomination and did not impart a specific doctrinal expression to life or death. They were nonetheless suffused with religion. Graveside religious ceremonies were daily events and religious symbols abounded on monuments to the deceased. Visitors who came to enjoy the cemetery's parklike qualities almost always commented at length on the solemnity of the place. For some this led naturally to religious reflection: "The very ground on which we tread, the ancient forest trees that surround us, and the very air we breathe, are hallowed by holy associations. . . . Above all, God is here."[49] Whether this sensibility was particularly acute in Brooklyn's rural cemetery, as opposed to Boston's or Philadelphia's, we cannot say. But we should at least observe that Green-Wood was founded and thrived during the heyday of the City of Churches, when religious institutions rapidly multiplied, institutions opposed by religious people did not, and public discourse and public action were shaped by the dictates of a Protestant Christianity based primarily on religious traditions brought to Brooklyn from New England.

As Brooklyn grew so did the number of its churches, and at a somewhat faster pace—the sixteen churches in Brooklyn and Williamsburgh in 1835, for example, swelled to 142 by 1855, a nearly ninefold increase that compares with a sevenfold increase in the local population. This growth impressed contemporaries such as William H. Smith, who published a list of local churches in his *Brooklyn and Kings County Record*. The list, Smith concluded, fully justified calling Brooklyn the City of Churches, and he thought it "probable that there is not another city in enlightened Christendom that has as large a number of places for religious worship, in proportion to its population." That claim may have been bold, but Smith could at least point out that Brooklyn had a far greater number of churches, in proportion to its population, than New York City. In 1860 Brooklyn had a church for every 1,734 inhabitants, compared to one for every 3,070 in New York.[50]

FIGURE 2.6.   Green-Wood Cemetery (Wallach Division Picture Collection, New York Public Library).

These numbers tell only part of the story, and perhaps not the most important part, of the influence of Protestant religiosity over Brooklyn's day-to-day life. Cooperation among Protestants—increasing the force of Protestantism itself—was enhanced by refocusing many denominations away from fine distinctions of theological doctrine and toward devotional practices that emphasized the exercise of Christian piety at home, at work, and in the larger community. Denominational differences were by no means erased by this shift; nor was the relative power within the community of specific churches and church congregations. Methodists, for example, were less inclined toward influencing public policies, and the predominantly nonelite social status of Brooklyn's Methodist congregants (Black and white) made civic interventions less likely. Upper- and middle-class Yankee Presbyterians possessed a much stronger inclination and ability to intervene. Still, the grounds for cooperation were improving. Protestants of different denominations may have disagreed about specific ways to create a more Christian community, but they did agree that such a pursuit was necessary and legitimate. Absent from all was any scruple that demanded a wall of separation between the church and the state.[51]

As in many other American cities and towns, Brooklyn's religious people, Protestants in particular, played pivotal roles in creating and operating quasi-public organizations devoted to moral or benevolent reforms. Smith's 1855 *Record* includes nearly two dozen such organizations. Two YMCAs (one in Williamsburg), three Bible societies, a religious tract society, a city missionary society, the Protestant Orphan Asylum Society, the Church Charity Foundation, and the Brotherhoods of Episcopal and Presbyterian churches, had obvious ties to Protestant churches, but other, seemingly secular organizations, also expressed Protestant religiosity. Religious groups called for the founding of a city hospital for the poor during the mid-1840s, and at public meetings on this subject Protestant clergymen were among the most forceful advocates. When the cornerstone was laid in 1851, the Reverend Fred A. Farley of the First Unitarian Church spoke at length of the hospital as "a Christian institution . . . which had grown up under the benevolent spirit of Christ's gospel."[52] A similar spirit, and similar people, animated other institutions: The Brooklyn Association for Improving the Conditions of the Poor; the Brooklyn Society for the Relief of Respectable, Aged, Indigent Females; the Brooklyn Female Employment Society; the Brooklyn Industrial Schools Association; the Children's Aid Society.[53] These institutions were run by religious people, often for explicitly religious purposes and sometimes in connection with specific churches. A report of the Brooklyn Industrial Schools Association, for example, proposes a "solid religious education" for poor girls, and lists below its officers thirty-five "managers," all women representing different Protestant churches.[54]

Most of the founders and managers of Brooklyn's moral and benevolent reform societies were men, and even the seemingly all-female Industrial Schools Association had an Advisory Committee of seven males. But women played a significant role in church-related reforms, largely because they were active in the churches themselves, often constituting a majority of communicants. Women's activism may have been enhanced by the weekday absence of commuting husbands from Brooklyn's suburban neighborhoods, but women reformers appeared in many American communities of this era, including small ones where husbands worked closer to home. The City of Churches, indeed, was not unique in the extent and forms of its moral and benevolent reforms. More distinctive for one of the nation's largest cities was the pervasiveness and power of Brooklyn's resistance to secular institutions deemed incompatible with its Christian ethos.

Opposition to the theater remained one of the clearest examples of this resistance. Flourishing in the pre–Civil War era, New York's theaters provided Brooklyn's moralists with highly visible examples of urban evils they expected Brooklyn to avoid. Objections to the theater were threefold: the plays and skits that formed the typical mélange of nightly offerings were often frivolous and sometimes immoral in message and tone; some performers, male and female, had shady reputations; and, most troubling of all, New

York's theaters were closely intertwined with prostitution. Brothels were numerous in the vicinity of theaters, and inside the theater prostitutes hunted for customers in the lobbies and from their perches in the infamous "third tier." According to the New York journalist and author George G. Foster—no stranger to sensationalist exaggeration—"abandoned women" typically occupy fully one-quarter of the house, "in which they nightly and publicly drive their sickening trade."[55] The *Eagle*'s assessment was no calmer: "The theatres of New York and all our large cities are the rendezvous of the depraved of both sexes. Their lobbies are the resort of prostitutes and blacklegs; and the characters of actors and actresses could hardly be described without offending good taste."[56]

For all these reasons the theater threatened the public goals of Brooklyn's Protestant leaders, including many who commuted daily to businesses in New York and wished to maintain their domestic world as a respectable—even a cleansing—retreat from the big city.[57] Support for the church—the institution that was the focus of their lives during the one day of the week these commuters spent in Brooklyn—was the antithesis and the antidote to support for the theater, which threatened the respectability that was essential to the upper- and middle-class suburban ethos and, even more powerfully, the injunctions of post-Puritan Protestantism. As James H. Callender notes in his insider's history of Brooklyn Heights, "the community, made up of people of New England birth and upbringing, looked upon the theatre as a creation of the devil."[58] We may detect a whiff of hypocrisy as well as brimstone here, as the New York theaters were readily available just across the river, and we can imagine some of the most straight-laced Yankee Brooklynites enjoying an occasional evening at the Park, the Olympic, Niblo's Garden, the decidedly raffish Bowery, or even "the third tier." The point of the opposition, however, was not merely, and perhaps not even primarily, one of individual behavior, but of the Christian character of Brooklyn itself. All the better, in this reckoning, that New York had theaters—and brothels—while Brooklyn had none.

This attitude set limits on the realization of another, contradictory goal, no doubt embraced more fully by prominent Brooklynites who were not New York commuters—the enhancement of Brooklyn as a great and growing city. Could Brooklyn be both a suburb and a city when these two social worlds were defined in such antithetical terms? For fastidious Brooklynites one solution was to develop, or make more extensive use of, respectable institutions of leisure. The most widely available were series of evening lectures, offered by the Brooklyn Lyceum and one or two succeeding organizations each week through the autumn and winter months.

Such entertainment was not novel. Cities and towns of all sizes played host to a variety of itinerant lecturers, ranging from famous intellectuals such as Ralph Waldo Emerson to lesser-known scientists, authors, clergymen, and travelers. Topics varied widely, from "The Moral Law of Politics and of Our Political System" (delivered by the Hon. Daniel D. Barnard of Albany), to "The Sidereal Heavens," (Professor William A. Norton of Newark College in Delaware), to "The Wonders of Science Compared with the Wonders of Romance" (Rev. Edward Hitchcock, who was also a professor of geology at Amherst College), to "The Distinction between Taste and Fashion" (by no less a figure than Rev. Horace Bushnell of Hartford), to the history and topography of Macedonia (by a Mr. Pedicaris of unspecified credentials).[59] Brooklyn's press did its best to promote these lectures with favorable reviews and reports of large and appreciative audiences composed of "the intellect, beauty, and fashion of our city."[60]

Although an element of boosterism motivated this coverage, the lectures did provide an important alternative to less respectable entertainments, and in Protestant Brooklyn clearly carried a moral burden. In 1853 the *Eagle* praised the Brooklyn Institute for providing not only "a splendid course of popular lectures for the improvement and occupation of our winter evenings during the week," but also an annual series of six Sunday evening lectures, endowed by Augustus Graham, "on the power, wisdom and goodness of God, as manifest in His works."[61] A better antidote to the theater could scarcely be imagined. Surprisingly, only a few years later the *Eagle* complained of boring lectures that attracted small audiences. "The lecturing business has degenerated into verbiage and twattle, never rising above common-place truisms, too silly to instruct and too stupid to amuse." The ulterior motive of this rebuff, however, may have been to promote an alternative, noting that the "musical taste of our citizens is almost a passion; and concerts are always well attended."[62] The music Brooklynites most often listened to, the *Eagle* implied, was just as respectable, and morally just as safe, as lectures on the goodness of God or the topography of Macedonia.

Much of that music was experienced in churches, not only as the weekly programs of church choirs but also for a time as the evening public concerts of the Brooklyn Sacred Music Association.[63] Outside the churches, in venues such as the Lyceum, the Athenaeum on Atlantic Street, and Duflon's Military Garden, concerts offered secular music of various kinds—popular ballads, symphonic selections, even an occasional opera. A Mozart Association performed at the Lyceum in 1843, and there was a Mendelssohn Society, led by none other than John Greenwood, who also happens to have been the organist at the First Unitarian Church. In April 1857, the very moment the *Eagle* called for a shift from lectures to concerts, leading men in the city, including Greenwood, founded the Brooklyn Philharmonic Society.[64] Before then musical events beyond the churches had been sporadic. Another new organization still on the horizon—the Brooklyn Academy of Music—would help change that and, to a degree, reduce Brooklyn's resistance to nonmusical theater.

Before the founding of the Academy of Music, there had been several attempts at founding a theater in the City of Churches that would be entirely free of the sins associated with the theaters of Manhattan. It was an uphill battle. In 1850 John Cammeyer built the Brooklyn Museum on Fulton Street as a thin disguise for a theater. The second-floor museum "contained a fine collection of stuffed birds, old pennies, . . . musty coats, deformed skeletons, wax figures" and other attractions, while the third-floor "lecture room" was actually a theater, operating at first under management that included New York's Frank Chanfrau, famed far and wide for his portrayal of Mose the Bowery B'hoy at the Olympic and Chatham theaters.[65] Chanfrau, whose Mose thrilled New York's working men and women but drove away genteel audiences, may not have been the best choice for overcoming the suspicions of Brooklyn's self-respecting Protestants. The *Star* greeted the museum as "a beautiful little place of amusement," deeming its performances "of a character well calculated to draw full and fashionable houses," while conceding that to date they did no such thing.[66] The theatrical company soon gave way to performances by horses (coaxed somehow to the third floor!), and then to renewed attempts at human theater, before the building was converted to a regimental armory.[67]

Editors tried to soften opposition by publishing lists of current productions under titles such as "Brooklyn Entertainments" or "Amusements Tonight," implying that entertainment and amusement were worthy in their own right, apart from considerations of morality and decorum. The problem, and not just at first, was that most of the offerings remained well within the nontheatrical canon. On December 1, 1841, for example, the *Star* listed four "entertainments" in Brooklyn. Three were lectures and the fourth was a concert of sacred music at the First Presbyterian Church.[68] The "amusements" listed on October 6, 1855, included six theatrical productions, but five of them were at New York theaters, while the sole Brooklyn item was a performance by child actors at the Athenaeum.[69]

But things were changing in Brooklyn, in part because they were changing in New York, with some theaters aiming for greater respectability by excluding prostitutes, and by extension the men who came to the theater in search of them. If New York could make drama more respectable, why couldn't Brooklyn relax its guard a little and admit first-class drama to its evenings? This question was raised in the context of the building in Brooklyn of an impressive new concert hall, intended primarily for opera and symphonic music, and located on the morally safe ground of Montague Street in Brooklyn Heights. The hall was intended to house an entirely respectable institution, which the *New York Times*, with some amusement, reported as the Brooklyn Conservatory of Music, "a most excellent name, and one which cannot possibly prove offensive to the nice religious feelings of our excellent neighbors across the East River."[70] The actual name, of course, was the Brooklyn Academy of Music, which gave offense to no one, and elicited no additional ribbing about Brooklyn's religiosity from the New York press. The project began in 1858 with a call by the Brooklyn Philharmonic Society for a hall large enough for its own concerts. Following public meetings and a successful drive for stock subscriptions, the state legislature incorporated "the Brooklyn Academy of Music, for the purpose of encouraging and cultivating a taste for music, literature and the arts."[71] A mixed Gothic and Moorish design was supplied by Leopold Eidlitz, construction began in earnest in the autumn of 1859, and the building delivered its inaugural concert in January 1861.[72]

Following the overture to a concert that consisted mainly of selections from well-known operas, S. B. Chittenden of the academy board gave a welcoming speech that night in which he spoke approvingly of "the Puritans"

FIGURE 2.7. The Brooklyn Academy of Music, Montague Street (Library of Congress Prints and Photographs Division).

before assuring the packed audience that the new building would not be used for theatrical productions, and that every performance that occurred within its walls would be "pure and innocent."[73] He was implicitly acknowledging the visible and vocal opposition to the new institution, especially among the Protestant clergy—the Rev. Benjamin Cutler of St. Ann's was a particularly adamant foe—on the grounds that this attractive new venue was a Trojan Horse, establishing a theater despite all the efforts of right-thinking people to exclude it.[74] Among the academy's subscribers, too, were those whose support was predicated on the banishment of theater from the building. Intended to reassure both groups, Chittenden's remarks were perhaps also a warning to subscribers who favored the introduction of spoken drama on some of the many evenings when operas or concerts (or balls, or horticultural exhibits) were not offered. They had heard Chittenden say there would be nothing disreputable in or near the splendid new Brooklyn Heights facility and that every production would be under strict supervision, as to content and personnel, by management and a board of directors of unimpeachable respectability. They may have wondered whether this justified classical and other responsible theatrical productions. If the academy board could approve of Verdi's La Traviata, might they not also approve of the plays of Shakespeare and Sheridan?

"It has been given out that theatrical representations are to be remorselessly tabooed," wrote the Eagle a week after the opening, a statement that presaged a long battle.[75] In December the academy board announced a series of four plays to be performed just before and after Christmas, stiffly justifying a clearly controversial decision: "That while the Board are opposed to letting the building for theatrical purposes generally, they will permit it to be used for such select dramatic representations as they or a special committee of their body may approve, subject to such regulations as they may prescribe." The plays—Hamlet, Othello, and two comedies, Sheridan's School for Scandal and London Assurance by the popular Dublin-born playwright Dionysius Boucicault—prompted the Eagle to declare it "wonderful that such a fuss should have been made about so small a matter."[76] Less than a month later, though, the Star revealed that the academy had "declined to permit Mr. Wm. M. Fleming, the well-known manager, to give a series of dramatic entertainments in so chaste a place as the Montague street temple," the proposed plays being, in the board's view, "too light and frivolous for the 'Hemisphere of Brooklyn.'"[77] So the "small matter" was not fully resolved. Academy members and others who wished to bring the theater to Brooklyn as a legitimate and permanent institution won but a partial victory in the early 1860s. That it would later become a rout—the Brooklyn Academy of

Music eventually became and remains today a renowned venue for dramatic arts—should not obscure the strength and tenacity of Protestant leaders, clergy and laymen alike, determined to protect Brooklyn from error.

The Christian Sabbath was another battlefield over the purposes and power of Yankee propriety. From the early days of the village era Brooklyn passed and enforced, with variable success, Sabbatarian laws prohibiting activities ranging from playing ball to selling alcoholic drink. A new Sunday closing law passed in 1852 led to renewed enforcement efforts by temperance mayors Edward A. Lambert and George Hall. A particularly energetic advocate of a dry Sabbath, Hall enjoyed touring Brooklyn on Sundays with several policemen in tow to test whether the side and back doors of taverns and groceries were tightly closed.[78] Perfect enforcement was impossible, of course, but skirmishes between violators and public officials, often based on differences in social class and ethnicity, rarely became public controversies.

One Sabbatarian issue that did become a public battle emanated from the Common Council's decision in 1853 to withhold from the newly formed Brooklyn City Rail Road Company the right to run horse cars on Sunday. Apart from an almost instinctive tendency to forbid any secular activity on the Sabbath, the council was responding to the fear that "rowdies" from New York would come to Brooklyn on the ferries, ride the cars, and disturb the quiet observance of the Sabbath, not only in the churches but on the private lands of farmers and suburbanites in the outer wards. Almost immediately, this decision met with opposition, especially from those who sensed a motive based as much on social class as on religion. It would not necessarily be rowdies who would fill the Sunday cars, they argued, but sober workingmen who, with their families, sought the simple pleasure of green fields and open sky after six days of toil in the confinement of Manhattan workshops. Seeking not just a rural retreat but the ability to attend churches distant from their homes—not a violation of the Sabbath but its very fulfillment—Brooklyn's own workers would suffer as well. Wealthy Brooklynites could take their carriages to attend any church in the city, visit Green-Wood, or go wherever they pleased, without any restriction on their movement. Why should the poor be circumscribed?

These arguments appeared in 1854 in a long letter to the *Star* from Walt Whitman. Warming up, perhaps, for the following year's publication of *Leaves of Grass*, Whitman wrote: "The citizen must have room. He must learn to be so muscular and self-possessed; to rely more on the restrictions of himself than any restrictions of statute books, or city ordinances, or police. This is the feeling that will make a great, athletic, spirited city, of noble and marked character, with a reputation for itself wherever railroads run, and ships sail, and newspapers and books are read."[79] Not realizing they had a great poet in their midst, most Brooklynites—save for one who wrote a send-up of Whitman's prose three days later—appeared to have ignored his eccentric essay. But opposition to the council's decision was not ignored. Meetings were held and petitions filed, including at least two from South Brooklyn arguing that the 8th ward would become nearly uninhabitable if horse cars ran through it on Sundays.[80]

The arguments for and against the Sunday cars raged on for nearly three years, coming to a head in the spring of 1857. Pious men such as ex-mayor Lambert argued at a public meeting in March that Brooklyn's Sabbatarian law "was at the foundation of all our institutions, and that the common law recognized the binding obligation of the Christian Sabbath." Sundays in Brooklyn already saw more crime than any other three days of the week, according to Lambert, and the Sunday horse cars would destroy the "quiet and sanctity" which made Brooklyn a desirable place to live. He and his family walked two miles to church each Sunday; they did not need or want horse cars to get there. Fisher Howe, a City Rail Road Company director and the owner of land in the outer wards, reminded the assembled gentlemen that the "green fields" some proponents of the Sunday cars spoke of as valuable resources for urban working people were also private property whose owners did not welcome trespassers. Livingston Miller, a former resident of Staten Island, amplified the reasons for Howe's concern, reporting that the New Yorkers who came to the island on Sunday "kept up such a perpetual riot, as to interrupt public worship, and committed such depredations as greatly to diminish the value of property. People had to stay away from church to watch their property."[81] The Eagle's response, especially to Lambert's remarks, was scorching: "In one breath, Sunday in Brooklyn is a saturnalia of crime; in the next it is so quiet and heavenly that people live in it on that account. It is unnecessary to reply to arguments like these; we prefer to let them demolish each other." As for his family's weekly two-mile trek to church: Fine, and they can "wear peas in their shoes" if they want to, but "they have no right to demand that everybody else shall do the same."[82]

The Eagle's conclusion cut a little deeper than defenders of Brooklyn's Sabbatarian laws might have wished: "If the Creator had intended the Sabbath to be on the Puritan plan he would have prevented the sun from shining, the odorous breeze from blowing, the musical brooks from murmuring, the birds from singing on that day; . . . But he made a lovely and cheerful world to live in, and no man has a right to make a Hades of it."[83]

This sentiment may not have eroded in any significant way the influence of Yankee Protestantism in Brooklyn, but it is worth noting that the Eagle was on the winning side of this dispute. In April 1857 the Common Council agreed to permit the Sunday cars. But the City Rail Road Company at first demurred, Fisher Howe and seven other officers voting not to run them. A month later the company reversed course, but only as a three-month experiment, with a limited number of cars running on Sunday.[84] On May 17, 1857, the first Sunday horse cars ran, and according to the *Eagle* (perhaps not the most unbiased source), they were filled with respectable people—churchgoers in the morning, and in the evening perfectly peaceable working people, evidently returning from visiting friends. "The rowdies, thieves, and rascals, who frightened the pious and timid souls of Gowanus, . . . were creatures of the imagination."[85] On the following Sunday cars ran full time and continued to do so after the end of the three-month experiment. In February 1858 the Rev. J. L. Hatch, a proponent of both Sunday cars and a joyful Sabbath, wrote to the Superintendent of Police and the president of the Rail Road Company to affirm the success of the experiment. Both responded that rowdiness had never appeared on the Sunday cars, President A. P. Stanton going so far as to declare that "there is better order, more decorum and quietness in the cars on this day than any other of the week."[86] Interestingly, two of the original opponents of Sunday horse car service, having seen that their fears were not realized, explained three years later that this experience helped change their minds about the danger of introducing theater to the Academy of Music.[87] Apparently, Brooklyn was more secure from the devil than some of its citizens realized.

Along with the battle over the theater, the horse car controversy displayed the determination of Brooklyn's conservative Protestant leaders to define and maintain a Christian community on their side of the East River—to give real meaning to the title "City of Churches." They lost these battles, but only because others in the community, including devout Christians, thought them mistaken, not about their goals and values, but about the probable outcomes in each case. Brooklyn would remain a City of Churches if it had respectable forms of theater; its Sabbath would not be imperiled by allowing horse cars to run on Sunday. The controversies provoked some impatience with stern Yankee culture, but on the whole the editors of the *Eagle* and the *Star*, and presumably most of their readers, remained supporters of, not dissenters from, Brooklyn's Protestant hegemony.

The battle over Sunday horse cars was fought over a private company's service on the public streets of the city. Another phenomenon that occupied the seam between the private and the public was the celebration of the founding of the Brooklyn Sunday School Union Society in 1816. In this instance there was very little controversy. The annual commemoration involved much of Protestant Brooklyn and, when fully developed, imparted one of the most tangible public expressions of Protestant domination. Many of Brooklyn's new institutions—and the conflicts some of them generated— echoed in other, usually smaller cities, particularly within New England and in the path of New Englanders' westward migration. The Sunday school march belonged to Brooklyn alone, echoing nowhere except on its streets and in its churches.

It is not certain when this celebration was initiated, but brief reports in the local press began to appear in the late 1830s, referring without elaboration to an afternoon procession of Sunday school children and their teachers from, say, Willow Street in the Heights to a not-distant church (in 1837 the Second Presbyterian) for a religious service.[88] As the years went by the event and descriptions of it grew more elaborate and enthusiastic. "Our City wore yesterday a joyous and triumphant appearance," the *Star* reported in 1850; "the children of the Sunday Schools turned out in their gay holiday clothes and their innocent fresh faces to attend the celebration of the Anniversary." Flags floated from City Hall, while students from thirty-two schools marched through the streets behind their own banners toward a service that began with a prayer from one of Brooklyn's leading divines, Rev. Richard Salter Storrs. After the service the children sang an anthem as they marched in separate formations toward their own schools.[89] The sheer size of the event in subsequent years—more than twenty thousand children in the 1856 celebration—required holding the service in different churches, which meant an even more extensive appropriation of Brooklyn's streets.[90]

An inclusive, city-wide celebration might be said to justify this appropriation of public space, but its boundaries were as important as its size. The parade was, by design, a Protestant—more specifically, an evangelical Protestant—event. None of Brooklyn's Roman Catholic Sunday school children marched and services were held only in Protestant churches. Brooklyn's Unitarians and Universalists were also excluded, although this boundary was not at first clearly drawn. In 1841, a member of the celebration's committee of arrangements asked Rev. F. W. Holland if the children of the Unitarian Society would like to march. The invitation was accepted but quickly withdrawn when several pastors threatened to forbid their own students from participating. For decades afterward, Brooklyn's Sunday school anniversary celebration remained the exclusive property of evangelical Protestants.[91]

This celebration occupied some of the city's public space on one afternoon each year. Another space—not quite public, not quite private—was occupied each day (except Sunday) by Brooklyn's Protestants. Brooklyn's newspapers, like those of other American cities and towns, were the organs

FIGURE 2.8. Anniversary Day in nineteenth-century Brooklyn (Wallach Division Picture Collection, New York Public Library).

of political parties; conveyors of local, national, and international news; community bulletin boards; printers of official government proceedings and announcements, and of presidential and gubernatorial speeches; presenters of poetry and fiction; and compendia of advertisements ranging from real estate to patent medicine. They also printed the opinions of editors and correspondents. In many of these roles, and not just the last, each paper maintained a certain tone and style as it explored and expounded upon a range of topics that editors believed would—and should—interest readers. In Brooklyn these topics, and to some extent the tone and style, varied, but the role of religion in the pages of the *Star* and the *Eagle* is striking.

Controversies and celebrations, extensively covered as they were, formed only a portion of the religious reporting and editorializing in the two main newspapers of this period of Brooklyn's history. Articles on the founding and opening of new churches were omnipresent, and were often long, detailed, and prominently placed. The arrival and departure of ministers were also significant news items. Sermons were printed often, again prominently and in detail; some sermons elicited correspondence and editorial comment for weeks and even months. As Brooklyn's clergy played a significant role in the founding of institutions and in public meetings, they were often featured in the press. And editors as well as correspondents maintained, as a matter of necessity as well as conviction, a tone of piety and a favorable attitude toward religiosity. For a time during the mid-1850s the *Star* published a lengthy article each Monday titled "Sunday," written by a reporter who had attended several Protestant churches on the previous day. "We are much gratified to know," wrote the *Star* at the close of one such piece, "that our Sunday articles are well received by our readers, which arouses to further efforts for their pleasure and gratification." The goal was to visit and report on *all* of Brooklyn's Protestant churches as a matter of public concern.[92]

The many articles on religious affairs, as well as the letters of correspondents, contain a discernible language of respectable Christian piety. This language was not always abandoned or compromised by discussions of topics that did not explicitly evoke "the worship of the most high" or "the path of Christian duty." The *Star* and the *Eagle* were rival political papers, yet the exchanges between editors (and correspondents) concerning partisan combat, victory, and defeat during the political campaign season were far less prone to the denunciation and ridicule that characterized newspapers in many other American cities and towns.[93] In these as well as other secular contexts, Brooklyn's editors sought to maintain a decent and, if possible, elevated tone. And when the topic turned to Brooklyn itself, editors and correspondents alike rarely wandered far from the city's religiosity. Whig and Republican writers were supposedly more prone to pious effusion during this era, but here is a typical example from the Democratic *Eagle* in 1844:

> That we [in Brooklyn] are a sober, moral and religious people is manifest in every one who has eyes to see with, and makes use of them. The holy Sabbath here is a proud day for the moralist and Christian, as they behold, all around them, the sure evidences of the triumph of their faith. In what other city, of our numbers, are seen so many tall spires pointing upward to the sky from the temples of the living God?[94]

The authors of testimonials of this sort did not ordinarily call attention to themselves as a cadre of the pious, as most signed their pieces with an initial or pseudonym. This meant that the most frequently identified carriers of faith and good works were the clergy whose names appeared within articles and editorials. "The parsons are our chief citizens," wrote the *Eagle* in its report on the opening of the Academy of Music. "We take their advice in everything; they teach us religion, and, (some of them) politics; we cannot open a school [nor even, evidently, the controversial Academy of Music] without enlisting them in the good work."[95] Credit was duly given for these highly visible roles in religious and civic leadership. Two names appeared most often. These men were most responsible for introducing Congregationalism to Brooklyn, though this mattered less than their individual intellects, eloquence, and personalities. Simply put, they were Brooklyn's religious superstars. One was Richard Salter Storrs, Jr. The other—*The Most Famous Man in America*, to cite the title of Debby Applegate's fine biography—was Henry Ward Beecher.

Storrs was born in Braintree, Massachusetts, in 1821 into a family of clergymen stretching all the way back to Richard Mather (through Increase and Cotton Mather), probably the most distinguished lineage possible for a New England Congregationalist. Educated at Amherst and the Andover Theological Seminary, he was ordained in 1845 and appointed to the Congregational Church in Brookline, Massachusetts. A year earlier, a group of Brooklyn's New Englanders had formed a Congregationalist society and began building what would become the Church of the Pilgrims on the corner of Henry and Remsen streets in the heart of Brooklyn Heights. When the building was completed the call went out to Storrs to become Brooklyn's first Congregationalist pastor.[96]

Storrs arrived in 1846 and never left. But spiritually and as a practical citizen, he never left New England either, and probably did more than anyone to justify and maintain the transplanting of post-Puritan Calvinism and a belief in the special civic responsibilities of the clergy from New England to the once-Dutch world of Brooklyn. An extraordinary speaker, Storrs was called upon on countless occasions, including as Brooklyn's principal orator at the most memorable celebration in the city's history, the opening ceremony of the Brooklyn Bridge in May 1883.[97] (It is worth noting that Brooklyn selected Storrs, a clergyman, while New York chose Abram Hewitt, a business and political leader.) The Rev. Joseph Kimball of the First Dutch Reformed Church described Storrs' talent: "I have heard all our great speakers, but for sustained eloquence, never forgetting for an instant the dignity of his theme, Dr. Storrs surpasses any man I ever listened to. I heard him speak for more than two hours without a note and he fairly electrified me."[98] This is an extraordinary statement, especially as it elevates Dr. Storrs' eloquence over that of Beecher, whose fame as an orator was far greater. But what Kimball was surely expressing was a widespread appreciation in Brooklyn for the substance and gravitas that accompanied Storrs' eloquence. He might also have had in mind his civic activism. More than any other, this was the man Brooklynites pointed to when they wanted to justify the role the clergy played as chief citizens of the City of Churches.

VIEW IN REMSEN STREET, BROOKLYN.

FIGURE 2.9. Church of the Pilgrims, Remsen Street (Milstein Division, New York Public Library).

Unlike Storrs, Beecher was more than a local religious superstar—he was a national celebrity. Born in 1813 in Litchfield, Connecticut, Henry was the eighth of thirteen children of Lyman Beecher. An unpromising youth gave way to studies at Amherst and then at his father's Lane Theological Seminary near Cincinnati, after which he held two pastoral posts at Presbyterian churches in Indiana, the first in the small town of Lawrenceburgh, the second in Indianapolis. Beecher thrived in Indiana, to some extent as a pastor but also as a leader of revivals, and when a New York merchant named William Cutler came through Indianapolis in the fall of 1846 and heard Beecher preach, a new opportunity arose. Cutler knew of several Brooklyn men who wished to break off from the Church of the Pilgrims to form a more progressive Congregational church than the one just placed in the hands of the conservative Richard Storrs. Brooklyn's First Presbyterian Church was moving to new quarters, and these men were arranging to purchase the Cranberry Street property for what would become Plymouth Church. Beecher was invited to New York City to address the Home Missionary Society the following May and crossed the river to talk to the new Brooklyn congregation. Plymouth

FIGURE 2.10. Richard Salter Storrs (Cassell's Universal Portrait Gallery).

Church was formally organized in June (with a sermon from Storrs), and by October Beecher was its pastor.[99]

Beecher was a sensation. His passionate preaching and magnetic personality drew crowds that were too large for the Cranberry Street church, and he filled even the larger building that replaced it when, in 1849, it was (some said providentially) gutted by fire. The rebuilt church was designed to give its pastor a stage and not just a pulpit to preach from, and Beecher made the most of it. Some years later, Samuel Clemens made the almost obligatory tourist's visit to Plymouth Church and described Beecher as "marching up and down the stage, sawing his arms in the air, howling sarcasms this way and that, discharging rockets of poetry, and exploding mines of eloquence, halting now and then to stamp his foot three times in succession to emphasize a point."[100]

Beecher was highly entertaining, and his audiences greatly exceeded his Plymouth Church parishioners. The East River ferries were crowded on Sundays, and soon earned the nickname "Beecher boats." But Beecher was no circus clown. His sermons addressed serious political issues—slavery and abolitionism above all—and conveyed as well, though not without some

FIGURE 2.11.   Plymouth Church, Orange Street (Wallach Division Picture Collection, New York Public Library).

puzzlement among his auditors, his own theological vision. That vision gradually but decisively departed from his father's Calvinism, and in particular from the Old School doctrines that Lyman himself had abandoned.[101] Beecher arrived fairly early at the notion that " 'Love should be the *Working Principle*' of religion—not blind obedience, abject submission, or cold justice." As he elaborated on this idea over the years he was sometimes accused of being a Methodist or, more horrifying still to Calvinist Congregationalists, a Unitarian or Universalist. For many years Beecher insisted he was just updating the old religion to suit modern times, but in 1882, only five years before his death, he explicitly renounced Calvinism and resigned from the New York Congregational Association.[102]

Beecher mattered because of his talent for promoting religion as a proper and productive preoccupation for individuals and society. He magnified religion's already exalted presence in Brooklyn, in no small part by making attendance at Sunday services an event to enjoy, as well as to perform a religious duty. He may have asked his congregation to accept an interrogation of

FIGURE 2.12.   Henry Ward Beecher statue, Cadman Plaza (photo by Stuart Blumin).

traditional Yankee doctrine, but by elevating his own status he helped elevate as well the status of Storrs and other more conservative clerical colleagues, a process abetted by Beecher's amiability and the friendships he maintained with Brooklyn clergymen. The 1870s scandal surrounding his alleged adulterous affair with Elizabeth Tilton diminished his influence, but we may find in the extraordinary Beecher both a force for religious observance and a force leading away from the doctrines that had long given substance to Protestant hegemony in Brooklyn.

As notable as religiosity was in the City of Churches, it did not pervade every corner of Brooklyn's life. Many Brooklyn men left home for work each day and returned to their families without "wearing peas in their shoes" or in any other way attending to the state of their souls. Many women found other things to do besides attending church auxiliary meetings or instructing the poor on how to make soup and become good Christians. And a few secular institutions were not inaugurated with a prayer or oration by Storrs. Masonic lodges appeared in Brooklyn, as did a larger number of Odd Fellows' lodges.

Although some of the former imagined mystical ties to ancient cosmologies (and proved attractive to a number of religious men, including some of the cloth), they shared no explicit agenda with Brooklyn's churches.

An interesting set of secular institutions were the New England, St. Nicholas, and St. Patrick societies, organized nominally as ethnic benevolent associations that met once a year shortly before Christmas for sumptuously catered dinners. Religion at these dinners was secondary to the larger goal of enjoying a long evening of ethnic-based conviviality. The first of these was the New England Society, which met for many years in New York City before Brooklyn's temperance advocates, "dissatisfied with the 'wine guzzling' celebrations" in New York, formed a separate organization for Brooklyn in 1844 "on the cold water principle."[103] The first meeting appears not to have been a dinner, or an occasion for joviality of any sort; rather, it was a lecture by Rev. Horace Bushnell at the First Presbyterian Church excoriating the Anglican Church, and by extension the American Episcopal Church, for their excessive rituals and church hierarchy.[104]

Later events conformed to the New York model in all respects except, presumably, the guzzling of wine: the dinner, an oration, the election of officers for the coming year, and a series of toasts, each followed by a response from an appropriate person. Clergy were present, were not silent, and some of the toasts referred to the religion of the Pilgrims, but the focus was mainly on secular matters, and the tone was invariably lighthearted. At the 1853 dinner, Rev. Beecher, responding to a toast to his home state, spoke of the Connecticut blue laws: "It is said that in this code of blue laws . . . on the Sabbath and on fast-days, no man should kiss his wife and children. (Applause.) This I regard as slander, for I have made all due enquire, and have been credibly informed that it is not so. (Laughter.)"[105]

Two years after the New England Society of Brooklyn established its annual dinners, Dutch-descended Brooklynites formed the St. Nicholas Society. Before the decade was over, there was also an Irish St. Patrick's Society, which differed from its predecessors only in holding its annual dinner in March, on or around the traditional anniversary of its patron saint. The three societies professed to be sisters rather than rivals and invited representatives of the other two to sit at the head table and join in the revelry. At the 1852 St. Nicholas Society dinner the eighth toast was to "Our Sister Societies— May the friendship of St. Nicholas for St. Jonathan and St. Patrick be ever on the increase, and meet with a warm response." The response by John Greenwood, the perennial representative of the New England Society, was certainly warm. Greenwood "was glad that Jonathan had been sainted, as it showed that he was improving his morals." He spoke approvingly of the

mingling of New Englanders and the Dutch in Brooklyn and, almost shock-
ingly for a judge and church organist, "knew from experience that the full
rounded form of the Dutch girl was very welcome to the embrace of the
spare Yankee." Not forgetting his other sister society, Greenwood concluded
by toasting "the daughters of the Isle of Erin."[106] Such was the tone and
purpose of these societies. Tensions among the groups, including the Irish,
were avoided, and religious differences were muted on behalf of an evening
of conviviality and good will.

Although the New England Society and its sister organizations may have
occasionally moderated the presence and force of religion during these evenings, they more frequently complemented Brooklyn's religious mores. Serious dissent is difficult to find within any of the city's secular institutions,
or in the written record of the attitudes and behavior of the respectable
upper- and middle-class people who were expected to populate the Protestant churches each Sunday. Perhaps the most amusing discordant note is
recorded in James H. Callender's *Yesterdays on Brooklyn Heights*. "The men
of the community," writes Callender, "usually claimed Saturday evening as
their own, a reaction perhaps from the Friday evening prayer meeting, and
a preparation for the solemn and somewhat depressing Sundays which were
then the order of the day." This meant an escape to "one of the numerous
chop houses" for dinner, cigars, and an occasional walk to a nearby stable
to witness and wager on a cockfight or boxing match. Callender relates the
story of "one very old gentleman, long an Elder in the First Presbyterian
Church," who attempted to sneak away from a police raid on one of those
illegal contests by squeezing through a rear stable window. "Portly of mien
he stuck half way, and for a time was sure his doom had overtaken him."
Fortunately, he got himself out of the window and "never again could . . . be
persuaded to stray from the straight and narrow path, at least so far as cock
fighting was concerned."[107]

The historical record also includes a few departures from Sabbath observance; for example, the practice among some welled dressed "young men
about town" of loitering on church vestibules before and after Sunday services they had no intention of attending, so they could offer unaccompanied
ladies a tip of the hat and an arm for their walk home.[108] And while many
congregants no doubt found the frequent ringing of Sabbath church bells
beautiful, others found them annoying. "This bell-ringing business is a growing evil," wrote one, "and I do not know what right any congregation has to
offend the ears of a whole city, many times in a day or of an evening, merely
to announce that they are about to worship, lest some careless sinners of
that congregation should forget it." "Cannot our Common Council," asked

another, "adopt some means to prevent the incessant clangor of church bells on Sundays, and at other times"?[109]

These behaviors and complaints posed no threat to the rule of Yankee Protestantism in Brooklyn. A somewhat more serious dissent was registered by the church-going Yankee, Alden Spooner, who sometimes tied his complaint about the weakness of Brooklyn's civic culture to the dominance of churches. "It is said," he wrote even before the conferral of a city charter, "that in Brooklyn our public spirit and liberality runs in a single channel— that of *churches*—and if we should divert some of this toward a City Hall, Court House, Jail, Market, public walks, parade, Society Library, Athenaeum, &c., we should be doing a little service to ourselves and posterity."[110] While noting the absence of a city library in 1837, Spooner allowed himself the nearly heretical comment, "We have churches enough," before calling for a diversion of resources to "our literary and scientific advancement."[111] This sentiment appeared again in 1839, when the Lyceum building was put up for sale. A steadfast backer of the Lyceum, Spooner feared that the building would be converted to a church: "There are certainly five churches now in the progress of building in Brooklyn—perhaps more. These are not called for by the wants of the community. . . . We hope hereafter some of them may be converted into Lyceums!"[112]

Spooner would not be the last to question whether Brooklyn had too many churches, or whether the outsized role of religion tended to weaken other aspects of its institutional and civic life. But dissent of this sort was limited in Brooklyn, and "City of Churches" was spoken far more often with pride than regret. As time wore on that phrase was frequently modified to "City of Churches and Homes," which not only calls to mind the large suburban component of Brooklyn's population but also suggests a vital connection between its religious and domestic life. As we noted earlier, the church was the institution commuters to New York used on the one day of the week they remained on the Brooklyn side of the East River. It was natural (the more Calvinistic among them might have said predestined) that they should invest their money as well as their time in building up this institution, both physically and culturally—as they were also doing with their suburban homes.

Does this suggest a more secular than spiritual motive for magnifying Brooklyn's religious life? Serious religiosity, shaped crucially by post-Puritan ideas and practices familiar and acceptable to both New Englanders and the Dutch, was without doubt very powerful in mid-nineteenth-century Brooklyn. But apart from this striking aspect of the life and culture of a rapidly growing city that was also a suburb, there was also the sheer numerical dominance of Anglo and Dutch Protestants, especially throughout the city's sprawling suburban areas. Even those among them who were not drawn to religion—who might have wished with their Connecticut relatives to kiss their wives and children on the Sabbath—regularly encountered people all around them who looked, sounded, and acted just like they did. These large parts of Brooklyn were, in other words, ethnically and culturally homogeneous. A numerical dominance undergirded the Protestant hegemony.

But Brooklyn was a city as well as a suburb, and men, women, and children who were not Anglo or Dutch Protestants also called it home. Some of them were sprinkled through the suburban parts of the city, but most lived and worked where the suburban dwellers generally did not venture. To find them we must go to the waterfront.

CHAPTER 3

On the Waterfront

Very few Brooklynites escaped the influence of the East River and its waterfront. Commuters to Manhattan enjoyed the brief passage across the river in good weather or cursed the ice and chill of winter. They were as attentive as they wished to the sights and sounds of an urban waterway filled with large ships that sailed the world, along with barges, ferries, scows, and lighters that traveled from wharf to wharf, landing to landing, ship to shore, within the smaller world of the river itself. Shoppers and theater-goers—often the wives of those commuters—were only slightly less connected to this lively avenue of trade and human travel.

That the experience could be special—even magical—was captured by two mid-nineteenth-century literary lions. In "Crossing Brooklyn Ferry," Walt Whitman, whose editorial office once overlooked the "incessant stream of people" flowing to and from the Fulton Ferry landing, wrote of his mystical connection to all those who would experience, in generations to come, his own depth of feeling during the seemingly humdrum act of crossing the river:

Others will enter the gates of the ferry, and cross
 from shore to shore,
Others will watch the run of the flood-tide,
Others will see the shipping of Manhattan north and

FIGURE 3.1. Steam ferry entering South Ferry slip (Wallach Division Picture Collection, New York Public Library).

    west, and the heights of Brooklyn to the south
       and east,
   Others will see the islands large and small,
   Fifty years hence, others will see them as they cross,
       the sun half an hour high,
   A hundred years hence, or ever so many hundred
       years hence, others will see them,
   Will enjoy the sunset, the pouring in of the flood-
       tide, the falling back to the sea of the ebb-tide.

And to those future river crossers he could sense but not see:

   Just as you feel when you look on the river and sky,
       so I felt,
   Just as any of you is one of a living crowd, I was one
       of a crowd,
   Just as you are refreshed by the gladness of the river,
       and the bright flow, I was refreshed.[1]

To Herman Melville, too, nothing about this waterfront experience was humdrum. In the first pages of *Moby-Dick*, his Ishmael marvels at the lure of the water to Manhattanites "of week days pent up in lath and plaster—tied to counters, nailed to benches, clinched to desks." Freed from their confinement "of a dreamy Sabbath afternoon," they flock to the East River waterfront "from Corlears Hook to Coenties Slip, and from thence, by Whitehall, northward. What do you see?" asks Ishmael of the reader who might follow this crowd of landsmen to the water's edge:

Posted like sentinels all around the town, stand thousands upon thousands of mortal men fixed in ocean reveries. Some leaning against the spiles; some seated upon the pier-heads; some looking over the bulwarks of ships from China; some high aloft in the rigging, as if striving to get a still better seaward peep. . . . Yes, as everyone knows, meditation and water are wedded for ever.[2]

As everyone knows, Ishmael soon went to sea.

Occasionally, these evocations of the magnetism of the waterfront were matched in the real lives of Brooklynites and New Yorkers. On two frigid January days during the 1850s an incoming tide pushed masses of harbor ice into the already icy East River, creating a solid bridge from shore to shore, and drawing thousands, not to quiet reverie, but to the thrilling experience of walking back and forth between Brooklyn and Manhattan. On the second of those two days, some twenty-five thousand men and women, according to the *Brooklyn Evening Star*, scrambled down hastily provided ladders (at two cents per person) from dock to solid river, just to prove to the river it could be tamed in this way. Crowds assembled on the two riverbanks, too, "shouting and hurrahing and having a good time generally, and the utmost hilarity prevailed" for some five hours, until the tide turned and detached the receding ice from both shores, stranding hundreds of revelers on an ice floe heading back into the harbor and toward the open sea. Hilarity turned to panic, but the shrinking ice permitted boats to come to the rescue and not a life was lost. The cheering from the shores resumed after the last straggler was saved.[3] One of those stragglers was the Reverend Henry Ward Beecher.[4]

Missing from these accounts of water and ice, tides and sunsets, yearnings for the sea and the magic of a river crossing is the drudgery of loading and unloading ships, filling and emptying warehouses, and manufacturing rope, white lead, glass, and dozens of other products. Missing too are the people who performed this work day after day; the shanties and tenements in which they and their families lived; and the ethnic, racial, and religious identities that differed from those of middle-class and wealthy commuters and shoppers, and of poets, novelists, and adventurous clergymen.

The public prints and private chronicles of this era do not ignore the working world of the Brooklyn waterfront, but there is a striking imbalance of attention between the suburban City of Churches and the less lovely—and decidedly less Protestant—workplaces and neighborhoods that lined the river from Red Hook to Williamsburgh and beyond. Newspaper and magazine editors were by no means indifferent to Brooklyn's economic development, but their articles focused most often on the need for retail shoppers to spend in local stores such as the dry goods dealers Journeay & Burnham on Atlantic Street rather than to travel across the river to the grander and better-known emporia of New York.[5] Most of those local stores were on the major streets—Fulton and Atlantic most notably—that led away from the ferry landings toward suburban Brooklyn.

After the construction of the Atlantic Basin in the 1840s, editors paid more attention to wharfage and warehousing, acknowledging that manual labor and a resident working class were vital components of the city's economic life. In the process they raised the profile of ethnic minorities, conflicts between ethnic groups, and struggles between capital and labor, with coverage of an 1846 strike of Irish workers at the Atlantic Basin, and attacks by strikers on German immigrants who were hired to replace them.[6]

Brooklyn's newspapers also examined manufacturing, although they did so significantly less frequently. As late as 1859 the *Star* admitted that it only "occasionally referred to the subject of manufacturing in this city, more with the hope of directing attention to it for a future effect, than in the expectation that any one would be led to adopt our suggestions now and turn their capital immediately into any prominent manufacture."[7] With respect to commerce, too, the *Star* wrote more often of the future than the present, hoping the New York City side of the river, "bristling with piers" and lined with a "forest of masts," would yield at least some its treasure to the as yet underdeveloped landing and storage places of the Brooklyn shore. New York, after all, was once, like Brooklyn, a city of dwellings, "before commerce drove away the dwellings for the more profitable occupancy of space, and thus it will be with our splendid city."[8]

What is curious about these assessments of Brooklyn's bright commercial and industrial future is that a good deal of it had already arrived. The immediate and continuing success of the Atlantic Basin stimulated the expansion of Brooklyn's commercial waterfront, along the gently rising shores of the old downtown and Williamsburgh, and in the narrow strip of land under the high bluff of Brooklyn Heights. By the 1850s Brooklyn was providing a significant and growing portion of the warehousing of the Port of New York, a fact only occasionally recognized in the press. In assessing Brooklyn's industrial sector, the public prints were also behind the times. The lists of manufacturing firms that occasionally appeared in newspapers, city directories, and gazetteers are far less complete than the official tabulation of such firms in the New York State census of 1855, which lists no fewer than 386 factories and workshops employing 8,604 workers.[9] Most of these firms were small shops with a handful of employees, but a sufficient number of

FIGURE 3.2. The Atlantic Basin in 1851, ground-level view (Wallach Division Picture Collection, New York Public Library).

larger units, located on or near the East River, gave the Brooklyn waterfront a distinctly industrial cast.

Just as in the early days of the City of Olympia and Vinegar Hill, many of them provided the ships, rope, and iron needed for maritime commerce—only there were more of them, and they were larger: ten ropewalks employing 677 hands, six shipyards with 540 workers, five iron furnaces with 602, a steamboat finishing plant employing 64, a lifeboat factory with 60. Five brass and copper foundries and smithies employed 236 people. Also located on or near the river were two hat and cap factories (666 workers), two glassworks (282), a white lead factory (195), seven distilleries (215), three gasworks (278), two porcelain factories (128), and numerous others significantly larger than the traditional artisan shops that operated on a much smaller scale.[10] And the 1855 list of Brooklyn's industrial firms was compiled a bit too early to capture what became the biggest of them all. In 1857 Frederick C. Havermeyer, Jr. moved his family's Manhattan sugar refinery to a much larger property on the Williamsburg waterfront. Competitors soon followed, and by the time the *Star* suggested that industrial capitalists might want to invest in Brooklyn, the City of Churches was on its way to becoming the world's largest producer of refined sugar.[11] The 1860 United States census reported an industrial workforce in Brooklyn that was half-again as large as the one detailed on the state census of 1855, establishing Brooklyn as the fifth most productive industrial city in the nation.[12]

Foreign immigrants were an essential part of the story of Brooklyn's commercial and industrial development and an increasing presence in the waterfront and downtown wards. Immigrants, mainly from Ireland, helped build the docks and warehouses, loaded and carted goods to and from the river, worked in local manufactories and workshops, and dug and hauled away some of Brooklyn's hilltops to fill in and straighten the waterfront itself. Their numbers were already sufficient by 1822 to justify the purchase of eight lots in Vinegar Hill for the building of Brooklyn's first Roman Catholic Church. That same year the First Presbyterian Church appeared in Brooklyn Heights. St. James, however, was not the center of influence and affluence that was established on Cranberry Street. As Brooklyn's chronicler of these years has written, Catholicism "came as an exotic, a part of the unfamiliar and unwanted cultural equipment of newly arrived and uncouth foreigners."[13] "Exotic," though, did not necessarily mean "repulsive." The *Star's* report on the founding of St. James was no less respectful than those describing the founding of Protestant churches, and Alden Spooner soon advertised Catholic books for sale in the shop adjoining his newspaper's offices.[14] During the next few years Spooner wrote approvingly of a procession of the Hibernian Provident Society of Brooklyn, St. Patrick's Day celebrations of the Erin Fraternal Association, and a meeting of the Friends of Ireland that forwarded $200 to Daniel O'Connell to further his struggle against English rule.[15] Spooner also objected to "a friend who was talking violently against the influx of Irish emigrants, whom he styled the '*low* Irish.' "[16]

As this exchange suggests, there were local Protestants who worried about the foothold in Brooklyn of the Irish Catholic community. But the people who brought their strong backs and distinctive brogue to Brooklyn, and who founded St. James (which took three years to acquire a resident priest) were, after all, small in number and among the least influential in the local population. Nativism and anti-Catholicism did not flourish in Brooklyn for a few more years.

By the mid-1830s, Spooner's tolerance toward the Irish was joined to the largely futile task of attracting them to the nascent Whig Party. The *Star* published pieces complimentary to the Irish as part of a larger strategy of convincing them that Democrats were false friends. "The Irish are a noble, generous, confiding, warm-hearted people, of hasty temperament, and an extremely quick sense of injury," the editor wrote in 1836. And if that latter trait made them susceptible to Democratic demagoguery, it was still true that "every importation of Irishmen is a real treasure to the country." Accompanying this praise, to be sure, was the recognition that an increasing number of Spooner's fellow Protestants had come to feel differently: "Why, then, are they hated and despised by our countrymen?" he asked, "and why is every fresh importation viewed as a calamity to the country?"[17]

This chasm between "treasure" and "calamity" is visible as well in the responses to a Thanksgiving Day sermon delivered in 1835 by Rev. Evan M. Johnson, rector of St. John's Episcopal Church.[18] Emphasizing the common Christian faith of Protestants and Catholics, Johnson called for toleration of Brooklyn's immigrants. Although Johnson was widely respected among Brooklyn's clergy and laity, the sermon ignited a controversy that lasted for months, not only in Brooklyn but in Protestant journals published as far away as Boston and Philadelphia.[19] A long letter in the *Star* eleven days after the sermon was delivered called it "an apology for the errors of the Roman Catholics," an attack on "the pilgrim fathers," and an inexcusable avoidance of the threat Irish Catholic immigrants pose to liberty and morality. The author of this unsigned letter described himself in the text as a Protestant minister.[20] By this time a Brooklyn branch of the nativist New York Protestant Association had been created, giving rise to meetings debating such questions as "Are the Roman Catholic Priests justified in prohibiting the people to read the Holy Scriptures?" "Are the Papal indulgences consistent with the Christian religion?" and "Is Popery compatible with civil liberty?"[21] Catholic priests were invited to attend these debates, given the chance to explain and defend the practices of their church, and generally treated with respect. But if in a formal sense the Protestant Association meetings fostered toleration, their content—a variety of Catholic practices that most Protestants found troubling if not abhorrent—widened the chasm between those who could and could not accept with equanimity an Irish Catholic community in the City of Churches.

A degree of ambivalence existed on both sides of this chasm. In 1835, James Watson Webb, editor of the New York *Courier and Enquirer*, helped form America's first anti-immigrant political party, the Native American Democratic Association, which soon spread to Brooklyn. An outspoken critic of Catholicism and Irish immigration, Webb nonetheless deemed Evan Johnson's sermon on toleration "eminently calculated to assuage the furious zeal, and cool the fiery bigotry of those who believe . . . that there is but one solitary path to Heaven, and they the only guide."[22] Spooner gave space in the *Star* to this surprisingly tolerant message, but a few months earlier he, like Webb, gestured to the other side, dangling the possibility of supporting the Native Americans if they focused on denying the vote to those immigrants whose poverty, ignorance, and illiteracy made them "the dupes of political knaves."[23] These departures, along with the failure of the Native American Democratic Association to gain much traction in Brooklyn's politics, suggest that some fluidity of opinion remained during the 1830s, despite an undeniable increase in nativism and anti-Catholicism among American-born Protestants.[24]

Attitudes hardened during and after the 1840s, when the potato famine in Ireland and political and economic upheaval in German states in the remnants of the Holy Roman Empire unleashed a huge migration of refugees to the United States. During the 1820s, an average of 12,850 immigrants entered the United States each year. In the 1830s that average increased more than fourfold to 53,843; it increased again to 85,733 during the first half of the 1840s. After the Irish famine began, and events displaced Palatines, Saxons, Hessians, and others in the still disparate German states, American immigration increased even more dramatically. The fifteen years between 1845 and the start of the Civil War averaged 258,742 immigrants, three times the average of the pre-famine 1840s, and twenty times the average of the 1820s.[25]

Brooklyn took in its share of the immigrant stream. By 1855 nearly fifty-seven thousand Irish-born people resided in Brooklyn, along with some nineteen thousand who had been born in Germany. Nearly half (46.6 percent) of the newly consolidated city was listed on the census as foreign-born—just under 28 percent from Ireland, 9 percent from Germany, and another 9 percent from Great Britain and other countries.[26] These populations stabilized in absolute numbers in the latter 1850s, and their proportions to the overall population declined somewhat as Brooklyn grew from the continuing influx of native-born Manhattanites and other domestic migrants to the city, as well as from the American-born children of the immigrants themselves. The young New Worlders were no doubt counted among the ethnics of the city by those who claimed an older native vintage, but it's worth noting that by 1860 the foreign-born in Brooklyn had been reduced to 39 percent of the city's population and the Irish-born to 21 percent.[27]

Many of the Irish immigrants were famine refugees and the hardships they fled stimulated some sympathy as well as fundraising for food shipments to Ireland. An announcement of a meeting for December 1, 1846, stressed the obligation of those with "superabounding blessings" to care for the needy and, perhaps inadvertently, drew a boundary between the Irish refugees and "us": "If any people may be said to have stronger claims upon our sympathies than another, surely those of Ireland are that people—their kindred are among us, and of us." Two men with Irish surnames joined six prominent Protestants in signing this appeal, the latter including the once-and-future mayor George Hall, a founding member of Brooklyn's Native American Democrats, who was best known for his crusades against mostly Irish-owned grog shops and his enforcement of Brooklyn's Sunday closing laws.[28] Whatever the mixture of feeling and intent toward the Irish, the appeal was a failure. Twelve days later the *Star* reported with unaccustomed brevity: "IRELAND. It is stated that the whole amount raised in Brooklyn to send food to Ireland, is only $220." At a meeting ten days later, funds were submitted from only three wards: ward 1, where Irish shanties clustered around Furman Street, contributed $50 (less until reporter Robert A. Lyon drew on his own funds to bring it to that amount); from downtown ward 2 Michael McNamara and J. Mahoney reported $23.50; and from ward 6, John Shields submitted $4. Ward 6 was the home of many of Brooklyn's new suburban neighborhoods, but this minuscule collection almost surely came from the Irish tenements and shanties along the waterfront near the Atlantic Basin.[29]

On February 6, 1847, the *Star* attributed these early failures to skepticism about the extent of the crisis. But proofs of the Great Hunger "come to us now with overwhelming weight. Vessels should be loaded and despatched with liberal contributions, and such a city as ours, with its fifty churches, should show, that its christian symbols will be followed by the exercise of the greatest of all the Christian virtues,—Charity." Another meeting was held ten days later and yet another, better organized and larger, ten days after that. At this meeting, sponsored by 347 signatories in addition to a highly influential Committee of Thirteen, a collection proposed by the ubiquitous John Greenwood yielded $700. An even more significant achievement was a formal plan to extend the appeal to all churches in Brooklyn and Long Island. The final result in dollars raised and food shipped is unknown, but we can certainly point to a serious effort on the part of some Brooklynites, including a number of its Protestant leaders, to relieve the suffering in Catholic Ireland.[30]

Although the organizers and attendees of these meetings may have been perfectly sincere, their sympathies toward the Irish in Brooklyn were not the same as those they extended across the sea to Ireland. The local Irish, after all, had escaped starvation, and in the process brought troublesome attributes to Brooklyn, including the Catholicism some Protestants could not abide. Only two days after the *Star* called for "the exercise of the greatest of all the Christian virtues," Alden Spooner admitted to the not-so-charitable motive of using relief to reduce the flow of migrants to Brooklyn: "If we would detain them at home, we must contribute to feed them there."[31]

Spooner's attitude toward the local Irish appears to have hardened. Even while lauding their hard work and high spirits, he had always had critical words for the rowdy and the drunken (to say nothing of the many Democrats) among them, but in 1848, a few months before he left the editorial chair of the *Star*, Spooner added a screed against the Catholic Church worthy of the harshest critics of Evan Johnson. "How finely does the Catholic religion, in its purest and fervent attributes, harmonize with human weakness," he wrote, in an uncharacteristically sarcastic mode:

> How seductively it speaks to the senses—how forcibly it operates on the passions—how strongly it seizes on the imagination—how interesting its forms—how graceful its ceremonies—how awful its rites. What a captivating and picturesque faith! Who would not become its proselytes, were it not, as some say, for the stern opposition of reason, and cool suggestions of philosophy.[32]

Anti-Catholicism, an important driver of nativist sentiment, was growing more strident in America, and the City of (Protestant) Churches was no exception. As the local immigrant population grew, new Catholic churches were founded in Brooklyn, mostly in Irish neighborhoods. In 1853, Archbishop John Hughes of New York established the Diocese of Brooklyn, with John Loughlin its first bishop and St. James its cathedral. By 1855 there were fifteen Roman Catholic churches in Brooklyn, at least three of which served German neighborhoods.[33] The local press continued to report the founding of Catholic churches with the same respect they afforded new Protestant churches, but in the hands of Alden Spooner's son Edwin the *Star* became increasingly vitriolic in its editorial treatment of Catholicism.[34] After the national and local collapse of the Whig Party, the paper served briefly as the organ of the nativist American ("Know Nothing") Party before swerving again to support the new Republican Party. In May, 1855, while a Whig-Know Nothing coalition was enjoying a brief majority on the Brooklyn Common Council, Edwin Spooner wrote of the "sheer delusions" of the "followers of Popery" and the "blindness and ignorance, that takes idolatry for religion, and upholds a hierarchy which is now, and has ever been corrupt and blasphemous from the sixth century."[35] "Irish Papists" became part of the vocabulary of the *Star* during these years, although not of the *Eagle*, which needed to frame its complaints in terms that would not threaten immigrant ties to the Democratic Party.[36]

Conflicts between Brooklyn's Protestants and Catholics occurred beyond the editorial pages of local newspapers. The late spring of 1854, a peak time for both Irish immigration and political nativism, was particularly productive of ethnoreligious conflict on the streets of both New York and Brooklyn. The return of warm weather encouraged Sunday outdoor "street preaching," located in spaces large enough to accommodate crowds of worshipers. In Brooklyn a preferred venue was the corner of Atlantic and Smith streets, where a burned-out building had been razed to leave a large open lot, and where Methodist minister John Beach was able to reach a far bigger audience than could fit into his little frame church on Bridge Street. In New York City a preacher of more dubious credentials, a sailor who named himself the Angel Gabriel, held forth on the steps of City Hall, his congregation gathered in the park below. This angel's preaching was fervently anti-Catholic, and on May 14 a sermon by his second in command (and accordion accompanist), one Samuel C. Moses, attracted the attention of Irishmen, who turned the meeting into a brawl. Smaller conflicts occurred on the following Sunday in New York, and in Brooklyn as well, where quick action by the police averted a riot.

On the Sunday after that the two weekly events merged. Rev. Beach delivered a sermon the *Eagle* described as "anti-sectarian and void of any of those sentiments which are calculated to give offence to a large portion of our foreign population." His large audience listened with quiet attention, but before Beach's sermon ended "a delegation of New Yorkers arrived, headed by a man with an accordeon [sic]." Three hundred strong, they declared they had come over the river "to help their Brooklyn friends: whether to pray or to fight" they did not explain. After much strutting about (and no praying) they marched back to the ferry at Main Street, in the midst of a mostly Irish neighborhood, where they were set upon by a large crowd. With no ferry in the slip there was time for a proper brawl, and "thus ended a Sabbath day in Brooklyn."[37]

The following Sunday, June 4, a large gathering at the lot on Atlantic and Smith streets heard a sermon (its text: "And this man receiveth sinners") worthy of Evan Johnson in its inclusiveness. But another delegation from New York appeared, bent on confrontation with Brooklyn's Irish. The *Eagle* labeled them Know Nothings and estimated their number at 150 and the *Star*, improbably, at two thousand. This time as they marched toward the ferry, they were confronted by Mayor Lambert, who had beefed up the police presence and secured the readiness of several militia units. Lambert ordered the New Yorkers to cease marching, but even if they approached the ferry in a less defiant posture it made little difference. Passing Fulton Street into the downtown, they were pelted by projectiles thrown from houses, while a large crowd on the street attacked them with stones, clubs, slingshots, and whatever else was handy. This time the New Yorkers answered with pistols, firing shots into the crowd while they retreated. The police were overmatched and the militia arrived too late to have any effect. Many people were injured, but no one was killed. More than forty men, all Brooklyn Irish, were arrested on what might well have been the most violent day Brooklyn had seen since the American Revolution.[38]

Within a few days Mayor Lambert issued a proclamation outlawing street preaching in Brooklyn, provoking complaints that he had no authority to forbid religious services on the Sabbath and was blaming the peaceful assemblies of Protestant worshipers while letting Irish rioters off the hook.[39] Street preaching continued for a time despite the mayor's order, but the Sunday following the June 4 conflict was peaceful, and so was the next, despite the return of a Bridge Street Methodist preacher to Atlantic Street, where he addressed about two thousand people. "In the crowd," the *Star* admitted, "we noticed a large number of Irishmen, who behaved themselves with propriety, and were not molested."[40] "The street preaching excitement has entirely subsided in this locality," noted the *Eagle* on July 10, while reporting on outdoor preaching in Brooklyn, Williamsburgh, and New York.[41]

Street preaching was by no means the only stimulant for sectarian and interethnic conflict in Brooklyn. Later in 1854, in an election day riot in Williamsburgh, one native American man was killed. In another confrontation two days later a Catholic and a Methodist church were threatened with destruction.[42] Aside from the battle in 1846 between Irish strikers and German strikebreakers at the Atlantic Basin and several smaller and perhaps more spontaneous skirmishes between the two major immigrant groups, the hostility between Irish Catholic immigrants and organized Protestant nativists was the primary source of ethnic public violence in Brooklyn.

To many native Protestants interethnic riots confirmed the violent character of the Irish, which manifested itself as well in the day-to-day misbehaviors associated with excessive drinking. The Irish were infamous for their love of drink, and tabulations of licensed taverns in Brooklyn assigned far greater numbers to Irish owners than to other groups—175 of 300 in the fourth police district in 1853, for example, with Germans far behind with 79, and "Americans" with 26.[43] And these were just the licensed places. American-born Brooklynites were as aware of the numerous unlicensed grog shops and liquor-dealing groceries in Irish neighborhoods as they were *un*aware of the Irish custom of the *shabeen*, which temporarily transformed the tenement or shanty of any new widow into a barroom where the men of the neighborhood were obliged to buy drinks, thereby providing the widow with a timely bit of financial assistance. Crimes were tabulated too, and in at least one case—Williamsburgh in September 1854—were listed in the newspapers by nativity as well as by the nature of the offense. More than half (226) of 415 offenses that month were for drunken and disorderly behavior and almost the same number of crimes (232) were attributed to natives of Ireland (in part, no doubt, because municipal authorities singled them out for arrest and prosecution).[44] Even though not all those hauled into court as disorderly drunkards were Irish, native-born Brooklynites who read the two lists found confirmation of a widespread anti-Irish prejudice.

Against this association of the Irish with mayhem and drink were many complaints in the Brooklyn press of rowdiness that strongly suggested native transgressors. Two articles from the early 1840s mention "Soap Lock" ruffians or rowdies, invoking even before Frank Chanfrau's famous stage depiction the character of the native-born working-class tough looking for a "muss" ("Soap Lock" refers to the Bowery b'hoy's signature hair style, straightened by soap or grease to protrude stiffly downward from his tall hat). Another warns young, well-born men who loiter on streets in Brooklyn Heights every evening in order to insult young women, particularly "the girls at service," that "a public exposure shall strip them of their pretensions of gentility."[45] The volunteer fire companies, and particularly the gangs of young men and teens who ran to fires with them, were another source of public disorder, and here too discussions were not cast in ethnic or sectarian terms. The fire companies were generally well regarded, and though the firemen sometimes looked for a fight with rival companies on their way to, from, or even at a fire, the gangs caused most of the trouble, achieving considerable notoriety. One of them, the "Forty Acres," which ran with Engine 5, a downtown company, was lionized in the *Eagle* in 1903, half a century after the gang's battles with the "Bucks" and the "Cat Killers." The Bucks were from "Irishtown" in the second and fifth wards, but ethnicity and religion may not have been the organizing principle of these battles.[46] Like Mose the Bowery b'hoy—who ran with a fire company in New York—these "fire laddies" were looking for a "muss," not to preserve the purity of a native- and Protestant-ruled republic, but for the simpler joy of breaking other people's heads.

These forms of public disorder did not distract significant numbers of native-born Protestants from what they understood as the Irish Problem. The Irish, in their view, threatened the image of Brooklyn as a beautiful and peaceful domestic haven. Their drinking and disorderly public behavior challenged the very core of that image, the quiet Sabbath devoted to the exercise of religious and familial duty. And they were, enduringly, adherents of a Roman Catholic Church that remained the bane of militant Protestantism. This issue was never far from Protestant Brooklyn's response to the Irish. In the aftermath of the "street preaching" riots of 1854 the *Star* published two letters blaming Roman Catholic priests for secretly encouraging their parishioners to attack the Know Nothings who had come across the river to taunt them. To these correspondents, the riots were not spontaneous community uprisings but the result of a priestly cabal.[47] And the Church, more than the Irish as a people, was condemned from the pulpits of the loftiest of Brooklyn's Protestant clergy. The *Eagle* described Presbyterian minister Samuel H. Cox, for example, as "one of the most popular and accomplished divines in Brooklyn," noted for "his inexhaustible fund of anecdote and ready wit and humor." Cox's amiability did not extend to Catholicism: "The Roman Catholic Church he denounces as 'the woman arrayed in purple and scarlet color—she that sitteth upon the seven hills, drunken with the blood of saints.' "[48]

Sitting on the border between sympathy and condemnation, another aspect of Irish immigrant life challenged Brooklyn's self-image as a beautiful and peaceful city and suburb. Arriving in America with few resources and surviving off the very low pay they received from menial labor, many Irish during these years lived in shanties and crowded tenements along or close to the East River waterfront, and away from the river in peripheral areas where rents were lower and opportunities for squatting were greater. Some lived downtown in the old second and fifth wards—the latter included the original Irish settlement of Vinegar Hill—or just beyond them in the seventh ward, particularly along Myrtle Avenue, an emerging thoroughfare that ran toward Williamsburgh. Where Myrtle ran along the north side of the new Washington Park (Fort Greene), a collection of shanties earned the names New Cork and Little Ireland, as well as the attention of writers whose descriptions combined amusement with contempt. "Descending Fort Greene," wrote the *Eagle* in 1847, "one comes amid a colony of squatters, whose chubby children, and the good-natured brightness of the eyes of many an Irish woman, tell plainly enough that you are wending your way among the shanties of Emeralders." A less jolly correspondent complained two years later of the "hundred or more miserable shanties, formerly occupied by the families of hogs and Irishmen." The hogs had been removed to a pound by the Common Council, leaving the Irish to make themselves "a special subject of remark and objection on the part of the decent and orderly inhabitants of this section of the city."[49]

Equally visible, especially to the commuters of Brooklyn Heights and South Brooklyn, were the poor Irish in neighborhoods near South Ferry and the Atlantic Basin, living in four-story tenement houses and other structures built primarily for the occupancy of dockworkers and their families. In 1856, a committee appointed by the state legislature to examine tenement housing in Brooklyn found cramped, dingy, leaky (and in basement apartments, regularly flooded) living spaces. A five-story building at 800 Hicks Street housed eighty-six families "occupying each a room and a dark bedroom of the most meager dimensions." Nearby were the so-called State Street barracks, twenty four-story houses offering equally deplorable accommodations. Kelsey's

Alley, a twelve-foot-wide passageway from Columbia Street to the river, was perhaps the most notorious slum street in Brooklyn, but it was typical of the area. On each side were eight four-story tenement houses providing two small rooms for each of 128 families.[50]

Had the committee ventured a short distance inland from the South Brooklyn waterfront they might have found less wretched but still troubling housing amid seemingly middle-class neighborhoods. In one of a series of articles written in 1844 for *The Columbia Spy*, Edgar Allan Poe described Brooklyn's suburban development in terms at odds with observers who had praised the homes and tree-lined streets that expanded the beauties of Brooklyn Heights well to the south of Atlantic Street. Recently arrived New Yorkers, Poe argued, had "contrived very thoroughly" to spoil the natural beauty of Brooklyn by erecting foolishly designed and poorly built suburban houses. "What can be more sillily and pitiably absurd than palaces of painted white pine, fifteen by twenty? . . . I really can see little difference between putting up such a house as this, and blowing up a House of Parliament, or cutting the throat of one's grandfather." And Poe lampooned unsophisticated city fathers for refusing to pave their streets with "Kyanized" [chemically treated] wood, claiming it had no equal "in point of cheapness, freedom from noise, ease of cleaning, pleasantness to the hoof, and durability." In the "next instance," he predicted, Brooklyn's Common Council might well "experiment with soft-soap or sauer-kraut."[51]

FIGURE 3.3. Workers' houses near the South Brooklyn waterfront (Brooklyn Museum Archives, Lantern Slide Collection).

Although Poe had just moved to New York, had little money in his pocket, and was clearly hiring out his pen in service to a newly fashionable mode of urban satire, his criticism should not be entirely dismissed. Eleven years later, the *Star* offered a disturbingly similar critique of South Brooklyn houses that had been built for tenants and were poorly maintained. Worse, "certain neighborhoods" of these houses "become exceedingly disagreeable from the influx of foreigners who are generally speaking, filthy to the last degree about their premises and who are almost strangers to soap and water." Landlords who do not look to the comfort of their respectable tenants "may be sure their property will depreciate, until it comes into the possession of 'Nix com rouse' and 'Be jabers.'"[52] Even a small immigrant presence in neighborhoods of this sort brought home—literally—the problems presented to Protestant Brooklyn by a growing and more visible diversity of peoples.

The fear of new peoples was focused mainly on the Irish. But the reality of Irish life in Brooklyn was more complex than some realized. The Irish community in Brooklyn traces back to at least the late eighteenth century, and by the 1820s possessed sufficient resources to found not only a Roman Catholic Church and several benevolent institutions, but other organizations intended to enhance the standing of the Irish in the larger community and embrace Irish identity. The Erin Fraternal Association, for example, was created in 1823 mainly to organize local celebrations of St. Patrick's Day. The association's founders, George S. Wise, Jr. and George L. Birch, illustrate the dangers of generalizing about Brooklyn's Irish, especially before the large migrations of the famine era. Born in Virginia to Irish parents, Wise came to Brooklyn in 1812 as a purser in the Navy Yard. Birch was born in Ireland but was a Methodist. Soon after arriving in New York in 1798, he became active in politics, moved to Brooklyn to edit a short-lived Democratic-Republican challenger to Alden Spooner's *Star*, and was appointed Brooklyn's postmaster in 1821.[53]

The Erin Fraternal Association's celebrations established a legitimate Irish presence on the streets of Brooklyn even before local Protestants did the same with their Anniversary Day parades of Sunday school children. These celebrations, along with outdoor meetings organized in support of Irish independence, lent purpose as well as presence to an Irish community that was still small in comparison to the Protestant majority. Significantly, the association and several successor organizations marched not just on March 17, but also on July 4, as prominent participants in Brooklyn's annual affirmation of American patriotism. The St. Patrick's Day marches helped build a more cohesive Irish community; participation in the Fourth of July celebration served notice to nativists and anti-Catholic militants that these Irish Catholic Brooklynites would not allow themselves to be treated as an alien and subversive element within this overwhelmingly Protestant city. They would continue to fight against English oppression in Ireland, but they would do so as liberty-loving Americans, at once strengthening their Irish identity and the legitimacy of their claim to American citizenship. This assertion was powerful in the early 1820s, with the mortar hardly dry in the walls of St. James; it became more powerful as Irish participation on the Fourth continued into and beyond the period of famine migration and rising political nativism. The local press approved: "The Erin Association, as usual, indicated the constancy of their attachment to the principles of the Revolution by coming out as a man to take part in the ceremonies," reported the *Star* in 1841. Descriptions of subsequent July 4 marches almost always validated the Irish presence in this most American of events.[54]

Organizations formed in the 1840s and beyond responded to the challenge of maintaining Irish respectability in the face of increasingly harsh native attitudes toward poor immigrants. One proclaimed an Irish elite. Of the eighteen men who formed the St. Patrick's Society (out of the earlier Emerald Association) in 1850, ten can be traced to the Brooklyn city directory. Among them were a doctor and a lawyer, two Fulton Street merchants and a Fulton Street hotel owner, an Atlantic Street grocer, the owner of a marble yard, a schoolteacher, a livery stable owner, and a mason.[55] Some of these men, surely, were the native-born children or grandchildren of Irish immigrants and were Brooklynites of long standing. They maintained an Irish identity, however, and were respectable enough within the dominant Protestant society of Brooklyn to dine and rub elbows with the New Englanders and Dutchmen whose New York counterparts laughed heartily at an Irishman's toast to Plymouth Rock as the "Blarney Stone of New England."[56]

Organizations such as the St. Patrick's Society pointed to a degree of diversity in the Irish population. The city directory helps confirm it. Of the sixty-seven men in the 1850 directory who were named Kelly, for example, thirty-three were listed as laborers or as stevedores, carmen, and other workers at or near the lowest rung of the economic ladder. But twenty-five men worked at artisanal trades—blacksmiths, carpenters, and masons accounted for fifteen of them—and nine were nonartisanal businessmen, including two, a broker and a wine merchant, who commuted to New York. The directory undoubtedly underrepresents unskilled workers (there may not have been much motivation to find and record shanty-dwelling squatters), and its simple occupational nomenclature obscures important distinctions—between masters and wage earners within the trades, between masters who earned tidy profits and those who worked close to the bone, between genuine grocers and those who did little more than sell cheap whiskey by the glass.[57] But it is clear enough that not all of the Kellys (nor the O'Reillys, Fitzpatricks, and Sullivans) of Brooklyn lived at or close to the bottom of the economic order. None of the Kellys listed in the 1850 directory were policemen or political appointees of other sorts, but we know from other sources that these public sector occupations were important avenues of upward mobility among the immigrant Irish. (Irish policemen were a significant enough issue in Brooklyn that Know Nothing aldermen of the mid-1850s made a determined and temporarily successful effort to replace them with native Protestants.)[58] There was, in sum, enough diversity within Brooklyn's Irish population to belie the stereotype of a monolithic underclass—poor, ignorant, hard drinking, and "almost strangers to soap and water." Yet the stereotype endured among many native-born Brooklynites, including those owners and managers of waterfront factories, warehouses, and construction sites who found in it justification for paying Irish laborers a pittance for their work.

These prejudices hardly pertained to Brooklyn's German-speaking immigrant population. Many of the Germans who were victims of political or economic upheaval quickly established themselves as artisans, shopkeepers, and in some cases professionals, in Brooklyn and Williamsburgh. The potato famine that devastated Ireland hit continental Europe as well, but famine refugees from Prussia, Bavaria, and other German-speaking regions were not numerous enough to define the larger stream of German immigrants. Noting the large number of Germans arriving in the spring of 1848, the *Eagle* commented on their "habits of industry, temperance, and economy, which are certain to make them thrifty and good citizens. Most of them bring money to purchase land and some of them a large supply."[59] This was a common perception; indeed, it is difficult to find demeaning characterizations of German immigrants by native-born commentators.

Germans themselves boldly reinforced that positive perception. In a speech to a local *Turnverein* festival in 1857, a Dr. Bauer boasted: "The Germans do not come as paupers or beggars among you, but bring along with them means of considerable amount." Referring to German immigrants generally, and not just the better-off '48ers, Bauer claimed: "In all branches of industry, manufacture, commerce, art and science of this country, the German hand and mind make themselves felt, and they occupy an honorable position."[60] Appropriate to the occasion and the audience, these rhetorical exaggerations were not far off the mark. The *Eagle* printed his speech with approval, and there was no objection on the occasion by the mayor of Brooklyn, who, touching upon the sensitive issue of temperance, noted that the Germans, even in their beer gardens, had taught "our people to understand that they could be convivial without becoming drunkards, and enjoy themselves without enfringing upon the rights of others."[61] The implicit contrast with the Irish could not have been missed.

The relatively solid economic status of Brooklyn's German immigrants can be gleaned from the city directories of the early 1850s. Among 104 Hoffmans, Kleins, Mullers, Schmidts, and other identifiable Germans of Brooklyn and Williamsburgh we find 18 workers in menial occupations, 68 masters or workers in 28 different manual trades, and 18 white-collar businessmen and professionals, including 3 who commuted to New York.[62] A majority of "Brooklyn's" German immigrants lived in Williamsburgh, fully four of ten (7,800 of 19,000) in a single Williamsburg(h) ward in 1855. Ward 16 of the newly consolidated city lay a dozen blocks and more from the East River, and the Germans reinforced its character as a neighborhood of small workshops and stores rather than of waterfront warehouses and factories. The neighborhood would soon change somewhat when the German-descended Havermeyers built their new sugar mill at exactly that latitude of the river; indeed, it appears they did so in part because "Dutchtown," as ward 16 was called, offered them many potential German workers. But this was not a working-class—and especially not an underclass—neighborhood. The German immigrants who lived there, and in Brooklyn more generally, displayed an occupational profile that clustered more to the center than the bottom of the economic order. The directories surely missed many German laborers and do not indicate the number of German artisans who lived close to poverty. But Brooklyn's Germans were mostly better situated than its Irish and gave the native-born population much less cause for alarm.

One reason they did not is that so many of them, almost surely a majority, were Protestants. The three German parishes of the Roman Catholic Church in 1855 were more than balanced by eight Protestant churches specifically identified as German. Some of these churches were smaller than their Catholic counterparts, but it is telling that nearly all the anti-Catholic sentiment expressed in the Brooklyn press during this era focused on Irish, not German, immigrants. And because the Catholic Church hierarchy in America was almost entirely Irish, German Catholics largely escaped the odium that resulted from the battle over public aid to parochial schools and the use in them of the Catholic Douay rather than the Protestant King James version of the Bible. In Brooklyn the only publicized instance of a German educational initiative was an uncontroversial project of the Turner's Association of the Eastern District to establish a private school for German children. "Religion will not be inculcated," reported the *Eagle*, "and will only be referred to incidentally, as facts relating to it appear in history."[63]

On rare occasions, the Brooklyn newspapers did aim invective or ridicule at German immigrants. In 1847, the early days of famine emigration, the *Star* criticized Germany, not Ireland, for sending "their pauper hordes" to America. Eight years later an extraordinary bit of condescension toward Williamsburg's German working class appeared in the *Eagle* under the title "Ball of the Strawberry Girls." These girls gained "a livelihood by crying berries and vegetables in the streets, a very large number of whom reside in the Eastern District of the City known as 'Dutch town.' . . . The male portion of the company consisted of butcher-boys, wagon boys, Germans, shoulder hitters, a few loafers and a sprinkling of shanghais." The fare was abundant but limited to boiled ham and mustard salad, coffee and bread. The next such occasion, eagerly awaited "among certain circles," will be "the ball of the 'bone-hunters,' alias rag-pickers."[64] These articles, especially the latter, were stark departures from the usual treatment of Germans, which was respectful even when discussing their one significant challenge to the dominant (Anglo) Protestant culture of Brooklyn, drinking alcohol on the Sabbath.

A central and much-loved institution in German society, the beer garden, was a pleasant place to take one's family and meet friends for a convivial Sunday afternoon. There would be music, typically from German brass bands, conversation for the adults, play for the children, and, of course, lager beer. The strengthening of the Sunday closing laws in Brooklyn during the 1850s was aimed primarily at taverns, groceries, and other places of alcoholic consumption, including the beer gardens, even though it was not yet widely believed that lager beer led to intoxication. But just as workers objected to the closing of horse car service on the one day they could take their families into the country (or to Henry Ward Beecher's church), Brooklyn's Germans objected to the peculiarly American idea that nothing but churches should be open on the Sabbath. Soon after the passage of the 1852 law they met in large numbers "to defeat the attempt to render the Sabbath a day of universal gloom." In speeches delivered in German they emphasized that "in Germany the Sabbath was not merely observed as a day of rest, but of social and intellectual intercourse." Men who worked six days in seven "met on Sunday to discuss social problems and political questions, and for intellectual intercourse and enlightenment," a claim no doubt intended to deflect attention from the fact that the places they repaired to for these discussions served beer along with ideas.[65]

Unlike the Sunday horse car controversy, the debate over German beer gardens appeared only occasionally in the local press and was rather muted when it did. More than a year after the 1852 German protest meeting, the *Star* rose to the bait offered by a New York City German paper: "In Brooklyn alone," wrote the *Turn-Zeitung*, "the sleeping chamber of New York, are 400 churches, the sleeping berths for the dulness of the Anglican Sabbath." The *Star* admitted that Brooklyn was New York's "sleeping chamber," noted that the claim of four hundred churches was "rather premature," and then defended the "Anglican Sabbath," however dull, as a truer route to happiness. It was, indeed, "our best American Institution."[66]

Scarcely convinced, Germans continued to denounce the Sunday closing laws as "despotic in the extreme, and an outrage upon individual rights," and continued to patronize such popular places as "Schneider's Mammoth brewery and beer garden in the 16th ward."[67] They could do so, even during the years of vigorous Sabbath law enforcement, for various reasons. Beer gardens were popular institutions, even among non-Germans. "The sixteenth Ward was in full blaze of glory," wrote the *Eagle* after the end of an August heat wave in 1857 brought crowds of Sunday customers from "a throng of nations" to Dutchtown beer gardens. Music was a big attraction, along with the beer, which the *Eagle* deemed relatively harmless. Closing the gardens down in the face of this popularity would have been difficult. As an institution, moreover, the beer garden was "far less objectionable to rigid moralists than the taverns and corner groceries" so clearly associated with the Irish population. Native Protestants were free to imagine it as a family institution, patronized by good citizens after a Sunday morning spent in church. That beer gardens did not breed either hard drinking or violent disorder allowed native Protestants to tolerate the German Sabbath, not only on its own terms, but also as a way of justifying their intolerance of the Irish. The *Eagle* observed that the "closing of all other places on Sunday has given the gardens a lift." It might well have reversed the causal sequence; the smooth and unobjectionable functioning of the German beer gardens lent strength to the policy of closing down those less reputable, mostly Irish, places.[68]

There is, finally, a more purely political explanation. Unlike the Irish, Brooklyn's German immigrants did not always gravitate to the Democratic Party. Their views (freely discussed each week at the beer gardens), were diverse, their circumstances less dire, and many among them found that remaining open to recruitment by both parties better protected their interests. In noting that there had been no attempt to close the beer gardens, the Democratic *Eagle* might have pointed to partisan as well as social and cultural reasons why "it will be as well to let them alone."[69]

There were, in sum, significant differences in the circumstances and experiences of Irish and German immigrants to Brooklyn in the years before the American Civil War, and a tangible divide in the reactions of native Protestants to each group. Much of this divide was based on the economic roles and well-being of each group, and on the behaviors that seemed to characterize each as a people. But it was shaped as well by numbers and by differences in visibility to the native-born, which was partly a function of urban and suburban geography. Far fewer Germans than Irish lived in Brooklyn, and most of them were concentrated in Williamsburg, away from the river and the suburban neighborhoods of Brooklyn Heights and South Brooklyn. Many of the Germans lived above the store in artisanal and retail neighborhoods, which made their housing less visible even to passersby, quite unlike the Irish shantytowns and tenement houses in and near Columbia Street and Furman Street, so close to the path of large numbers of commuting suburbanites. If they chose to, Brooklyn's commuters, including those who used the downtown ferries, could *see* the largely Irish waterfront world of work and domestic life as they crossed the East River each day. So much a part of the geography of Brooklyn from its earliest days, the river continued to influence the life of the city, even in the ways some Brooklynites reacted to the new and different people who complicated their increasingly less homogeneous City of Churches.

Not all the Brooklynites who differed from the dominant population were newcomers. African Americans had lived in Brooklyn for generations, almost entirely in bondage. At the turn of the nineteenth century they constituted 27 percent of the population of mostly rural Brooklyn. But as the number of slaves diminished in anticipation of the emancipation set by the state legislature for 1827, and as the free Black population modestly increased, the growth of the overall African American population was vastly outpaced by white in-migration, both domestic and foreign. By 1820 the now mostly free African American community was reduced to less than 12 percent of the total population. By 1840, now entirely free, it was down to 5 percent, and by 1860 the 4,313 African Americans of Brooklyn constituted only 1.6 percent of the city's residents.[70]

The small-farm slavery of rural Brooklyn had been less brutal than the slavery of Southern plantations and the long process of emancipation in New York State, though contested and grumbled over, was acquiesced in by even the most conservative slaveholders. But neither of these conditions paved the way to racial equality. White racism, in Brooklyn and elsewhere in the antebellum North, was firmly embedded in the culture of European Americans, few of whom were willing to assist propertyless former slaves in their transition to freedom. The New York State constitutional convention of 1821, for example, eliminated property qualifications for white male voters but maintained an onerous requirement for free Black males. Nearly all the freedmen lacked capital for investing in land or artisanal or commercial proprietorships, and most faced discrimination in the search for employment commensurate with the skills they possessed. Isolated successes—in barbering, undertaking, teaching, preaching, and other trades and professions where white practitioners refused to provide their services to Black people—did not reflect tolerance in the larger community but a potent form of racial animus.

These limiting circumstances applied to free Black communities all over the North. But New York City and Brooklyn offered additional obstacles stemming from the vital role New York merchants, brokers, shippers, and bankers played in the shipping and financing of Southern cotton, sugar, and tobacco. The importance of the South to New York commerce led many of the city's most influential businessmen, and not a few political leaders, to oppose an aggressive national policy toward Southern slaveholders, and made New York a reluctant supporter of the war to preserve the Union. Some of these Southern-connected merchants were residents of Brooklyn, and the storage and processing of sugar, tobacco, and cotton were important components of the development of waterfront warehousing and manufacturing on the Brooklyn side of the river during the 1840s and 1850s. The effect of these connections on white Brooklynites' attitudes toward the local Black population is difficult to separate from the more general racism of the antebellum era. But they could not have helped build racial tolerance, especially when so many livelihoods depended on a system, however distant, of racial subjugation.[71]

In the decades preceding the war, Brooklyn's free African Americans established independent institutions, and even an independent community, in response to the limited opportunities afforded them within the dominant white society, and the insistence by whites of separation as the normal relation between the races. Black churches were the most prominent example. The first of these, as we have seen, was founded by African Americans who separated from the Sands Street Methodist Episcopal Church in 1817.[72] For some years this Wesleyan African Methodist Episcopal Church was the only Black church in Brooklyn, but by 1855 there were at least ten, most of them founded in the late 1840s and early 1850s.[73] Separate institutions in benevolence and education trace back to Brooklyn's village period. An African Woolman Society "of colored people, for benevolent purposes" was formed in 1824. Among its projects was the founding in 1827 of a school for Black children. In 1830 a meeting presided over by white clergy at St. Ann's

Episcopal Church called for extending Brooklyn's venture into public education by opening a second public school for African American children, apparently by moving the Woolman Society school into the public sector. The *Star* approved of this effort on behalf of "a poor and laboring population." It may also have been an attempt to reinforce the segregation of the children of the two races. A letter to the *Star* in 1833 signed by "A Colored man who pays school taxes" complains of the diminution of public financial support for the "Colored School of this village," and closes with a warning: "I sincerely hope that our school will be taken more into notice, as we are aware of the disagreeable feeling that is likely to take place, if we were to send our children to the regular district school of this village."[74] Apparently, adult book reading, too, required segregation. In 1841 a public meeting of African American citizens resolved to form a library "for the benefit of the people of color in the city of Brooklyn."[75]

The most striking initiative in racial segregation, though, was the forming of the African American settlement of Weeksville (and of Carrsville, which adjoined Weeksville, and was only occasionally described as separate from it). In 1832 an African American chimney sweep named William Thomas purchased thirty acres of land along the hilly glacial moraine about three and a half miles east of the settled portion of Brooklyn, a site at once remote from Brooklyn and accessible to it by means of the Atlantic Street tracks of the Long Island Railroad. Samuel Anderson, a preacher, bought seven acres in the area in 1833, and two years later Henry C. Thompson, a manufacturer of blacking and president of the Woolman Society, bought a parcel of thirty-two lots. In 1838 Thompson sold two of these lots to James Weeks, a Brooklyn stevedore, whose name became attached to what would grow over the next few years into an almost entirely Black community.[76]

By 1840 Weeksville was home to twenty-seven families, twenty-four of which were African American. Most farmed the hilly land, but others commuted to work in Brooklyn, even as far as the waterfront. Weeksville soon attracted more families, many from other cities and states, and by 1855 had a Black population of 521. Not an especially large number—only about one in eight of Brooklyn's African Americans lived there—it was enough to make Weeksville the second largest distinctly Black settlement in the New York area (the largest was in Seneca Village on the upper west side of Manhattan) and a center of African American Brooklyn's political life. As part of a protest in 1852 against the exclusion of Black riders on Brooklyn's omnibuses, "sundry individuals of color, residing in the Ninth Ward" (i.e., Weeksville) drafted a petition and presented it to the mayor. The derision with which the Common Council rejected this petition testifies to the courage required to

FIGURE 3.4. Wood-frame house, Ralph Avenue, Weeksville (Milstein Division, New York Public Library).

make even so simple and just a claim upon white Brooklyn.[77] Rejection and amusement were the most common responses, but at least one by the *Star* in 1859 described Weeksville as a community deserving respect: With a church (there were actually two), a schoolhouse, dwellings that "compare more than favorably with those of a large class of the whites who have more privileges and much better opportunities," and many residents who commute to good jobs, including even in "the large stores of New York."[78] By this time, too, Weeksville had become "significant statewide and nationally as a center of activism against slavery and for the rights of free people of color." Its residents were active in the Underground Railroad and would later provide refuge for African American victims of New York City's 1863 draft riots.[79]

Some white Brooklynites joined the residents of Weeksville in opposing slavery and promoting the rights of African Americans. Not all New York businessmen who lived in Brooklyn engaged in Southern commerce, and not all were supporters of the slave system. Lewis Tappan was not active in Brooklyn's reform and philanthropic societies, but he maintained his credentials as a leader of the antislavery movement through his New York-based American and Foreign Anti-Slavery Society. A founding member of

Plymouth Church, he was a friend and supporter of Henry Ward Beecher. On the famous occasion when Beecher presented a young slave woman to his congregation and challenged its members to purchase her freedom, Tappan rose to announce that he and several other men would contribute whatever was needed to meet the price.[80] The coterie of well-to-do slave sympathizers that gathered around Beecher was not small, and Beecher himself hammered away frequently at the evils of slavery. He was also active in local reforms and benevolent efforts relevant to the local Black community, promoting, for example, the New York Colored Orphan Asylum to his congregation, this time using a performance by the children to raise funds.[81]

Southern secession and the outbreak of war shifted the balance of sentiments away from the South and, by extension, the slave system. Some white Brooklynites who opposed or were indifferent to abolitionism rallied to the call to defend the nation against the rebels. Brooklyn's existing regiments marched off to war, and new ones were formed, trained, and prepared for battle. American flags and expressions of patriotism were seen and heard everywhere. Even the *Eagle*, which had steadfastly opposed attacks on the South and its slave system (and ridiculed local efforts to address the rights of African Americans), accepted the necessity of the Union war effort. This was no trivial adjustment. Before the war, and in its early days, the *Eagle* fiercely attacked Beecher's full-throated call to arms and warned of destruction that would make it impossible to preserve a single nation. Four days after the attack on Ft. Sumter an editorial deemed abolishing slavery as feasible as "turning back the Mississippi to its fountain head. . . . No; even if conquered, the South must be let go and set up for itself." Less than a week later, however, it admitted that calls for peace were now fruitless: "Let it now be war determined and decisive." Within a few months, under new editor Thomas Kinsella, the *Eagle* established a policy of supporting the war and the Union while criticizing President Lincoln's management of both.[82]

A few years later the *Eagle*, by then well established as Brooklyn's newspaper of record, published long reports on the city's most significant home front effort, the Sanitary Fair of February and March 1864. The US Sanitary Commission had been created by federal law early in the war to supply and sustain military hospitals, inspect army encampments, and in other ways provide support for sick and wounded Union soldiers. Its role in mobilizing support from the civilian population for these efforts culminated in a series of large fundraising fairs in major cities. Brooklyn's fair was proposed by the Woman's Relief Association of Brooklyn and Long Island, which had been formed under the leadership of Marianne Fitch Stranahan at a meeting held at Richard Storrs' Church of the Pilgrims late in 1862. The Women's Relief Association "desired the cooperation of the men of influence" for the Sanitary Fair project, but the women did not surrender leadership when many of Brooklyn's male leaders endorsed the proposal. Mrs. Stranahan was appointed co-president of the fair's governing body, along with A. A. Low, and a large executive committee contained a few more women than men. The former included Mrs. Henry Ward Beecher and Mrs. Henry E. Pierrepont; the latter included Pierrepont's husband, as well as Stranahan's—James S. T. Stranahan, owner of the Atlantic Basin and a leading proponent of public works in Brooklyn. Some two dozen committees were structured the same way, and a glance through the long lists of names of committee members reveals a catalog of Anglo-Dutch Brooklyn Protestantism: Mrs. John Greenwood (Refreshments), Richard Storrs (Art, Relics, and Curiosities), Fisher Howe (Manufactures and Mechanic Arts, Western District), Mrs. J. A. Harper (Publications and Printing), and John J. Van Nostrand (Grocers and Hardware Merchants). There is a slight sprinkling of Irish names, but like the Stranahans (James was a Presbyterian born in New York State into a family that had migrated there from Connecticut) some or all these people were Protestants. The only recognizably German name is Havermeyer.[83] In its report on the opening night of the fair the *Eagle* described the crowd as "clergymen, authors, editors, actors, singers, lawyers, physicians, men of leisure, old men and very young ones also; the ladies turned out in large force, and added greatly to the charms of the occasion by brilliant toilette and still brighter eyes."[84]

Emblematic of the roots of this crowd, and even more of the organizing committees, were the two eating establishments at the fair: Knickerbocker Hall and the New England Kitchen. The *Eagle*, less closely attached to Brooklyn's Yankee Protestant elite than had been the *Star* (which ceased publication in 1863), poked gentle fun at the attempt to replicate an old-fashioned New England kitchen, with its offerings of beans, cheese, pies, and apple cider: "If the establishment was a fair specimen of New England living in the olden time, we should say of New England what Dr. Johnson said of Scotland, that it was a capital spot to go from, and we don't wonder now that so many New Englanders immigrated to Brooklyn." It also observed that on display at the Kitchen "were two very old Bibles, an article not peculiar, we believe, to New England, although they seemed [to] be exhibited as a special feature of that region."[85]

The fair was a great success, attracting large crowds each day and raising the immense sum of $400,000 for the Sanitary Commission. But this elite-led affair did not attract Brooklyn's immigrant and African American

Figure 3.5. Brooklyn's Sanitary Fair, 1864 (Wallach Division Picture Collection, New York Public Library).

workingmen and their families. Indeed, as the fair approached its scheduled closing date the executive committee considered "the propriety of opening the buildings again next week at a reduced rate, for the common people." The price of admission was reduced by two-thirds for two days of what the *Eagle* called "The Poor Man's Fair," but it still did not draw much attention from the working class.[86] This much-publicized event of the Civil War home front expressed the class and ethnic fault lines within Brooklyn's society as clearly as it did any general mobilization of support for the Union cause.

The war itself complicated these divisions at the same time it increased racial tensions *within* the laboring population. Many Irish workers were at best conflicted about working alongside African Americans, fearing that a general emancipation of Southern slaves would unleash a huge migration northward of competitors for their own precarious livelihoods. There were Irish brigades in the Union forces, to be sure, including at least one from Brooklyn, and their contribution to the war effort helped moderate native Protestant antipathy toward the Irish in the postwar era. But for Irish workers on the home front a Union victory was as much to be feared as fought for. The call for new conscripts in the days following Gettysburg made prominent an equally clear distinction between them and those Sanitary Fair attendees who could afford to buy their way out of the draft.

Tensions boiled over in Brooklyn nearly a year before the infamous draft of mid-1863. On Saturday afternoon, August 2, 1862, a fight broke out between an Irishman and an African American in front of a grog shop near the waterfront in South Brooklyn. The two men were reportedly workers at a nearby resin factory, but the antagonism that built up after the fight focused on two tobacco factories, Lorillard and T. Watson & Co., near neighbors on Sedgewick Street in the heart of this Irish working-class neighborhood. About one hundred African American men, women, and children worked in these two factories, along with nearly twice as many whites, with the two races divided by task. At Watson's, each crew had a foreman of its own race. All the Black employees lived outside the neighborhood in either New York City or the peripheral wards of Brooklyn, commuting to work on the South Ferry or, if Weeksville was their home, on the Long Island Railroad. Interactions between the races in these factories were limited, and during that day and the next inflammatory rumors spread through the immigrant neighborhood.

On Monday morning the advance guard of a gathering mob approached Lorillard's to demand entry, only to be turned away by the foreman, a Mr. Hignet, who had already sent the African American workers home to avoid violence. He advised Watson's to do the same, but most of the Black male employees were already on the other side of the city at an emancipation rally, and the twenty or so who were at work, mostly women and children, decided to stay. By the time the mob attacked Watson's factory, the white employees had gone home for their mid-day meal, which left the commuting Black workers at the mercy of the mob. The police showed up in time to turn away the attackers and stymie an attempt to burn the building down. In the end, the damage was confined to a few minor injuries, some broken windows, and Brooklyn's self-image as a place where such things did not happen. The *Star* (still active in 1862) "could scarcely credit the report that a riot had actually taken place" in this "city of Churches and noble charities," before admitting that it did. It concluded that the assault was the work of "half-drunken, ignorant white men and women."[87] The *Eagle*, too, was appalled by "one of the most disgraceful riots, which has ever happened in this city." After placing blame on the "considerable ill-feeling" that had long existed between the African American tobacco workers and the Irish of the surrounding neighborhood, the *Eagle* insisted that no serious conflict between them had occurred before the Monday assault.[88]

The military draft law of the following year provided the occasion for even more violent conflict. The National Conscription Act of February 1863 required male citizens and male aliens who had applied to become citizens between the ages of twenty and forty-five (thirty-five for married men) to enroll for possible conscription into the armed forces of the United States. Draft quotas for each Congressional district were to be set by the president, with the process of enrollment and conscription supervised by a Board of Enrollment headed by a provost marshal. The act specified in detail who would be eligible, and how the process was to be carried out. It allowed for exemption from the draft upon payment of a $300 fee or the provision of an acceptable substitute.[89] Given the Supreme Court decision six years earlier in *Dred Scott v. Sandford* that ruled African Americans ineligible for citizenship, only white men would be enrolled.

The new law proved explosive when the conscription lottery began that July. The $300 exemption payment, which was about a year's income for unskilled labor, and the exclusion from risk of African Americans, sharpened the class and racial grievances of large numbers of white workingmen, especially those whose commitment to the war was already weakened by President Lincoln's recently implemented Emancipation Proclamation and the now undeniable fact that this was a war for the liberation of more than four million slaves. It was now easier for these workingmen, including a very large number of natives of Ireland, to perceive a "rich man's war and a poor man's fight," as well as a conspiracy to drive down their wages by freeing masses of Black workers to compete for their jobs. Neither of these perceptions was particularly accurate: the rich, the modestly well off, and the poor all fed the bleeding grounds of the Civil War, and the great migration of African Americans from the rural South to the urban North would not begin for at least another generation. Arguing these points to the men and women who marched from Central Park to the provost marshal's draft lottery headquarters in New York City on Monday, July 13, 1863, however, would have been a dangerous thing to do.

The events following that march during the next three days are well known: the burning of the draft headquarters and the Colored Orphan Asylum; the stalking, beating, and in some instances lynching and mutilation of Black men; the attacks on the homes and businesses of wealthy supporters of the war; the storming of police stations and armories; the battles with police and the few soldiers who remained in the city (most had been called earlier to the bigger battle at Gettysburg); the destruction of African American churches and properties of all kinds; the barricading of streets. The arrival of five regiments of troops from Gettysburg eventually ended the carnage, with more than a hundred dead (some say a good deal more), the flight of thousands of African Americans from the city, massive property damage, and a shredded political community only partially repaired by the dominant

Democrats who, with Lincoln's acquiescence, pursued limited reprisals against the rioters, prosecuting many but convicting few. The draft resumed without incident in August. Draft riots occurred in other cities, but New York's was the largest civil disturbance the nation had ever seen.[90]

It was Brooklyn's good fortune that the draft that provoked the riots in New York City was scheduled to begin in Brooklyn on Wednesday, July 15, two days after the authorities became fully aware of what might lie in store for them. On Tuesday they postponed the draft indefinitely. Brooklyn's Democratic leaders quickly followed up by reminding restive citizens that Governor Seymour had already announced a plan to challenge the constitutionality of the Conscription Act in court. The *Eagle* reported precautionary measures by the mayor and sheriff to prevent New York rioters from invading their city, including moving weapons stored in the armories to safe hiding places and fortifying the Navy Yard.[91] On Wednesday a meeting in Williamsburg organized a citizens' "Law and Order Brigade," which attracted more than two hundred volunteers. At another meeting Col. Edmund Powers persuaded Williamsburg "artisans, laborers, and others" who might have been inclined to start a riot that they would be safe from any draft. When one of the six hundred people at that meeting called for "three cheers for Jeff Davis" he was met with "shouts of derision and groans," and cheers for Governor Seymour, General McClellan, and the Union.[92]

This combination of effort and good timing spared Brooklyn the terrible violence experienced by New York City. To be sure, isolated attacks on African Americans warranted the temporary abandonment of several well-known Black streets and neighborhoods, and tensions were unquestionably high elsewhere in the city. A fistfight in Williamsburg on a Wednesday evening drew a thousand onlookers, and though the fight "was hardly a mentionable one, as not even a whortleberry-colored eye was bestowed," the fact that the draft was discussed for another hour before the crowd dispersed "is most significant of the heated condition of the public in this district."[93] But few if any lives were lost anywhere in Brooklyn. The most significant episode of property destruction appears to have been unrelated to the draft, or to racial and class tensions associated with the war. On Wednesday, around eleven o'clock at night, two grain elevators at the Atlantic Basin were destroyed by fire. It was generally understood that the fires were set by grain shovelers angered by the introduction of machinery that would cost many of them their jobs.[94]

This episode of American Luddism, no less perhaps than the tensions generated by the nation's most serious domestic conflict, speaks to the threat posed by the workers and the ethnic and religious minorities of the

East River waterfront to the dominance of Brooklyn's Protestant upper and middle class. That dominance was still plain to see in the City of Churches, and disruptions at Watson's tobacco factory and the Atlantic Basin were announced in the public prints as shocking aberrations, events that should not disturb a quiet and beautiful city that delighted in tracing its religious and cultural genealogy to the Pilgrim Fathers. Was that a pretense wearing thin? Few would have said so in the generation leading up to the Civil War. But further challenges would arise in the generation that followed, and grow beyond denying in the generation following that.

CHAPTER 4

Toward a New Brooklyn

In April 1865 the people of Brooklyn, along with countless others, celebrated the end of the Civil War, and then mourned the death of a president, as epochal events in American history. But if a local legend is true, Brooklyn would soon experience its own epochal moment, known at the time to only a few. On the bitterly cold evening of December 21, 1866, the city's leading public works contractor, William C. Kingsley, visited State Senator Henry C. Murphy in his Bay Ridge mansion. Kingsley's mission was to convince Murphy, a powerhouse in the Democratic Party, that the time had come to realize a long-discussed but elusive project—the building of a bridge, not a temporary dam of ice on a cold winter's day, but a real and enduring span of iron, steel, and stone, across the East River. The project was enormous and expensive, and Murphy was skeptical, but when Kingsley won him over one of the most iconic events in Brooklyn's history was fairly launched. The state legislature passed Senator Murphy's bill authorizing the building of the East River bridge, a company was organized, and the accomplished engineer, John A. Roebling, was hired to plan and supervise the immense undertaking. But three years passed before construction began and another fourteen before the bridge was completed. Appomattox and the assassination of Abraham Lincoln were distant if still-vivid memories when what was soon known as the Brooklyn Bridge opened to traffic on May 24, 1883.[1]

The ceremony on that day was like nothing ever seen in Brooklyn's long history. Even before the festivities began the *New York Times* called it, with customary condescension, "the greatest gala day in the history of that moral suburb."[2] It was indeed a gala day of school and business closings, marches, speeches, receptions, dinners, a massive evening display of fireworks, and ceremonial cannon fire from Governor's Island, the Navy Yard, and an armada of Navy ships. Governor Grover Cleveland was there, as was the president of the United States, Chester A. Arthur, who once had run the Custom House of this very port.[3] The *Eagle* devoted the entire front page and four interior pages of a twelve-page edition to the event and followed up with two more pages (nearly half of the paper) the next day. "*UNITED!*" its headline proclaimed in the paper's largest type.[4]

When the smoke from the fireworks and cannons cleared, the bridge went about the business of proving itself worthy of the celebration. In the days, months, and years that followed, many thousands of people crossed the river each day on foot as well as in carriages and wagons, and many more boarded the bridge trains (they were cable cars) when that service to and from Manhattan began in September. By 1885 the trains were carrying twenty million passengers per year, and in 1888 the bridge trustees reported

FIGURE 4.1. Brooklyn Bridge opening celebration, May 24, 1883 (Wallach Division Picture Collection, New York Public Library).

more than thirty million rail passengers and nearly three million pedestrians. Carriage passengers were not counted, but the revenues from this source were four times as large as those from the pedestrian promenade.[5] In its fifth year of full operations, about one hundred thousand people crossed the Brooklyn Bridge each day.

Dubbed by locals the Eighth Wonder of the World, the bridge, and Brooklyn itself, attracted the admiration of many who did not need statistics to know something grand had happened. Writing in *Harper's New Monthly Magazine* a decade after the opening, the journalist Julian Ralph could hardly contain his astonishment at the throngs that flowed toward the bridge from the New York City side each workday evening. The crowds of London or Paris, he wrote, are nothing in comparison:

> Here come the elevated railways that carry three-quarters of a million souls a day, the surface vehicles of the million and six hundred thousand people of Manhattan, the streets leading from the densest population in America, all meeting in one little square, all pouring out people, and all the people streaming into a great trumpetlike mouth of iron in order to be shot across a hanging cobweb of metal threads into a city that has not its mate or counterpart on earth—Brooklyn![6]

Brooklyn's rapid growth and its continuing attraction to those who worked in New York City in the years following the completion of the bridge earned that exclamation point. Between 1880 and 1900 Brooklyn's population more than doubled from more than five hundred thousand inhabitants to well over a million, about twice the growth rate of all the other major east coast cities, including the very big one just across the river.[7] The bridge no doubt played an important role in Brooklyn's remarkable growth. But Brooklyn's population had also doubled during the twenty years before the bridge was completed, and its decade-to-decade rate of growth was about the same—an impressive 42–48 percent—from just before the Civil War until the end of the nineteenth century. The growth of the 1860–80 decades is especially impressive because it had been quite slow during the war years.[8] Brooklyn added more people in the decades following the opening of the bridge, but the *rate* of growth was greater in the years just before the speeches, the fireworks, and the cannons of May 24, 1883, than it was after they had all quieted down.

More important than these statistics is the kind of place Brooklyn was before and after the bridge was built and the role this robust city played in the expansion of a much larger metropolis. Ralph's celebration of Brooklyn as "a city that has not its mate or counterpart on earth" did not contradict the *Times*' more modest and less appreciative "moral suburb." Despite its

FIGURE 4.2.   Brooklyn's transportation system: horse cars, elevated railroad, Fulton Ferry terminal, Brooklyn Bridge (Wallach Division Picture Collection, New York Public Library).

size Brooklyn was still a "town across the river" from a still larger place, its industrial waterfront (extending now as far north as Greenpoint, and around the southern shoreline to Gowanus Bay and up the now-canalized Gowanus Creek) continuing to serve as part of an industrial periphery of Manhattan that also reached across the Harlem and Hudson rivers to the Bronx and New Jersey. And its role as a suburb was by no means eclipsed by Brooklyn's expanding industrial zones or its own downtown. On the contrary, much of Brooklyn's post–Civil War expansion was in its residential neighborhoods and in new areas that became residential as the city—both cities—reached out to incorporate them. Brooklyn "is like a city in some things," Julian Ralph wrote. "It is a vast aggregation of homes and streets and shops, with a government of its own. Yet many things it has not got—things with which many a little town could put it to the blush. And every other city earns its own way, while Brooklyn works for New York, and is paid off like a shop-girl on Saturday nights."[9]

What made Brooklyn so notable, then, was its size and significance as a gigantic suburb within the nation's greatest metropolis, a place whose role could be best understood by watching hordes of commuters returning across the bridge to their homes. "What is Brooklyn to which all these persons go?" Ralph asked. "It is the home of the married middle people of New York, Manhattan Island being the seat of the very rich, the very poor, and the unmarried. It has been called the sleeping-room of the metropolis." This time-worn image—the "sleeping-room," the "bed-chamber," the "dormitory"—of the real city across the river, had been spoken for many years by those who sneered at Brooklyn and accepted by those who extolled it. All that had changed by Ralph's era was the scale. There were many towns across the river and many others with no river to separate them from nearby larger cities, but no suburban town anywhere in America was remotely comparable to Brooklyn. Nor did any other place have a dual identity as one of the largest cities and industrial centers in the nation and, at the same time, a suburb of an even larger and more powerful city. "Nine hundred thousand persons call Brooklyn 'home,'" wrote Ralph in 1893, "though, as a rule, they write New York opposite their names on the hotel registers when they travel. . . . These men are far more interested in New York than in Brooklyn. They do not know in which ward of Brooklyn they live, they cannot name the sheriff or their members of the Assembly."[10]

Brooklyn was large and industrial enough even before the bridge was built to present this same anomaly. But its massive growth in the post–Civil War period presented new challenges, including to the way prominent Protestants shaped the public policies and quasi-public initiatives that gave character to this "moral suburb." Continuing urbanization was itself a threat to Brooklyn's old order. New and proliferating urban institutions expanded life choices that could and did compete with older rules and values. And an equally important challenge arose not from Brooklyn's thickening urban fabric but from the physical spread of its suburbs, both within the existing boundaries of the city and beyond them into the neighboring towns of Kings County. Could the old order maintain its influence over a much more widely spread population? Had the moral suburb reached its physical limit? The story of Brooklyn's physical expansion is also the story of its cultural and political evolution.

Brooklyn's post–Civil War expansion reflected the interplay of population pressure, the projects of real estate developers, and the continuing construction of the city's system of mass transportation. Pre–Civil War horse cars left many areas of the county well beyond the range of feasible daily commutation to either New York or downtown Brooklyn. These distant and largely agricultural areas might have continued to thrive outside of the metropolitan orbit, but real estate investors, developers, and transportation planners saw the Kings County townships as future suburbs and accepted the notion that Brooklyn would sprawl, not concentrate.[11] The bridge helped advance this suburban vision, at least with respect to potential commuters to New York.

FIGURE 4.3.   St. Mark's Place, Bedford, 1893 (*Harper's New Monthly Magazine*, April 1893.)

But other improvements were needed, and the most significant of them were not only in the air above the river but on and just above the ground, stretching far inland. The growth of post–Civil War Brooklyn, and especially its physical expansion, was stimulated and controlled by horse cars, elevated railroads, street-level "steam dummies," and electric trolleys, as much as by its spectacular new bridge.[12]

The horse cars had served Brooklyn well when the outer reaches of the city were no more than a mile or so from the East River ferries. But in the postwar period settlement pushed well beyond the practical limit of horse car commutation. A striking example was the village of East New York in the Town of New Lots, on the eastern edge of Kings County. More than five miles from the Brooklyn waterfront, East New York traced its origin to the 1830s, when John R. Pitkin, a wealthy Connecticut businessman, bought several farms, laid out streets and small building lots, and built a shoe factory. Then, through advertisements in the press, he invited artisans and small manufacturers from New York and Brooklyn to escape "the ruinous effects of a crowded city, where vice and immorality exist to a great extent, alluring the young and inexperienced."[13] Unfortunately for Pitkin, the enticement of a presumably more moral atmosphere in easternmost Kings County did not rescue his plan from the sin of bad timing. It was offered to the public at the beginning of the economic depression of 1837, and though Pitkin did his best to create a community among the few residents he attracted to East

New York, he did not advertise his project again. Pitkin soon surrendered much of the land he had bought.[14]

Later entrepreneurs revived Pitkin's plan, but their efforts were limited by the village's distance from Brooklyn and the East River ferries. The Fulton Avenue horse car line of the Brooklyn City Rail Road Company extended as far as East New York, but the five-and-a-half-mile trip consumed more than an hour, and most cars went out only as far as Bedford, itself an expanding suburb two miles closer to the ferry.[15] New Lots, including East New York, contained nearly ten thousand residents by 1870, but significant growth awaited three developments: The introduction of steam to street railways in 1877; the extension to East New York of an elevated steam railway in 1885; and the replacement of street-level steam dummies and other types of steam cars with electric trolleys in the early 1890s. The Brooklyn Bridge became part of this system when it was connected to the elevated, but without steam- and electric-powered ground transportation it would have done little to integrate East New York, along with neighboring villages Brownsville and Cypress Hills, into the maturing New York/Brooklyn metropolis. In 1886, the Town of New Lots, including these villages, was annexed by the City of Brooklyn, becoming its 26th ward. The population of New Lots in 1890 was 29,505. A decade later it exceeded 66,000.[16]

Brooklyn's spread through the whole of Kings County involved the annexation of a good deal of land that remained rural and sparsely populated, as well as villages that, unlike East New York, had been on the map since the European settlements of the seventeenth century. Agriculture was by no means in decline in most of the rural townships; 1880 was the peak year of production on Kings County farms as most producers plowed under their grain fields in response to the rising and more profitable market in New York City and Brooklyn for fresh vegetables. This transition, which included the increasing use of urban waste to fertilize fields of cabbages and potatoes, was also a sign that Brooklyn's suburban sprawl was growing ever closer. Some Dutch farmers, whose families had been on the land for generations, sold their farms, at first to other farmers, many of them first- and second-generation Irish and Germans eager to get a foothold on the land. By 1880, 35 percent of the farm owners and tenants in Kings County were Irish or German. (Only one Black farmer was recorded on the census of that year, an ironic postscript to distant days when slaves tilled the soil on so much of this land.)[17]

By the 1890s, farmland passed mostly into the hands of suburban real estate developers, which in turn increased the likelihood of annexation to Brooklyn. Nowhere was the transformation of farm to suburb more dramatic than in Flatbush, which also happened to be the place where op-position to annexation was the strongest. The village of Flatbush had been the Kings County seat until the 1830s, and the township was still the home of many of the county's wealthiest and most venerable Dutch families. These families retained a strong sense of local identity, and with it a resistance to be-ing merged into Brooklyn. Resistance was rooted as well in anticipated land use restrictions and higher taxes to pay for street extensions, paved roads, and streetcar lines. In the face of local opposition, the Brooklyn City Rail Road did not extend a single horse car line to Flatbush until 1860, and steam was not introduced for another two decades—for a railroad that ran through Flatbush from Prospect Park to Coney Island, the opposite direction from downtown Brooklyn![18] By the mid-1880s several railroads crisscrossed the township, and some of them led to Brooklyn. The population of Flatbush increased from about 7,600 to over 12,000 during that decade, and it became increasingly clear, even to the most diehard Dutch, that the future of this old rural community lay in suburban development.

Many of the old families sold their land during the 1890s to the Germania Real Estate and Improvement Company, which transformed land that had been farmed for 250 years into newly platted suburbs whose only crops were houses, sidewalks, roads, and people, that last crop increasing to more than twenty-seven thousand during the decade. Any remaining resistance to sub-urban infrastructure in Flatbush was overcome by commuting newcomers, including affluent Anglo-Protestant and German families, whose interests lay in rapid transit and other modern services. Some of the Dutch farmers who sold their land remained in Flatbush to become members of the nonag-ricultural business elite, but others relocated further east, beyond the Kings County line to Jamaica, Flushing, and North Hempstead. Flatbush became Brooklyn's 29th ward in 1894.[19]

To the south and southwest of Flatbush and constituting the western end of the Atlantic shore of Long Island lay two more original European settle-ments, Gravesend, which included Coney Island, and New Utrecht. Along with Flatbush, Brooklyn absorbed these two towns in 1894, leaving only Flat-lands, at the far southeastern end of the county, outside the city's borders. Gravesend and New Utrecht were seaside and bayside towns, distant from the city, and their earliest appeals to city folk were as weekend resorts and sites for summer homes rather than as year-round suburbs. Henry C. Mur-phy was one of a small number of Brooklynites who made their year-round homes there, and it was for the long journey to his mansion overlooking the water in New Utrecht's Bay Ridge that William C. Kingsley may have bundled up on that cold December night in 1866.[20]

During the 1880s New Utrecht was often described as a pleasant summer resort, developing its waterfront attractions despite what "the Yankees call pigheadedness" among resisting Dutch farmers.[21] The New York and Sea Beach Railway had been carrying weekend and summer visitors as far as Fort Hamilton at the southwest corner of the island since the 1870s, but improvements in the new 30th ward came only after the 1894 annexation. Changes included a more extensive wealthy community in Bay Ridge and more modest settlements of year-round residents in Fort Hamilton and a few other places, all facilitated by steam and electric connections to downtown Brooklyn, the ferries, and the bridge.[22] Still, this tilt toward the Yankees in the distant towns of Kings County was far from fully realized. At the end of the century New Utrecht remained more rural than suburban and more oriented to the sea and the bay than to the city.[23] And when Flatlands became Brooklyn's final acquisition in 1896 (and its 32nd ward), it was a collection "almost exclusively of farmers and fishermen."[24]

Gravesend, Brooklyn's 31st ward, differed from the other annexed towns in one important respect. At its southern end lay a place unique within Brooklyn—Coney Island. Separated from the mainland by a narrow tidal strait, this popular seacoast island did not become just another suburb. "It is the people's playground of the Greater New York," wrote the *Eagle* in 1897, "and as such does not enter into the realty calculations of anyone."[25] Seventeen years earlier *Scribner's Monthly* counted sixty hotels and five thousand "bathing rooms," along with restaurants, food stands, dance halls, and facilities providing every other conceivable seaside amusement, omitting only the illicit ones left for advertisement in less genteel publications. Previously inconceivable developments were soon to come, including a hotel built in the shape of an elephant and the three vast and innovative amusement parks that shaped Coney Island's lasting popular image.[26] Coney Island was already a distinctive and very peculiar place, and Brooklyn swallowed it whole; not, however, without a certain amount of indigestion.

The difficulty came mostly from the more raffish Norton's Point on the western end of the island (now the exclusive and gated community of Sea Gate). By the 1860s it was "a haven for gamblers, confidence men, pickpockets, roughnecks, and prostitutes, who could ply their trades upon recreation seekers beyond the reach of New York and Brooklyn officials."[27] On the eastern end and in the center, in areas rechristened Manhattan Beach and Brighton Beach, a more respectable world of beachfront leisure was developing, especially with the construction between 1877 and 1880 of three large and elegant resort hotels, the Manhattan Beach, the Oriental, and the Brighton Beach, each accessed by railroads owned by the hotels' proprietors, and at the Brighton Beach by steamboats landing at its ocean pier. Wealthy New Yorkers, Brooklynites, and tourists from afar patronized these places, while the less well-to-do clustered in hotels, large and small, in West Brighton.[28]

Even in these more respectable areas of the island, a good deal of behavior did not sit well with Brooklyn's Protestant leaders. There were theatrical events of dubious merit, dances, alcoholic drinks, and betting on horse races—and much of this occurred on Sunday, the day of the week when Coney Island was the most crowded with people of all classes and conditions who were clearly not spending the Sabbath in church and quiet religious reflection.[29] The island itself had no churches until the construction of a Catholic Church in 1880 to serve a small Irish community. There was no Protestant church, unless one credits the "small frame church" lampooned in a newspaper account in the summer of 1868, in which a minister delivers an unsuccessful sermon to a congregation of thirteen adults and five children, the collection is an abysmal failure, and "no announcement is made of any preaching for next Sunday." Religion, this article concludes, "may be set down as at a discount on Coney Island."[30] Thirteen years later plans were announced for the island's first real Protestant church, a Union Church without any denominational affiliation.[31] Religious practice satisfactory to Brooklyn's Protestant leaders no doubt remained "at a discount."

Underchurched and oversupplied with brothels, saloons, gambling dens, and criminal characters, Coney Island was on the moral as well as the physical periphery of Brooklyn, a "Sodom by the Sea" that was an embarrassment

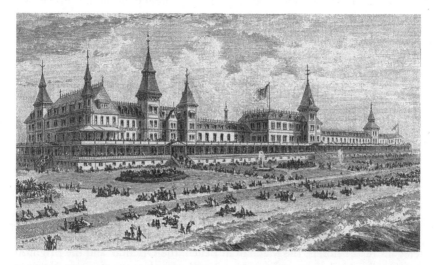

FIGURE 4.4.   The Manhattan Beach Hotel, Coney Island (Milstein Division, New York Public Library).

to the City of Churches. Part of the problem was the tolerant oversight of Coney Island's long-time Democratic political boss, John Y. McKane, who surrendered his seaside domain for humble riverside quarters at Sing Sing, not by coincidence only two months after Brooklyn took over law enforcement in Gravesend and its raucous resort.[32] But hopes that with the departure of McKane Brooklyn's police force would quickly enforce the city's sterner laws on Coney Island were not realized. An *Eagle* correspondent complained a year after annexation that "all parts of the Island are cursed (and have been ever since the McKane reign), with a superabundance of houses of ill repute."[33] "Immoral dances and shows" remained troubling during at least the next two years, despite assurances that public performances of the "couchee-couchee" and other such offenses would soon be squelched.[34]

Criminality and vice were ultimately reduced on Coney Island, but by events and developments that had little to do with law enforcement. Almost simultaneously with Brooklyn's annexation of Gravesend two large fires destroyed many of the illicit operations on the western half of the island. In a few years they were replaced by large amusement parks where excitements were legal and less morally offensive. A "New Coney Island" emerged, resolving some but by no means all of moral Brooklyn's objections. The exuberant commercialism remained, along with a relaxation of ordinary social constraints, especially between young men and women, and the unapologetic embrace of physical enjoyment away from any church on the Christian Sabbath.[35] Nor was Coney Island alone among Brooklyn's worrisome new children. Racetracks on the Gravesend mainland and in Queens just across the county border from New Lots attracted gamblers, and steam trains catered to factory workers on their way to a rowdy good time at Fort Hamilton, no doubt reminding some Brooklyn old-timers of their fears of Sunday horse cars.[36] Although none of these attractions, not even on Coney Island, unraveled the social fabric of New York's "moral suburb," Brooklyn's annexation of the five Kings County towns presented a challenge to those who had exerted moral leadership over a much smaller city.

Altogether, the annexed towns amounted to one hundred forty thousand inhabitants at the end of the century, about 12 percent of Brooklyn's population. Most of the city's post–Civil War growth, therefore, occurred within its older boundaries, thickening up some of the already densely populated neighborhoods near the East River waterfront and around a shifting and growing downtown, but for the most part extending the built-up parts of the city into wards that had been sparsely populated before the war. In the earlier days of Brooklyn's growth, the principal direction of physical expansion was southward toward Gowanus and Red Hook. Contemporaries celebrated

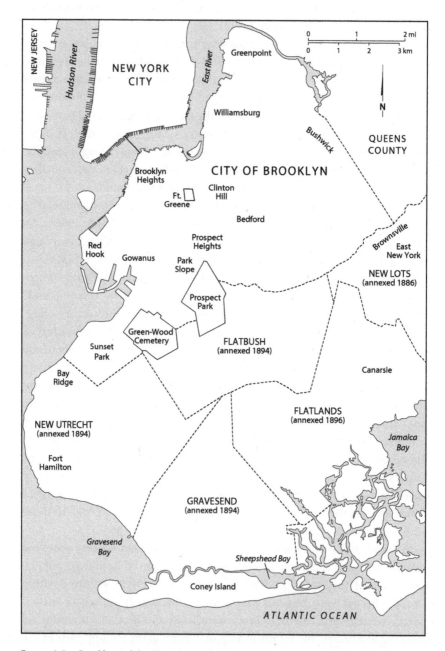

FIGURE 4.5.   Brooklyn and the Kings County towns, 1884 (cartography by William L. Nelson).

South Brooklyn (roughly the areas known today as Cobble Hill, Carroll Gardens, and Boerum Hill) as a wealthy and middle-class extension below Atlantic Street of the suburban world first established in Brooklyn Heights. But South Brooklyn also contained working-class neighborhoods adjacent to the bustling waterfront. These expanded as new docks, warehouses, and factories were built further south, down to and around Red Hook along Gowanus Bay. The huge Erie Basin, completed just after the Civil War, attracted much of the grain trade and a good deal of ship repair to the southern shore of Red Hook, while the Gowanus Canal pushed the commercial and industrial waterfront—a crowded array of factories and lumber, coal, brick, and stone yards—into what had been a bucolic area of marshes, ponds, and farms surrounding the meandering Gowanus Creek.[37]

Red Hook and Gowanus contributed to Brooklyn's robust growth during the post–Civil War years, but contemporaries were not quick to appreciate it. "The name South Brooklyn has not had a good favor with some Brooklyn people," wrote the *Eagle* in 1886, "the very name has been an injury to it as a residence district and tended to drive people away and to depreciate the value of property." Red Hook "enjoys the distinction of being . . . the dumping ground of the city and the shantytown of Brooklyn," while Gowanus is noted for the stench of its canalside factories.[38] The *Eagle* also complained of criminals who used Gowanus and the canal's docks and barges to store and transport stolen goods.[39]

Developers often established residential suburbs on open land beyond unattractive zones of docks and factories, once these areas were provided with good transportation to the city center. New Utrecht's Bay Ridge was already growing in this way, and between Gowanus and Bay Ridge was a tract within the old city boundary dubbed for a time "the real South Brooklyn."[40] This area, with hundreds of comfortable new houses, would soon be called Sunset Park, but despite the pretty name it attracted more waterfront workers than commuters after the new Bush Terminal docks and warehouses made the waterfront there as busy as any in the Port of New York. In general this southwestern region did not greatly extend the once-dominant southern axis of Brooklyn's suburban development.

During the post–Civil War decades that axis shifted decisively to the east.[41] When Julian Ralph described Brooklyn as "made up of hundreds of miles of avenues and streets lined with little dwellings," he no doubt meant new sections of suburban housing stretching eastward from downtown Brooklyn, Fort Greene, Clinton Hill, and Williamsburg, a large area known then as Bedford and East Brooklyn and today as Bedford-Stuyvesant, Crown Heights, and Bushwick. Ralph was intrigued by modestly situated New Yorkers "shot across" the East River each day: "Sooner or later such ones move to Brooklyn where there is elbow-room and a hush at night, and where they see trees and can have growing flowers. . . . There lies the secret of the suburb. . . . It is possible for a clerk to own a house in Brooklyn; it is easier for a clerk to fly than to own one in New York."[42] In New York clerks lived in boarding houses, tenements, or apartments. In Brooklyn, Ralph estimated, each of them could have a house for half the cost. This was Brooklyn's niche in the metropolis and why it spread so widely as it grew.

In Bedford and East Brooklyn, broad and elegant streets provided housing commuting clerks and even small businessmen could not hope to buy or rent. Yet within this extensive gridiron of streets there was considerably more modesty than opulence. As early as 1871 the *Eagle* pointed to the 21st ward, which encompassed much of this area, as "the banner ward of Brooklyn as to buildings," 550 houses having been built there in the previous year. Nearly all of them were reasonably priced two-, two-and-a-half-, and three-story row houses, some designed for two families.[43] The "builders' art" was soon applied to two empty square miles and to Bushwick just to the north, yielding a still wider spread of housing within the price range of Ralph's commuting white-collar workers. Four years later the state census tabulated nine thousand houses in this eastern end of the city, four-fifths of which were wood frame. They were valued about 20 percent lower than the average for the city. Some seventy thousand Brooklynites lived in this area in 1875, a number that ballooned to three hundred fifty thousand by the end of the century, about two and a half times the population of the newly annexed townships.[44]

Closer to the ferries, the bridge, and Brooklyn's downtown were three smaller neighborhoods, each more upscale than Bushwick and the farther reaches of East Brooklyn: Fort Greene, just south and east of Washington Park; a not-yet-named Prospect Heights, just north of the newly completed Prospect Park; and Park Slope, climbing the square mile toward the new park from the more settled parts of South Brooklyn, partly realizing Edwin Litchfield's dream of an elite neighborhood below his mansion at the top of the hill. Like Fort Greene and Prospect Heights, Park Slope was mostly middle class, with long, shaded streets and an almost even mixture of well-finished frame and brick or stone houses. But there was variation here, with more modest houses in the area closest to Gowanus and its infamous canal and far more pretentious ones at the top of the slope, on the avenues and streets closest to the park. Here in 1890 were the new homes of Thomas Adams, Jr., the manufacturer of chewing gum, Clinton L. Rossiter of the New York Central Railroad, and other corporate executives, merchants, and lawyers.[45]

Around the same time a different breed of men, whose fortunes were made in horse racing, built four adjoining five-story brownstones that were soon known as Sportsmen's Row and, for several years, "the most talked of houses in Brooklyn." But if these men of the turf threatened the tone of this new center of wealth and prestige, they did not do so for long. Three of the four quickly sold their houses, and judges, an ex-mayor, and the commissioner of jurors soon dominated the block.[46] To complete the rout of the disreputable, the First Dutch Reformed Church built its new home, "one of the handsomest church edifices ever erected in this city," on Seventh Avenue and Carroll Street, in the heart of the neighborhood.[47] Park Slope remained only partly built-up at the end of the century—one memoirist recalls a girlhood spent mainly among empty building lots—but clearly this was poised to be a center of wealth, and possibly prestige, to rival Brooklyn Heights.[48]

Fort Greene had its wealthy section as well. The neighborhood surrounded Washington Park, but the greater part of it lay south of the park as far as Atlantic Avenue. Brick and stone townhouses lined most of these streets, giving the area a distinctly upper-middle-class character. The most elegant part of Fort Greene, though, was on the two blocks facing the east side of the park. Shortly after the war William C. Kingsley established his home there, as did his partner in the construction business, Abner C. Keeney.[49] They soon had neighbors in elegant brownstones up and down the two blocks.[50]

In the 1870s a new neighborhood developed that soon became the only legitimate rival to Brooklyn Heights as a center of wealth and influence in the city. Before the war, Clinton Hill was largely undeveloped, though several expensive country villas were built on newly laid-out Clinton Avenue, five blocks east of Washington Park. After the war, rows of brownstones appeared on nearby streets, just as they did in nearby Fort Greene. But the area was truly transformed after 1874 when Charles Pratt made Clinton Avenue his home. Pratt was one of the latest of Brooklyn's successful New England immigrants. Born in Massachusetts in 1830, he moved to New York as a young man and almost immediately prospered, first in the paint and whale oil business, and eventually—and spectacularly—in the new business of refining petroleum. In 1867 he and his partner Henry H. Rogers established Astral Oil and built a large kerosene refinery on Newtown Creek in Greenpoint. This venture became part of John D. Rockefeller's Standard Oil Trust in 1874 and Pratt, now a member of the Standard Oil board, began construction of a large Italianate villa, a project that pleased him so much that he (and later his widow) built mansions on the same street for each of their four sons. By 1878 another dozen of "the 'golden guild' of the town" resided nearby and "the Hill" became a counterpoint to "the Heights" in

Brooklyn's lexicon of lofty neighborhoods.[51] "The Slope" would only later enter the conversation.

The appearance of Charles Pratt and other Gilded Age industrialists on Clinton Hill might suggest an old wealth/new wealth cultural divide between the Heights and the Hill and with it a significant challenge to the influence of post-Puritan New Englanders so long associated with the churches and the sober lives of Hezekiah Pierrepont's original suburb. But this does not seem to have been the case. Pratt himself, who is best remembered for the Pratt Institute, the Pratt Library, and contributions to Adelphi University, was not just another rich businessman and philanthropist who happened to be from New England. During his long residence on the Hill he was a leader (and had been a founder) of the neighborhood's Emmanuel Baptist Church. When he died in 1891 Emmanuel's pastor, the Rev. Dr. John Humpstone, eulogized him in terms that could have described any number of Brooklyn's Protestant elites: "His life from first to last was the fruit of that New England Puritan spirit which has truth for its staple and righteousness for its practical aim."[52] (It might have been no coincidence that Pratt's business partner, Henry H. Rogers, claimed descent from *Mayflower* Pilgrims.) Nor did the new residents of the Hill display their wealth with more ostentation than did those on the Heights. Without distinguishing between the rich families of the two neighborhoods, the *Eagle* described the tenor of their lives: "Our people, in the main, live moderately, no matter how wealthy they are, and the general tone is one of culture rather than display." New York City is where opulence and social climbing is to be found, "and it so happens that the current of Brooklyn's social life runs with a deeper and more even flow."[53]

The Hill did not disturb Brooklyn's social and moral order in large part because it so closely replicated the suburban ethos of the Heights and the upper parts of South Brooklyn. That ethos had long been linked to Brooklyn's Protestantism in ways that were not entirely distinctive; it was a widespread assumption in Victorian America that piety and good works were nurtured in just the kind of family settings that suburban homes provided. But the extensiveness of middle- and upper-class suburbanism in Brooklyn, and the imprint of the Protestant social and moral order on many Brooklyn suburbs, was unusual if not unique.

Not all of Brooklyn's growth took the form of individual houses. A degree of population concentration in a new domestic setting for middle- and upper-class families—the apartment house—proliferated across the city during these years, even in the most suburban neighborhoods. Apartment buildings were generally four to six stories, tended to cluster on main thoroughfares and near elevated railway stations, and offered comfortable housing to people across a broad range of income levels. Brooklyn Heights contained no fewer than seven luxury apartment houses by the 1890s, all with elevator service and other amenities, and all with imposing names such as the Montague, the Pierrepont, the Grosvenor, and the Berkeley, the grandest of them being the ten-story Margaret on Columbia Heights. Several smaller houses on the Hill rivaled Heights apartments in luxury. Concentrated housing of this sort, however, on the Heights, the Hill, and in less wealthy neighborhoods, did not threaten the suburban ideal. In most of Brooklyn's suburbs, apartment buildings were small and pleasantly designed, and fit comfortably into the fabric of areas dominated by single-family homes.

Tenements were another form of concentrated housing, long associated with poverty and squalor and with the bad behavior more fortunate people expected from the poor. Squalid tenement houses continued to be found in Brooklyn, particularly in the waterfront wards. But surprisingly, as the tenement population increased, the association between multiple unit dwelling and squalor weakened. An 1878 Sanitary Commission report was upbeat in its assessment of the cleanliness and healthfulness of Brooklyn's tenements, although its definition of "tenement" as a building housing three or more families included many structures that diverged dramatically from the structures we have described on the South Brooklyn waterfront. The commission found tenements in all of Brooklyn's wards, with by far the greatest number—more than 1,000 of some 6,700—in the 16th ward, Dutchtown, which was not a poor neighborhood. Many of them must have been three-family houses, or buildings with a floor or two of apartments above a store or workshop. In Dutchtown and in the city as a whole the tenements in the commission's tabulation averaged fewer than five families per building.[54] Brooklyn did have larger buildings rented out in single accommodations of two or three rooms, but some of them were "improved," according to the *Eagle*, and "the actual difference between the improved tenement and the apartment is one of degree" only. "There are a few in crowded portions, but not enough to be considered a feature. She [Brooklyn] leaves that phase to her twin sister at the other end of the big bridge."[55]

In this era, the tenements of New York's lower east side were becoming the subjects of searing social criticism; in nonfiction such as the journalist Jacob Riis' *How the Other Half Lives*, and in fictional accounts, none more powerful than Stephen Crane's *Maggie: A Girl of the Streets*.[56] In Riis' tenements successful domestic life was a heroic achievement; in Crane's it was an impossibility. Places in Brooklyn could have achieved the same notoriety, but none did. Throughout this period Brooklyn remained, in image and reality, predominantly suburban.

Public spaces that reinforced the controlled rusticity of spacious neighborhoods became important components of Brooklyn's suburban world. The two major parks, Washington and Prospect, both built on land that was in the path of suburban rather than urban or industrial development, were magnets for new residential neighborhoods. Prospect Park, by far the most significant public park in Brooklyn, had for years been on the minds of leading Brooklynites. In 1859, in response to the success of New York's partly opened Central Park, the state legislature appointed a commission to create a plan for a large park and parade ground for Brooklyn. The commission's proposal of three large parks and five smaller ones spaced across the city did not go over well, given the cost and the question of how it should be apportioned across the rapidly expanding municipality. In 1860 the legislature appointed a new commission, with James S. T. Stranahan at its head, which proposed a single park on Prospect Hill, a lovely spot with far ranging views in all directions and attractive woods, meadows, and ponds. Some residents from distant wards groused about the location, and some about the price tag, but objections were easily overcome, and the commission quickly appointed Egbert Viele as chief engineer and de facto designer. The outbreak of the Civil War considerably slowed progress on construction, however, and by the war's end a new design within a somewhat smaller footprint was developed by Central Park's designers—Calvert Vaux and Frederick Law Olmsted. Even before its completion in 1873 Prospect Park was uniformly celebrated as a great success. Brooklynites soon boasted that it was superior to that other park across the river.[57]

The city parks were not just popular public amenities and attractive front yards for contiguous suburban neighborhoods. Brooklyn's Protestant leaders, led by Stranahan, readily subscribed to Olmsted's claims that large urban parks were healthful and morally uplifting environments, where working-class people and others not trained in "respectable" social decorum could observe and emulate the behavior of those who were.[58] The leisure activities available in the park—boating, ice skating, picnicking, listening to brass band concerts, carriage driving, walking and resting in a beautiful natural setting—contrasted with the more suspect and downright illicit pleasures of Coney Island, and were embraced as moral counterweights to dangerous amusements in the city.

Vaux and Olmsted also envisioned parkways fanning out from Prospect Park, including one that would extend to and beyond the river to provide a natural corridor between the two great parks of the two great cities. They designed and built only two, however, neither of which goes toward New York or the urban parts of Brooklyn. Eastern Parkway heads from Prospect

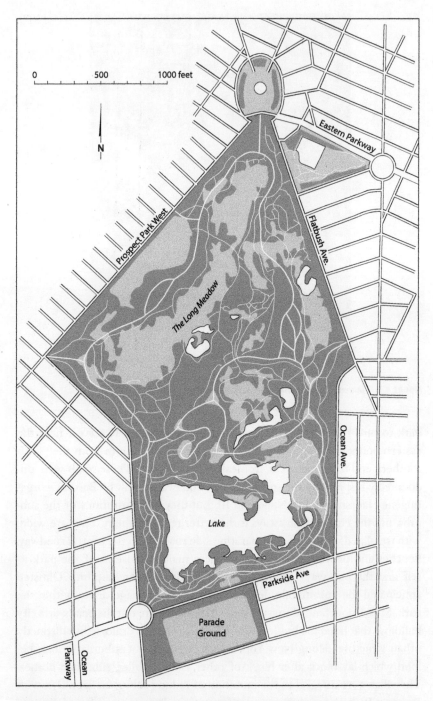

Figure 4.6. Plan for Prospect Park by Olmsted, Vaux & Co, 1871 (cartography by William L. Nelson).

Figure 4.7.   James S. T. Stranahan statue, Prospect Park (photo by Stuart Blumin).

Park toward Evergreen Cemetery and the Ridgewood Reservoir near the eastern boundary of the city; Ocean Parkway heads south from the park's southern end to the ocean at, ironically, Coney Island. These roads were undoubtedly inspired by the great Parisian boulevards built by Baron George-Eugène Haussmann and Napoleon III. But they are institutions of the suburbs, not the city, and parkways is the better term for them. They are wide, with tree-lined, grassy malls separating side roads from the central roadway. Benches and pedestrian paths make these malls extensions of the park itself and the parkways' central carriage roads (neither Vaux nor Olmsted anticipated the automobile) led naturally to the carriage drives within the park. Most important, alongside these parkways were not the beaux-arts city buildings that lined the boulevards of Paris (or the less uniform but distinctly urban structures along New York's Park Avenue), but suburban villas, behind which lay block after block of other, often smaller, suburban homes. The villas were integral to the intention of linking suburban Brooklyn with Prospect Park as a unifying secular institution. The construction of Eastern Parkway contributed to the obliteration of the once independent African

American communities of Weeksville and Carrsville, but there is no evidence of concern on the part of the promoters and planners of the larger project. Prospect Park and its parkways served the purposes and shared the moral ethos of the predominantly white City of Churches and Homes.[59]

Brooklyn's suburban development during the post–Civil War era is most notable, though, for its sheer extensiveness. A broad swath of upper- and middle-class residential neighborhoods spread across the city from the East River to the Queens County line, absorbing a large portion of Kings County's eighty-one square miles. Even more than before the war Brooklyn's townscape was dominated and defined by residences. It was in this era that the old sobriquet City of Churches was often expanded to City of Churches and Homes, suggesting that Brooklyn's brand of New England Protestantism and its suburban social world were two faces of the same thing. Did that claim retain its strength in the rapidly expanding city? Even leaving aside the increasing presence of a decidedly non-suburban industrial and commercial waterfront, and of non-Protestants within the suburbs themselves, we may question the nature and force of Brooklyn's long dominant religious leadership, especially in the more distant suburban neighborhoods. Suburban homes may have been the natural allies of Yankee Protestantism, but the spread of those homes beyond the old centers of influence presented challenges as great as the brothels and gambling dens of Coney Island.

FIGURE 4.8.   Bicyclists on the side path of Ocean Parkway, 1896 (Wallach Division Picture Collection, New York Public Library).

The incubation of religiosity in suburban homes was by no means universal; if a family was not pious the home was not going to make it so. More common among suburbanites of all stripes was the embrace of individual and family privacy as valued features of daily experience. More than in the crowded city center, the homes of the sprawling suburbs were separate enclaves, not precluding neighboring and a broader religious and civic engagement, but not encouraging them either. Rather, these forms of sociability and public responsibility occurred when they did despite an impulse to withdraw within the domestic moat and pull the drawbridge up. (Privacy was enhanced within the home, too, when steam heating allowed individual family members to withdraw from the family hearth to separate rooms.) Many suburbanites engaged in an active religious life outside the home, and for pious Protestants especially the privacy of suburban life accorded well with the doctrine that an individual's relationship with God exceeds the communion provided by the church. But privacy could lead in other directions.

When Brooklyn was a small city, it was institutionally thin.[60] The suburbanites of that era had little interest in replicating the secular institutions of New York, concentrating instead on building and maintaining the churches that served them and their families on the one day of the week they all gathered on the east side of the river. But as Brooklyn grew it acquired many new institutions, a significant number of which were offshoots of its churches. These did much to underscore religion's force, particularly among suburban women. The Brooklyn that Julian Ralph described in 1893 was "a woman's town." In the weekday absence of men from "those endless miles of dwellings," women not only ruled over "children, maids, nurses, shade trees, flowers, and pretty door-yards," but served outside the home as "the backbone of the churches, in which they sing and hold fairs." Even at the upper reaches of Brooklyn society women reached out primarily through their churches: "Instead of one crowning triumph of caste, society there is divided into church coteries, and out of these grow many sorts of little circles." They include "bowling clubs, whist clubs, euchre clubs, poker clubs, literary guilds, musical coteries, amateur dramatic companies, and dancing classes."[61] Clubs and coteries of this sort had little to do with religion, but even in these secular recreations the church remained an important source of life beyond the home.

Many women's institutions, not noted by Ralph, were closely related to the church's mission. Every church in Brooklyn had one or more auxiliary organizations in which women had a significant or exclusive role (in 1888 the *Eagle* listed nearly two hundred for a partial list of Protestant churches), and there were women's benevolent associations with looser ties to specific churches.[62] Men, too, were active in church auxiliaries, benevolent associations, temperance societies, and the YMCA. In all these ways, for both women and men, Brooklyn's institutional expansion magnified older forms of religious activity and influence in the City of Churches and Homes.

This is not to say that religion and the churches monopolized institutional life in post—Civil War Brooklyn. Organizations developed that had little or nothing to do with religion, including some that fostered exclusivity alongside and at times in competition with a more inclusive religious or civic engagement. The most significant of them were men's clubs devoted to sociability among a selective membership. Entirely independent from larger organizational networks, and lacking the regalia and rituals of the Masons, Odd Fellows, Knights of Pythias and other fraternal lodges, the new clubs also differed from the New England, St. Nicholas, and St. Patrick's societies in their possession of elegant clubhouses that provided the setting for year-round sociability. The first of these institutions in Brooklyn, the Union Club, was founded during the war "by certain of the most prominent gentlemen of the day" on principles that accorded well with the reigning Protestant ethos. Neither drinking nor gambling was permitted on the club premises, and "the 'sport' was denounced as a character to whom it would be impossible to grant the right of entry." This might seem a natural adaptation of the club idea to Brooklyn's dominant culture, but the Union Club failed on precisely these grounds. The "perfect fabric" woven in Puritan zeal was tattered by later entrants, mostly younger men, who "somehow or another, made their way into the sacred precinct." Drinking and gambling became common at the Union Club and in 1872 it disbanded, "leaving a chorus of 'bloods' to chant its requiem over their champagne cocktails."[63]

The fate of the Union Club points to a split between older members who sought sociability without violating religious principles and younger men with fewer scruples toward improper Christian behavior. A similar divide seems to have occurred, but without fatal consequences, in the Brooklyn Club, which was founded in 1865 and quickly became—and long remained—Brooklyn's most exclusive social organization. Its members were, as in the Union Club, selected from the most prominent businessmen and professionals in Brooklyn. Many were residents of Brooklyn Heights, the first president was a Pierrepont, and the clubhouse was a large and elegantly furnished affair in the heart of the Heights.[64] "The two conditions of wealth and social standing are imperatively demanded on the part of candidates applying for admission to its charmed circle," wrote the *Eagle*.[65] The Brooklyn had some of the same rules as the Union—no game of chess, whist, euchre, billiards, or pool was to occur between 11:55 on Saturday night and seven o'clock on Monday morning, and no gambling on these games was permitted at any time. The founders were at times derided as the "Old Men's Christian Association." But when younger members took control they created no serious schism in the ranks, evidently because the "bloods" among them were less impious than those at the Union, but also because the "OMCA" included men more interested in the enjoyment of exclusive sociability than in the enforcement of the club's "blue laws."[66]

Other clubs founded during this era sought the social exclusivity of the Brooklyn. The Hill had the Clinton, the Oxford, and the Lincoln, and Park Slope saw the building of a magnificent Venetian-styled clubhouse for the Montauk and the rebuilding in grand style of the Carleton. But many other types of clubs were established as well. The Long Island and the Constitution were places of resort for Democratic city and party officials (the Long Island for the higher ranks of the party, the Constitution for less exalted troops in the inner city's 5th ward), while the Union League did the same for local Republicans. The Faust was made up of journalists, actors, musicians, and artists. Poignantly for some, the old Hamilton Literary Association, no longer a young men's debating society, was transformed in 1882 into the Hamilton Club, an older men's place of quiet conversation. There was a Yacht Club and an Athletic Club, the latter occupying the old Second Presbyterian Church building on Brooklyn Heights. There were clubs in Williamsburg, South Brooklyn, Flatbush, and the distant 23rd ward. A social and literary club made up of printers was based in the 25th ward. The Columbian and the Manhasset were unusual in consisting (at first) only of Catholics and the Germania of well-to-do Germans.[67] A number of clubs were short-lived and some merged, but new foundations kept the numbers growing. In a Sunday paper at the end of 1893 the *Eagle* ran a full-page story, complete with portraits, of twenty-one presidents of Brooklyn's leading clubs.[68]

Pointing to the short life of several local clubs, the *Eagle* had claimed in 1877 that Brooklyn was not a "clubbable" city. It did not elaborate at the time, but seven years later it provided a very telling explanation: "In a community so largely domestic and so habitually religious as the Brooklyn of the past the secular club found little encouragement." Then "we really were a city of churches and the influence of the church was felt in social life as it is no longer felt."[69]

Clubs began to flourish, according to the *Eagle*, in response to the fading influence of the church, and their rise contributed further to the church's retreat. Was, then, a new generation of Brooklyn's clubmen turning away from what for many years had been the city's defining institution? Did the

FIGURE 4.9. The Montauk Club, Park Slope (photo by Stuart Blumin).

men's club encourage a pivotal transition in Brooklyn's history? A few years later, while noting that "Brooklyn is fast achieving popularity as a club city," the *Eagle* reported on the removal of South Brooklyn's Manhasset Club to palatial quarters on the corner of Clinton and Union streets. The Manhasset, an offshoot of the Young Men's Union of St. Stephen's Roman Catholic Church, installed an entirely nonsectarian and secular regime.[70] "At the present ratio of increase," the *Eagle* wrote a few weeks later in introducing the new Hanover Club, "the city of churches will, ere long, be able to lay claim to be the city of clubs."[71]

A City of Clubs did not necessarily efface a City of Churches, especially where clubs were linked to churches or adhered to religious principles. But most clubs had no religious connection and many challenged Brooklyn's traditional religious order with an alternative ethos of secular camaraderie that included violations of that order with respect to drinking, gambling, and Sabbath observance. The structure of clubs was also significant. It was private and exclusive, where the churches generally welcomed anyone who wished to attend. The two institutions could certainly co-exist and even command the loyalties of the same individuals. But these loyalties were, to some extent, competitive. The problem did not go unrecognized. At a Franklin

Literary Society debate on February 18, 1889, the subject was whether "the great social clubs are injurious to the morals of the community."[72]

A related trend of this era was the increasing separateness, assertiveness, and celebrity of Brooklyn's wealthiest and most prominent citizens. After years of insisting that Brooklyn's elites were interested in no more than a comfortable and pious life centered on their homes and churches—a "deeper and more even flow" than could be found among the opulent social climbers and claimants of New York—the *Eagle* began to cover the denizens of the Heights and the Hill as a distinct upper class. Exclusive clubs formed part of this new theme, but so too did events separate from them, such as the annual Ihpetonga and other fancy balls, private teas and dinners, and the comings and goings of elite families to Europe and fashionable domestic resorts. Begun in 1886, the Ihpetonga Ball served as a marker of who did and did not belong to Brooklyn's high society. "The proof is simple," wrote the *Eagle*. "If a person is in good society he goes to the Ihpetonga. If he is not he cannot get there."[73] Increasingly, the *Eagle* covered "Society Events" and by the mid-1890s the paper presented a regular page, "Brooklyn Society," featuring balls, weddings, receptions, and the comings and goings of the right people on the Heights, the Hill, and Park Slope: "Miss Maxwell, Miss Bowers, Miss Kenyon and Miss Suydam are Park Slope girls, and should give that section a winter of gayety, though they will frequently be seen in Heights parlors. . . . Debutante teas have, in great measure, been the events of the week that has just passed. . . . Mrs. E. H. Litchfield introduces Miss Marion Litchfield at 2 Montague Terrace."[74]

Also keeping up with the times was a new journal, titled *Brooklyn Life*, which bore the subtitle, *A Journal of Society Literature Drama and the Clubs*. The first issue, on March 8, 1890, announced its commitment to "the freshest gossip of society, club life, the theatre and politics," and presented the first of its "Portrait Gallery" of notable citizens: Mr. Arthur M. Hatch, a descendant of "sturdy Puritans," a partner in the New York brokerage firm of W. T. Hatch and Sons, and a "prominent figure in Brooklyn society" who recently organized the latest Ihpetonga Ball. "Among the Clubs" followed this portrait page. Mixed in with these recurring features were numerous pages of jokes and cartoons poking gentle fun at fashionable men and women.[75] Clearly and unapologetically aimed at high society readers, this journal remained in print for forty years.

It is interesting that *Brooklyn Life* chose for its first portrait a society leader who was also a descendant of "sturdy Puritans" and a member of Richard Storrs' Church of the Pilgrims. But despite this gesture to Yankee religiosity, the tone of *Brooklyn Life* was distinctly secular. Its editorial stance was often at odds with Sabbatarianism, the temperance movement, and some church-men's continuing opposition to the theater. Illustrated ads for luxury goods underscored an editorial embrace of the good life. The *Eagle*, too, increased its advertising during these years, though with less of a focus on expensive products. This was in part because Brooklyn's retail marketplace was itself expanding, with large dry goods and department stores such as Abraham & Straus, Frederick Loeser & Co., and Liebmann Bros. joining Brooklyn's origi-nal large retail dry goods store, Journeay & Burnham, on Fulton Street.[76]

Commercial expansion, on the ground and in the press, was hardly unique to Brooklyn. But the change in Brooklyn was more dramatic than in other American cities. It was so long in coming because Manhattan retail shops were within easy reach, a competitive situation unknown in other large cit-ies; and within a short period of time so many more customers appeared for the goods that defined and enabled the middle-class suburban life. Although Brooklynites did not suddenly turn away from their churches to worship Mammon at Abraham & Straus, elements of Brooklyn's secular life were expanding, along with the more complex array of possibilities that define any large city.

Commercialism was not confined to Fulton Street; nor was it solely di-rected toward the acquisition of material goods. As in any city, the perform-ing arts, sports, and other amusements competed for Brooklynites' attention and dollars. As late as 1857 the *Eagle* had bemoaned the absence of them in Brooklyn: "There is no other city in this country of the same population as Brooklyn as destitute of public amusements. There are no theaters, no concerts—except few and far between—nothing except courses of lectures, which have become a bore and are about to be discontinued."[77] The Philhar-monic Society and the Academy of Music soon addressed this complaint, at least for the wealthy, the academy becoming "a veritable home to Brooklyn society—yes, and its nursery, too; for up to this time there was hardly any-thing that might be regarded as organized society in the city. There were church circles, and neighborhood circles, and family circles," but virtually nothing beyond them to bring certain kinds of people together.[78]

Secular institution building did extend well beyond the Academy of Music and served a larger population than the embryonic upper class. In 1863, only two years after the Academy of Music opened with a hesitant policy toward theatrical productions, an elegant Park Theater appeared on Fulton Street just across from City Hall Park. Within a few years half a dozen theaters in Brooklyn offered serious drama, minstrel shows, and variety shows that catered to all classes of people. Lyceum lectures faded for a time but revived as evening entertainment for some, including working men and women.[79]

Organized sports—baseball and horse racing above all—provided daytime entertainment on days other than Sunday, a limitation that reminds us that religious leaders still cast a watchful eye over Brooklynites' use of leisure time. No church, however, appears to have supervised or objected to the tours of Green-Wood Cemetery offered by hack drivers, who delighted in pointing out the graves of murderers and their victims, an amusement not anticipated by Henry Pierrepont and Green-Wood's other founders.[80]

The growth of the theater in Brooklyn is particularly notable, given the long history of opposition from churches. That opposition appears to have become somewhat idiosyncratic. In 1869 the *Eagle* scorned the efforts of Rev. Mr. Boole, "a sensation preacher of the Methodist persuasion," to shut down Williamsburg's Odeon. "After he has entirely closed the Odeon," the *Eagle* suggested, "he may turn his attention to . . . the Academy of Music, and turn that building into a conventicle, preach down the Park Theatre, Hooley's Opera House, Donnelly's Olympic, and all the side shows." Noting the Methodist Church's practice of rotating ministers, the paper suggested New York, "a terribly wicked city," as the Rev. Boole's next assignment. Moreover, and ominously for Brooklyn, "In New York they have been turning churches into theatres, reversing Boole's programme entirely."[81] The *Eagle* subsequently proposed a more serious solution: "The church and the stage should be co-workers rather than antagonists," placing both on the same plane, perhaps not in a way either entirely appreciated: "Give us, O preachers and players, good, genuine, honest, legitimate work! Avoid, each of you in his specialty, the meretricious and the sensational, which degrade your several arts, corrupt your professions, and weaken your influence—or, what is worse, strengthens it for evil."[82] The church and the theater could and should be not only partners but co-equals in the fight against evil, a proposition that in an earlier time would have been inconceivable in Brooklyn.

Another sensational preacher was not nearly as easy to satirize as the Rev. Boole. Not long after assuming his post in Brooklyn, Henry Ward Beecher was invited to address the Boston Mercantile Library. His speech on "Amusements," in which he argued there should be more rather than less of them, caused a scandal in Boston, but was more popular closer to home. On other occasions Beecher railed against the theater as the devil's playground, but here declared that theater was not intrinsically evil but was too often driven and surrounded by evil people. Rid the theater of the pimps, prostitutes, and producers of salacious plays, and it becomes an innocent amusement and a site of possible moral uplift. Beecher had no quarrel, either, with the theater's commercial character. He embraced money making as a potentially positive force, and without qualms or apology pursued a profitable career of his own in lecturing, writing, and editing—and even as an endorser of consumer products, including Pears' Soap.[83]

Other Brooklyn preachers and Yankee Protestants more generally, were not so quick to recognize an alliance between commercialism and the church's mission.[84] At the very least, department stores and theaters were competitors for people's attention and could lead to enthusiasms that did not stem from religious feeling or belief. Sports were another competitor and became increasingly so as three horseracing tracks were built on Coney Island and the Gravesend mainland, and baseball developed as an amateur and professional sport. A club sport before the Civil War, baseball was quickly embraced in the press as America's national game. Its breeding ground was the New York metropolis (not Cooperstown), and Brooklyn was a full participant, forming at least twenty amateur clubs by 1858.[85] The clubs were private organizations, but their games were reported in the newspapers and lots of people attended them. Upward of five thousand attended a three-game series played in 1858 in Queens, between leading players selected from clubs in New York and Brooklyn. Tickets cost fifty cents, and the proceeds of this amateur event were donated to charity. This time, Brooklyn fans did not have to "wait 'til next year." After the New York team came back in late innings to win the first game, Brooklyn won the last two by wide margins. The *Eagle* reported after the first game that "the assembly was of the most respectable character. It was composed, in the main, of staid citizens, sober business men of various callings." A "large number of fancy characters" attended the second game but apparently did little betting.[86] None of these games, nor any of the regular games played by the clubs, occurred on Sunday.

After the war baseball evolved toward professionalism. A National Association of Professional Base Ball Players was founded in 1871, and three Brooklyn clubs joined it just a year later. One of them, the Mutuals, became a charter member of the new National League in 1876, although the team did not last the year. The Brooklyn Grays, briefly renamed the Atlantics, joined the American Association in 1884, and then, with the charming name Bridegrooms, moved on to the National League in 1890, winning the league's pennant in their first year. This team, in an odd homage to the city's ever-growing transit system (and pedestrians' need to dodge its ubiquitous trolleys), would ultimately be named the Brooklyn Dodgers. A popular activity for amateurs, baseball was praised as healthy and invigorating exercise and recreation for the young men who played it. Professional baseball partially transformed it into an amusement for the masses, however, something to watch and follow in the newspapers. As a spectator sport, even more than as a game to be played, it became another secular distraction in the City of Churches.

The prohibition of Sunday baseball was by no means trivial, especially to professional teams that had to forego their most profitable day of the week. In 1890 only one professional league, the American Association, scheduled games on Sunday. Its Brooklyn team played home games just over the city line in Ridgewood, Queens, without any interference from authorities on either side of the boundary. That summer the Brooklyn members of the Players' League attended a special Sunday service in their honor at Christ Church on Bedford Avenue, the Rev. Dr. Darlington pointing out with satisfaction that the league "had many opportunities to increase its wealth by Sunday ball playing, but out of respect for the day had always refused."[87] The Rev. Darlington was no doubt less pleased to know that certain amateur baseball clubs in Brooklyn had no such scruples. Near the northern edge of Red Hook regular Sunday contests drew upward of five or six thousand spectators, who did not pay an admission fee but were encouraged to enjoy a beer or two at the nearby saloons, which in all likelihood supplied the $10 or $20 stake that went to the winning team. "There is no church in the vicinity," wrote the *Eagle*, "and most of the residents not being at all Puritanical, there are no complaints." The police did not interfere with the game or the saloons.[88] No force was strong enough to overturn the Sabbatarian laws that had prohibited Sunday ball playing in Brooklyn since the earliest days of the incorporated village. But there were places in the city, and just beyond it, where those laws, as well as the old Yankee Puritanism that inspired them, were ignored. The offenders were not merely those who played the game. In far greater numbers they were people, no doubt including some Yankees, who came to watch.

Attending a Sunday afternoon baseball game was less of a violation than betting on a cockfight in a downtown stable or a bare-knuckle boxing match in a remote field. Enjoying some of the more innocent amusements of Coney Island, shopping in a fancy department store, attending the theater or a weekday ballgame, or reading about these activities in a local newspaper, was not a violation at all, but merely the act of private citizens availing themselves of the diverse offerings of the big city Brooklyn had become. Some of these offerings enhanced the sense of belonging to a larger community. But experiencing them accorded well with the withdrawal into private space that was a feature of Brooklyn's post–Civil War suburban sprawl.

As Brooklynites experienced these pleasures and opportunities, some of them began to question (and absent themselves from) the occasional transformation of city streets from their usual role—conveying persons and goods between homes, stores, docks, factories, workshops, churches, and places of amusement—into sites of public celebration. As in cities and towns across America, Brooklyn had for years celebrated the Fourth of July with parades that occupied many of the city's major streets for hours at a time. It also extended the privilege each March 17 to its oldest, largest, and politically most powerful ethnic minority on the traditional birthday of Ireland's patron saint. Additionally, and uniquely, residents of Brooklyn took to the streets near the end of the school year with Anniversary Day marches of thousands of children from the evangelical Sunday schools. This tradition endured and was generally applauded as a fitting celebration for the City of Churches, despite frequent criticism of the physical demands the marches made on small children and the continuing exclusion of Roman Catholics, Unitarians, and Universalists.[89] In 1897, in contemplation of the sixty-eighth celebration of Anniversary Day, the last Brooklyn conducted as an independent city, the *Eagle* looked forward to a time when "it will not be called upon to note that the sinful Unitarian children and the mistaken Roman Catholic children and the erroneous Universalist children have been debarred from orthodox ice cream and evangelical cake and that the pleasure of walking under Calvinistic trees and playing on Arminian grass has been denied to them."[90]

Missing from criticisms of this sort was any suggestion that the parade of Sunday school children should not occur at all.[91] St. Patrick's Day parades were also generally accepted as legitimate preemptions of public space, although the history of the event was complicated by a schism in the Irish Catholic community that resulted in no parade in some years and two separate parades in others. A different kind of complication was the extension of the privilege to other ethnic groups such as Irish Protestants, Germans, and, eventually, Italians. In 1871 a long letter appeared in the *Eagle* protesting the use of the city's streets for such parades because their ethnic and political character increased antagonisms between groups (Irish Catholics and Protestants especially), and slowed the development among immigrants of an American identity. "Far better . . . if street parades were abolished altogether, or strictly limited to national or municipal objects, in which all our citizens, native and adopted, could equally sympathize and participate."[92]

The celebration that clearly met this criterion was the annual Fourth of July parade. But this parade had been dispensed with by the city, along with the patriotic oration and the recitation of the Declaration of Independence. There had been a parade in 1865, but during the following two years the public celebration of the Fourth was limited to fireworks, the firing of cannons, and the decoration of public buildings. When the parade returned in 1868 objections were raised by militiamen who were forced to spend a holiday from work marching in woolen uniforms at the hottest time of the year.

Let them have "one day in the year which they may call entirely their own," wrote one sympathizer.[93] The Common Council complied. There was no parade in 1869, and in the following years the local press reported mostly on "the arrangements for celebrating the Fourth of July by private associated citizens."[94] Vast numbers of citizens left town for Coney Island and other resorts. Those who stayed behind enjoyed picnics, band concerts in the park, baseball games, and gatherings at home. Private celebration of the Fourth was probably for the best, concluded the *Eagle* in anticipation of the 1880 holiday.[95]

At least one of the institutional changes in post–Civil War Brooklyn did nothing to enhance the private amusements of suburban families or the exclusive sociability of upper-class men and women. On January 27, 1869, the Rev. Abram Newkirk Littlejohn, rector of the Episcopal Church of the Holy Trinity on Brooklyn Heights, was installed as bishop of the diocese of Long Island. "Brooklyn has long been known as the City of Churches," wrote the *Eagle*, not for the first time, and now it is a cathedral city, a See of the Episcopal Church of America. This seminal event allowed the paper to gloat about Brooklyn's significance as a religious center. The city continued to add new churches—nineteen in the previous year—and to attract distinguished clergy to its pulpits. Other cities might have one or two outstanding orators and theologians, "but taken as a whole, it is conceded now in the religious circles of every denomination, that Brooklyn leads the American pulpit, and that in the City of Churches throbs the brain as well as the heart of religion on the American Continent." Best of all, its thriving churches and its distinguished clergy account for "the almost entire freedom of Brooklyn from the disgraceful features of almost every other large city in the world."[96]

The *Eagle* found other occasions to praise the quality of Brooklyn's clergy and note the salutary influence of the church on its people. "Wherever else religion may have lost its hold," it wrote six years after Bishop Littlejohn settled into his new office, "in this city it has gained in strength—a fact doubtless due to the remarkable ability of Brooklyn's ministers as a class."[97] And yet, a far different strain of writing, by newspapermen and clergy alike, paints a darker picture of religion in Brooklyn—of half-empty churches, declining clerical influence, and unseemly attempts to reverse these losses. We have already seen the *Eagle*, while writing of the influence of secular men's clubs, refer wistfully to a time "when we really were a city of churches and the influence of the church was felt in social life as it is no longer felt."

The complaint that churches were half-empty on the Sabbath seems unexpected, given the rapid rise in Brooklyn's population. In 1874, the number of persons per church in Brooklyn was approximately 2,100, about 22 percent more than the 1,734 for 1855.[98] Brooklyn still had significantly more churches in relation to its population than New York City, but the pace of church construction had clearly not kept pace with population growth. It would have been a remarkable achievement if it had. According to the state census of 1875, Brooklyn's houses of worship could accommodate about 38 percent of the city's total population, a significantly higher proportion than New York's 28 percent, but hardly suggestive of a surfeit of seating.[99] Of course, we cannot expect to have found anything approaching universal attendance, even in a place with Brooklyn's reputation for religiosity. And we do not know how widespread church attendance really was in Brooklyn (or how many churches spread congregants out by conducting multiple Sabbath services) during this era or in earlier times when few clergy complained about preaching to empty pews. We do know that such complaints were common in the post–Civil War era and that Protestant clergy and pious laymen regarded the existence in Brooklyn of a vast unchurched population as a gravely urgent issue.

Some, including Bishop Littlejohn, blamed the common practice of selling and renting pews, which kept away people who could not afford the price or felt humiliated by the sexton's directing them to inferior seating or an unoccupied pew paid for by someone else. "Knock the doors off the pews," he argued, "and discard the little plated tablets which indicate ownership of a section of the House of God."[100] Others added that large numbers of poor people and young clerical workers at the start of a business career were intimidated by wealthy congregants who came to church to socialize and show off fine clothes. Still others pointed to Brooklynites who worked on Sundays, had family responsibilities that kept them at home, were simply too tired after six days of hard work, or were inclined to practice their religion in private. "I don't always go to mass, but I pray a lot to the Lord," explains Mimi in Puccini's *La Bohème*, and no doubt many in Brooklyn said (or perhaps even sang) the same.

More troubling were explanations that looked beyond the irregular church attendance of religious people to the rise of secularism, religious skepticism, and open disbelief. In an article referring specifically to Methodists, the *Eagle* observed a "profound change" in popular belief leading to "doubts and questions about the Old Testament, the miracles, plenary inspiration and other dogmas which were seldom asked and never answered in the days of Wesley and Whitefield."[101] This was, after all, the age of Darwin, not the Methodist founders, and of other advances in science that raised doubts and questions for some people, including those brought up in Biblical faith communities.

Was faith itself declining in the City of Churches and with it the influence of Brooklyn's eminent clergy? Half-filled churches seemed a symptom of a deeper problem that could not be solved by extinguishing pew rentals.

The problem itself may have been somewhat overstated or, in the matter of church attendance, misunderstood. In most identifiable examples of empty pews and financial unsustainability the church in question was located in one of Brooklyn's older neighborhoods, where the population was growing slowly if at all, ethnoreligious change in the local population made certain churches lose while others gained, or old schisms (over theology or pastoral practice) led to small congregations even before the decline of potential adherents.[102] The three wards of Brooklyn's original downtown grew by only 5 percent during the last four decades of the nineteenth century, while the city as a whole quadrupled. Within those inner wards some streets lost population to commercial and industrial expansion. In 1882, when Methodists tried to consolidate three downtown churches, this population decline (exacerbated by homes condemned and removed for the approach to the bridge) created the attendance problem, not an identifiable crisis of faith among those who remained in the neighborhood.[103] Some of those no longer filling these downtown churches may well have joined newer Methodist churches in Bedford, Bushwick, and East New York. As Presbyterian pastor J. Winthrop Hageman explained in 1889: "The Protestant Church is on wheels, running after the people who will support it. By the moving out of the population old churches are becoming stranded."[104]

A year earlier Rev. Hageman had offered a detailed (if somewhat tortured) rebuttal of the complaint that churches were losing attendees. Churchgoing in Brooklyn, he maintained, stood at about 63 percent of possible attendees, or even 80 percent if one excluded "the 'incorrigibles' whom the church cannot by hook or crook get hold of." These numbers are almost certainly too high, and in any event the chorus of complaints about half-empty churches did not stop. And when Hageman concluded that "the religious condition of Brooklyn to-day is better than it has ever been," he pointed to the good work of churches in home and foreign missions rather than to widespread Sabbath attendance.[105] Still, his optimism was perhaps a mild antidote to the prevailing gloom.

Rev. Hageman was joined at times by the *Eagle*. Noting the plan for a brief religious service (to be led by Bishop Littlejohn) at the ceremony opening the Brooklyn Bridge, the *Eagle* acknowledged "it may be deemed absurd if not superstitious to invoke the divine blessing upon the work in the presence of at least a respectable minority of atheists and agnostics." But never mind: "Considering that the vast majority of our citizens . . . still believe in a God, an invocation and a hymn of praise to Him would scarcely seem inappropriate. . . . Brooklyn is a theistic city," and the only expected complaint will come from sectarians who object to an Episcopal service rather than one from their own denomination.[106] Three years later the *Eagle* provided a similar confirmation of Brooklyn as a city of believers, again in the face of "the prevailing talk about the decay of religion and of the religious sentiment, about the growth of agnosticism, and about the rising power of science." Most of its readers, the editor claimed, believe "there is something good in religion," and "if the City of Brooklyn is to be kept right . . . the churches will not only be cared for, but made to keep pace in their progress with the progress of the city."[107]

Believing "there is something good in religion" may not have been a stronger answer to agnosticism and the embrace of science than Rev. Hageman's calculations were to perceptions of declining church attendance. But arguments of this sort did, like Hageman's, at least complicate an issue otherwise left entirely to those who claimed the influence of the church in Brooklyn was declining, a claim that was frequently found as well as rebutted in the *Eagle*. Vacillation between levels of hope and gloom on this critically important subject is perhaps not surprising, considering that the appraisal was not a simple one to make.

The paper was somewhat more consistent in its treatment of the more sensational style of preaching offered by some as an antidote to declension. In 1875 a month-long revival conducted by America's leading itinerant evangelist, Dwight Lyman Moody, and his assistant, the gospel singer Ira Sankey, drew nightly crowds of six thousand people to an auditorium set up in a downtown Brooklyn skating rink. The *Eagle* approved of their attempts to reach people who were not attending any church. Moody and Sankey left town, however, without firm evidence that they had converted many unbelievers or deepened the commitment of churchgoers.[108]

Brooklyn had its own evangelist in Thomas DeWitt Talmage, who preached in a more sensational style than Moody. The *Eagle*, for the most part, approved of him too. Talmage's base was the Brooklyn Tabernacle, where he regularly drew crowds that rivaled those that flocked to Plymouth Church to hear the theatrical preaching of Henry Ward Beecher. Perhaps sensing the need to outdo Beecher, Talmage reportedly opened one sermon by sprinting across the raised Tabernacle stage. As he reached the end and his audience gasped at the certainty of his hurtling into the crowd, he leaped upward, landed safely at the edge, and shouted, "Young man you are rushing toward a precipice!" "By many he was declared a pulpit clown and a mountebank," wrote the *New York Times* in 1902 on the occasion of Talmage's death, but "his preaching became the religious sensation of the time."[109] A back page story for the *Times*, Talmage's death was a front-page headline for the *Eagle*, even though the preacher had left his Brooklyn pulpit (and stage) for Washington, DC, eight years earlier.[110]

The *Eagle* approved of Talmage and Beecher mostly because they consistently drew large crowds, just as Moody did, and seemed to keep the church alive and relevant, even while departing from the more sober conduct of a Richard Storrs. But in emphasizing performance over denominational doctrine these preachers also threatened the old order. In an 1882 article assessing Brooklyn's clergy, Mary L. L. Bradford praised Storrs and other conservative preachers but gave short shrift to Beecher and was downright hostile to Talmage, whose influence, she argued, "cannot be considered as part of the living organism of the city. His activity is not functional, and is in the nature of an excrescence upon the body politic." He should be dismissed "rather as a sensation than as a motive power in the religious world of Brooklyn."[111]

FIGURE 4.10.   The Brooklyn Tabernacle (Milstein Division, New York Public Library).

In one respect the *Eagle* was entirely consistent. It used forests of news-print to highlight religion as a topic of primary importance to the City of Churches. Each Monday the paper's lead story summarized what had hap-pened in Brooklyn's churches on the previous day, and on most other days religious affairs occupied a good deal of columnar space. The Sunday paper contained a religious section along with potentially distracting summertime baseball box scores. And if its most frequent assessment was that the influ-ence of the clergy had in fact waned, the *Eagle* was not bashful in stepping up to fill the void: "The mantle of prophecy has fallen on the press; the Sunday EAGLE is regarded by the Christian people of Brooklyn as an Encyclical, and the alleviation of consciences is no inconsiderable part of our editorial function."[112]

The press had always been an important voice for organized religion in Brooklyn, and the laity, within and beyond the churches, had played a sig-nificant role in transporting religious values into the city's secular affairs. If the personal presence of the old Yankee leaders no longer reached as easily to the peripheries of the city, the movements these leaders had generated—temperance, Sunday schools, and others—continued to thrive, and Sabbatar-ian and licensing laws were still on the books and generally if imperfectly enforced. The extent to which the Yankee leaders of the old order were able to assert their moral authority and political influence in the face of new chal-lenges may be difficult to judge, but the continuing presence of that authority is beyond questioning. "City of Churches" continued to express that presence, even when tinged with nostalgia for an age that seemed to be slipping by.

During the latter decades of the nineteenth century the most active and visible of the New England-born Protestants to face challenges to their moral authority was a newcomer, and not at all the old type of Brooklyn leader. Born in 1844 in New Canaan, Connecticut, Anthony Comstock came to New York, as so many had before him, as a young man looking to climb the lad-der to a lucrative commercial career. By 1871 he had climbed high enough to marry, and established his nest in Brooklyn on Grand Avenue in Clinton Hill. He soon became a member of the Clinton Avenue Congregational Church. Comstock had joined the Sons of Temperance before he left Connecticut, and in his teens developed a penchant for vigorous freelancing in his enforce-ment of what he (and sometimes the law) considered immoral activity. In one instance he broke into a New Canaan barroom at night, opened the taps, emptied the bottles, and left a sign warning the owners that if they didn't close their business the building would be destroyed. The owners left town.

In New York City this penchant blossomed into a crusade against illegal drinking, gambling, prostitution, abortion, contraception, free love, and, most famously, the production and distribution of what Comstock considered to be salacious books, magazines, and works of visual art. In 1873 he became secretary and de facto head of the newly founded New York Society for the Suppression of Vice. Before the year was out he coauthored an "Act for the Suppression of Trade in, and Circulation of, Obscene Literature and Articles of Immoral Use," known throughout the land as the Comstock Law. Comstock was appointed an inspector and special agent at the Post Office, a position he used for thirty years to prevent the mailing of "obscene" materials.[113]

Comstock's most significant activity in Brooklyn was in Coney Island, where he focused mostly on illegal racetrack gambling. He was not popular there. One day in August 1884, a group of Kings County deputy sheriffs approached a "pool selling" club house on a civil matter that was quickly misinterpreted as an anti-gambling raid. One of the deputies resembled the famous reformer. A scuffle ensued and "the crowd which filled the place set up the cry, 'Comstock! Comstock!' and scampered helter skelter for the doors and windows." Those who remained gathered around the supposed Comstock and cried, "'Kill him!' 'Slug him' 'Hang the ___ ___ ___'!" The mistake was quickly corrected, and the deputy was spared. A witness reported: "If that had really been Comstock I don't think he would have left Coney Island alive, and his double would have fared badly but for a friendly voice saying 'That ain't Comstock.'"[114]

Anthony Comstock would serve nicely as an emblem of the decline of Yankee influence in the City of Churches if the narrative of declension were clear and uncontested. But as we have seen there is evidence of endurance as well as decline—of the continuing influence of the Lows, the Stranahans, and others among Brooklyn's lay leadership, and of the clergy as a body. Mary Bradford was particularly eloquent in her description of Brooklyn's cultural continuity. "The singleness of aim, the simplicity of life and the intensity of moral earnestness which characterize the beginnings of municipal life are still deeply felt in Brooklyn," she wrote. "The old time power in certain classes of society is still theirs, and the law givers of the social and intellectual life of the city sit in their time honored seats." Of the clergy, "nowhere else," not even in New England, are they "so dominating a force in the social and civil life of a community." If Beecher was tarnished and Talmage a mere sensation, dozens of others carried on the good work of decades past. "Brooklyn," she concluded, "is the city not only of churches, but of what gives churches their worth, a place where a high plane of living is possible, because the values by which life is tested are other than material ones."[115]

Bradford wrote about the Brooklyn she knew and cared deeply about, but in doing so she excluded such uncomfortable facts as emptier churches, the

FIGURE 4.11.   Anthony Comstock (Chronicle/Alamy Stock Photo).

spread of the city to places physically and perhaps culturally remote from the old centers of influence, and the development of a wide array of secular opportunities that included and even promoted those material values she rejected as measures of the good life. Nor is there anything in her essay that recognizes the strains that class and ethnic diversity placed upon Brooklyn's old pattern of influence. Her insistence on the endurance of that pattern is not easily dismissed. But it needs to find a proper context in the bigger and more diverse city Brooklyn had become.

CHAPTER 5

Newcomers

Julian Ralph's characterization of Brooklyn in 1893 as a vast suburb was shaped by his view of thousands of men crossing Brooklyn Bridge after a day's work in New York City—a nightly return to their wives and "the only female among our cities—the sister city to New York." But Ralph also reports from a different vantage point: "There is a view of Brooklyn which gives it the appearance of a smoky seat of manufactures. It is obtained from the east side of New York, looking over at the great sugar-refineries which tower like Rhenish castles beside the swift East River." This view led him to tabulate Brooklyn's industrial might—more than ten thousand manufacturing firms employing more than one hundred thousand workers—and a catalog of "very large hat-works, chemical-works, foundries and iron-works, candy factories, coffee and spice mills, and boot and shoe factories." Less easily characterized as female, this Brooklyn did not interest him. His essay quickly pivots to Brooklyn's excellent schools, the natural product of a "city of homes," and again of women's influence: "Whatever a mother would concern herself about is what thrives in Brooklyn, and everything else is poor or despairing."[1]

Ten thousand workshops and factories speak as much of dynamism as of despair, even if few of them resembled Rhenish castles. Many were small companies of men in the construction trades—carpenters, masons, painters, plasterers, plumbers—called upon to build homes, shops, churches, wharves,

FIGURE 5.1.   Havermeyers & Elder sugar refinery, Williamsburg (General Research Division, New York Public Library).

and factories for a rapidly growing city; others were small shops of bakers, blacksmiths, and custom tailors serving the neighborhoods construction workers had built. Still others were cigar makers, seamstresses, other artisans, and semiskilled outworkers who toiled in tenement sweatshops to feed goods into large networks of wholesaling and retailing on both sides of the river. Factories came in all sizes, and some industries combined factories, independent artisans, and outworkers. In boots and shoes, for example, Brooklyn at the end of the century was home to forty-four factories employing 3,500 workers and 1,250 shops with 1,260 proprietors and only 535 hired hands.[2] Many of the larger factories, including the sugar refineries, clustered along and near the waterfront, which now extended north to the city boundary with Queens County at Newtown Creek—Astral Oil was there—and south to and along Gowanus Bay and up the Gowanus Canal. Among the departures from this pattern, the Knox Hat Company factory, reputedly the largest hat factory in the world, was located well inland at the boundary of the suburban neighborhoods of Prospect Heights and Crown Heights.

The growth of manufacturing in Brooklyn was part of a larger story of industrialization in the United States. Once a minor contributor to a predominantly agricultural economy, manufacturing became the American economy's leading sector by the end of the nineteenth century, accounting for more than half the value of the nation's vast economic output. Brooklyn contributed substantially to this industrial revolution.[3] During the last four

FIGURE 5.2. The waterfront below Brooklyn Heights, 1906 (Wallach Division Picture Collection, New York Public Library).

decades of the century its industrial sector increased tenfold, outpacing the sevenfold growth in the entire country. In 1860 about 15 percent of working-age Brooklyn men held industrial jobs. By 1900 that ratio had increased to about 25 percent. Among women the increase was from 1 percent to 7 percent.[4] If Brooklyn's factories and workshops failed to overwhelm the City of Churches and Homes, along with its docks and warehouses they continued a robust transformation of the East River (and New York Bay) waterfront, sallying beyond it on occasion into the suburban world that seemed so distant from its purposes.

While Brooklyn's industrial sector was expanding so rapidly, the city's population grew more diverse, continuing a trend that began before the Civil War. In the 1840s and 1850s immigrants compelled to work for low wages helped stimulate the take-off phase of the city's waterfront development.[5] Many things contributed to this critical moment in the economic history of Brooklyn (and the United States), including a new rail and canal system of inland transportation that expanded markets at reduced costs, the stabilization of banking after the 1837–43 depression, and the implementation of more centralized modes of production. But just as crucial to industrial growth was the arrival of large numbers of Irish workers, their potato crops having failed just when American manufacturers and shippers were in particular need of cheap labor. German immigrants supplied some of this labor as well, although many arrived in America with enough skill and capital to operate their own small workshops.

Post–Civil War manufacturers continued to rely on immigrant labor, and for some years much of it came from familiar sources. Before the 1880s, Germany was the largest source of immigrants to the United States, and Great Britain was second, although Ireland probably would have ranked ahead of Britain if records reflected the ethnic Irish among the latter's emigrants.

FIGURE 5.3.   The Gowanus Canal (Milstein Division, New York Public Library).

After 1880, though, new sources added to and even surpassed the old. Scandinavia contributed as many immigrants to the United States as Ireland. Poland, Russia, and other countries of Eastern Europe outpaced them both, as did Italy during the 1890s.[6] The impact of these new immigrants on Brooklyn, however, would occur mainly after the turn of the new century. As late as the 1890s, the pattern of arrival and settlement was much as it had been for more than half a century.

The familiarity of the immigrant stream during the post–Civil War period helped calm native Protestants in Brooklyn, as did the partial assimilation of earlier immigrants and their American-born children. The proportion of the foreign-born within the local population actually declined from 39 percent in 1860 to 30 percent at the end of the century. (In 1855, near the end of the major burst of migration from Ireland and Germany, it was 46 percent.) But as the immigrant proportion decreased, the second generation expanded. By 1900 the native-born population with foreign-born parents constituted more than 40 percent of Brooklyn's population.[7] Ethnicity, if not place of birth, set them apart.

Within a brief period the Anglo and Dutch Protestants of Brooklyn had become a distinct minority in the City of Churches. Nonetheless, their dwindling presence did not fuel a revival of the nativist and anti-Catholic disturbances that had characterized the antebellum era. Surprisingly, perhaps, xenophobia and Protestant anxiety did not dominate in politics or public discourse, or on the streets of the city. At least temporarily, they had lost some of their power.

The presence of immigrants and second-generation Americans in Brooklyn's sprawling suburbs is an interesting aspect of this story of relatively calm interethnic relations. That presence can be traced in large part through the founding of Brooklyn's Catholic churches. Before 1860 twenty Catholic churches were built in Brooklyn, mostly in the downtown wards, Brooklyn Heights, and the 6th ward, the latter to serve the mostly Irish neighborhoods on and near the South Brooklyn waterfront. Five of these churches, though, among the last of those built, were located much further from the waterfront in emerging suburbs, a pattern that soon became pronounced. Between 1860 and 1900 the Diocese of Brooklyn more than quadrupled its parishes by building sixty-two new churches, forty-five of them in the new suburbs. Twenty-eight of these churches were built during the last two decades of the century. The Catholic Church was tracking—and in many instances leading—its faithful to Bedford, Bushwick, Flatbush, East New York, and Bay Ridge.[8]

Many of Brooklyn's suburban immigrants were domestic servants, living in houses they could not afford. But there were householders as well, especially among second-generation ethnics, and especially in the more modest suburban neighborhoods. Foreign-born householders, to be sure, were still more concentrated in the older wards, where many, particularly the Irish, worked at low-paying, waterfront jobs.[9] In a pattern similar to pre–Civil War days, Irish immigrants were overrepresented only in the least skilled occupations, while the German-born were overrepresented in skilled neighborhood trades such as baking and butchering and, to a lesser extent, in factory work and retail storekeeping.[10]

There was now, however, a greater occupational diversity within these groups, including the Irish. As in other American cities, immigrants achieved success in business, politics, and social and cultural leadership. Politics was a route upward for Thomas Kinsella, who emigrated from Ireland as a boy, became a printer in the upstate New York town of Cambridge, moved to Brooklyn in 1858, and ascended from typesetter to editor of the *Brooklyn Daily Eagle*, a position he held until his death in 1884. From his editorial chair, Kinsella functioned as a leader of Brooklyn's Democratic Party and was rewarded with terms in Congress and as local postmaster.[11] For Frederick A. Schroeder, a German immigrant, politics was not a route but a destination after a successful business career. Schroeder learned the trade of cigar making as a youth, opened a cigar factory in Williamsburgh, and became a tobacco importer. He was also a founder and long-time president of the Germania Savings Bank, which gave him a significant Dutchtown base for political office. He won his race for city comptroller in 1871, was elected mayor in 1875, and later served in the New York State Senate.[12] Dutch-born Martin Kalbfleisch followed a similar path, settling in New York as a young manufacturer of paint before moving to Greenpoint, where he opened a chemical plant. Elected alderman in 1854, Kalbfleisch became Brooklyn's first non-Anglo-Protestant mayor in 1862, went to Congress in 1863, and served as mayor again from 1867 to 1871.[13]

The success story of Charles M. Higgins, who was born in Ireland in 1854 and brought to America as a boy of six, is perhaps the most interesting of this era. Charles and his family settled into the South Brooklyn waterfront, where his father worked as a laborer and his mother as a housekeeper and later a teacher. As a young man Higgins found employment in a New York patent solicitor's office, where he filed patent claims for clients and his own inventions. The latter ranged widely, from window screening to shoe manufacturing machinery to a new kind of India ink, from which he made his fortune. Charles M. Higgins & Co., founded in 1885, produced ink and adhesives from a factory near the Gowanus Canal in the lower part of Park Slope. Higgins Ink became a highly profitable brand, known to school children (and their parents) well beyond the borders of Brooklyn.

Near the end of the century the Higgins family moved up the Slope to a brownstone mansion facing Prospect Park, a short walk from the Montauk Club where Charles was now a member. He was a member of other clubs as well, including the Brooklyn, which cemented his status among the city's elite. Higgins bought a sprawling country estate in Smithtown, Long Island, where he bred horses and show dogs, supported cultural and civic organizations, helped found a Kings County Historical Society, and involved himself in commemorations of the Battle of Brooklyn, which included building a war memorial in Green-Wood Cemetery, just in front of the burial plot he had bought for himself and his family. These activities may have been intended to enhance his social position, but Higgins was also iconoclastic. When he left the Catholic Church as a youngster, he announced himself a freethinker. Instead of joining a prestigious Protestant Church when he began his social ascent, he associated himself with a Brooklyn offshoot of Felix Adler's Ethical Culture Society, an organization springing from Reform Judaism. He often expressed interest in Eastern religions. Later in his life he became a leader of the national Anti-Vaccination League. Missing from the chronicle of his life is evidence of sustained interest or activity in institutions related to his identity as an Irishman.[14]

Higgins's life in Brooklyn is the story not only of rags to riches but also of the seemingly perfect assimilation of a poor immigrant boy into the ways of his adopted land. Higgins's story, however, should not unduly shape our understanding of the immigrant experience, for, apart from its atypicality, it posits assimilation—a progressive path from one definable way of life to another—as the overriding goal of immigrants and as the inevitable arc of their collective history.

In their classic study, *The Polish Peasant in Europe and America*, William I. Thomas and Florian Znaniecki offered a different perspective. The issue of any Polish immigrant's assimilation, they wrote, is entirely "secondary and unimportant. . . . The fundamental process . . . *is the formation of a new Polish-American society*, . . . which in structure and prevalent attitudes is neither Polish nor American but constitutes a specific new product."[15] The notion of a singular and superior American way of life and culture that immigrants and their children must aspire to was at bottom a nativist conceit. Most immigrants, even those eager to prove their American credentials, did not see their lives as a process of shedding one culture and adopting another. They made their way in America as Irishmen, or Poles; the lives, institutions, and social and political values they built were not Irish, or Polish, or American, but Irish-American or Polish-American, and that was different from simply becoming American as a fixed and prior cultural property. Nor was this process necessarily deliberative, an explicit program of retaining just so much of the old country's ways and values and adopting just so much of what American natives demand. It was an outcome—a set of outcomes, variable and even contestable—of predilections expressed in day-to-day life, identities shaped and reshaped by experience, and more and less persistent longings for the old country and acceptance by the new. Its result, as Thomas and Znaniecki insisted, and as is invariably the case as human societies pass through time, is both old in its traditions and new as circumstances dictate. In understanding immigration and ethnicity, the hyphen was, and remains, an indispensable tool.

The Irish-Americans of post–Civil War Brooklyn offer important insights into these identity-forming processes of shedding, retaining, and becoming. The country they left was different from the nations of the other immigrant groups. Ireland is a small and relatively homogeneous country in which long-standing parochial identities were increasingly joined to a vigorous nationalism bred by the struggle for liberation from British control. As early as the 1820s Irish immigrants in Brooklyn formed institutions that expressed a strong commitment to their country of origin, and on occasion gathered in support of Irish liberation and, when the occasion arose, famine relief. Their annual St. Patrick's parade was more secular than religious, a celebration not so much of a Catholic saint as of Ireland and Irish identity. During the last four decades of the nineteenth century older and newer immigrants supported the Fenian, Land League, and Home Rule movements in Ireland, while continuing to build local institutions that perpetuated a distinct Irish identity. By this time the roster of organizations named Erin, Emerald, Shamrock, Hibernian, St. Patrick, or Irish had reached impressive levels, with an Irish Convention of Kings County that was a kind of parliamentary meeting ground for two distinct societies, the Ancient Order of Hibernians and the St. Patrick Alliance. The latter, as the name suggests, was itself a federation of groups based in Brooklyn's Irish Catholic churches, while the Ancient Order of Hibernians was a collection of individual lodges, seventeen of which marched in the 1870 St. Patrick's Day parade.[16]

The Irish Convention of Kings County did not have a long or happy life. In 1874, in a dispute over policies toward the homeland, the St. Patrick Alliance walked out of a convention meeting and a few years later the Hibernians split into two factions.[17] Nonetheless the institutional density of Irish Brooklyn endured. Less than three weeks after the split-up of the Hibernians and the Alliance the St. Patrick's Day parade featured twenty-six Hibernian divisions, fourteen branches of the St. Patrick's Alliance, and six Catholic temperance societies, demonstrating on a rainy mid-March day "that the sons of Hibernia, like good Irish whisky, can, without diminution of spirit, stand a great deal of water."[18] The parades of the following two years were impressive (thirty Hibernian divisions and twenty-two Alliance branches marched in 1876), but they dwindled by the end of the decade.[19] In 1880 a decision was made to divert the funds that would have been spent on a parade to the Land League in Ireland, and for four years Brooklyn hosted no St. Patrick's Day parade. The turnout was large when the parade resumed in 1884, and it remained so for some years despite the division among the Hibernians that generally required two separate events.[20] When the factions reunited in 1894 a new dispute arose. Mayor Schieren, an immigrant from Germany, refused to fly the Irish flag over City Hall on St. Patrick's Day. After much wrangling his decision prevailed. "We would as soon think of employing dynamite to kill flies or a sledge hammer to repair a watch," the *Eagle* scoffed, "as to get excited over something just about the size of the flag question."[21] But the controversy testifies to the continuing presence of Ireland in the American lives of these immigrants and their children.

Hibernian lodges were located in many Brooklyn neighborhoods, as were church-connected associations. We cannot tell how many laborers, dock workers, carters, and other low-wage workers participated in them, but the sheer spread of these organizations indicates that they penetrated deeply into the Irish-American working class.[22] Other organizations did not. Founded in 1850 on the model of the New England and St. Nicholas Societies, the St. Patrick Society served for many years as a convivial club for Brooklyn's Irish businessmen and professionals, convening on St. Patrick's Day each year for a sumptuous banquet. Led by Irish-born men such as Thomas Kinsella, who was elected six times as president, the St. Patrick Society paid as much heed as the Hibernians to Irish affairs and the celebration of Irish culture, placing a bust of the poet and composer Thomas Moore in Prospect Park, for example, and raising $1,000 in response to Charles Stewart Parnell's appeal for funds for the Land League.[23] But there is little to indicate that it cooperated with the Hibernians, the St. Patrick Alliance, or any other broad-based group.

Formed in 1875 by relatively affluent second-generation Irish, the Irish-American Union also celebrated the big day with a dinner rather than by marching with other groups in a parade. Describing itself as a social, literary, dramatic, and musical society of young people of Irish descent, it modeled itself on native Protestant organizations such as the Hamilton Literary Society rather than any of the Irish societies. But if the Irish-American Union signaled an assimilationist turn among the second generation, the signal was not a strong one. The Union may not have lasted beyond its first anniversary dinner in 1876.[24]

More than any of these organizations, big or small, long-lasting or ephemeral, broad-based or elite, the institution that defined the Irish presence in nineteenth-century Brooklyn was the Roman Catholic Church. Unlike other immigrant groups, the Irish worshiped at a church that was singular and centralized, and in some ways—the schooling of children, for example—reached more deeply than Protestant churches into the daily lives of its adherents. Although a few Protestant Irish lived in Brooklyn—Kinsella was one of them—the overwhelming majority were Catholics, and they all came from a country where the Catholic Church exerted enormous influence over everyday life, a cultural inheritance that endured in the United States. There were, of course, German Catholics in Brooklyn, but many if not most German immigrants were Protestants of different denominations, and some were Jewish. By the 1890s, when Italians arrived in significant numbers, the Catholic Church in Brooklyn had become a more diverse institution in the ethnic composition of its parishioners and increasingly its priesthood. But through much of the nineteenth century the Church belonged to the Irish on both sides of the communion table.

The price the Irish paid for their ownership of the Catholic Church was virulent anti-Catholicism in the antebellum era, which was often inflected with scorn for the Irish as a people. Animus of this sort did not disappear

from Brooklyn, but it did not carry over in especially consequential forms
into the postwar period.[25] Indeed, the Catholic Church gained in stature
among Brooklyn's Protestant leaders, partly because of its growing physical presence in the city, partly because of the perception that it anchored
immigrant neighborhoods in ways that promoted peace and good behavior
among its parishioners, and partly for its role in advancing the moral and
benevolent agenda the Protestants endorsed.

On numerous occasions ministers and priests appeared together on the
dais at the opening of an orphan asylum or an old-age home. Bishop Loughlin
was widely admired, and Catholics as well as Protestants appeared on several
lists of notable Brooklyn clergy.[26] Among the favorites was Father Giuseppe
Fransioli, a small, quick-witted, and good-natured Italian Swiss appointed
rector of the new parish of St. Peter's by Bishop Loughlin in 1859. Serving an
Irish working-class neighborhood on the South Brooklyn waterfront, Father
Fransioli quickly overcame any hesitation among his flock, some of whom
no doubt saw him as an Irishman with a funny accent. He proved to be a
popular pastoral leader and builder of institutions. As construction began
on the new church he announced his intention of establishing a parochial
school, St. Peter's Academy, and then moved on to St. Peter's Asylum for or-
phans and the poor, which expanded into Brooklyn's first Catholic hospital.
Before he died in 1890, he added a Home for Working Girls.[27]

These institutions were central to Catholic life in Brooklyn, particularly
in poorer parishes such as Father Fransioli's St. Peter's. Churches also sponsored temperance societies, mutual aid societies, and social clubs for men
and women, while parochial schools spread all over Catholic Brooklyn. The
teachers in these schools were drawn mostly from nearly a dozen male and
female religious orders, several of which Bishop Loughlin brought directly
from Ireland.[28] Churches and church-related organizations were important
to Protestants, too, but most Protestants did not experience so strong a connection between the church and the school, and certainly not as a force for
perpetuating ethnic identity.

Like the Irish, German immigrants came to America from a region where
the politics of nationhood was of the utmost importance. German unification before and after the 1871 proclamation of the Prussian Empire gave
former Prussians, Saxons, Hessians, Bavarians, and others much to discuss
in the beer gardens of Brooklyn's 16th ward. But German immigrants were
not called on for financial or moral support against an external tyrant, largely
because unification was widely greeted as a positive event, and even Catholic
Bavaria quickly shed its qualms about domination of the new German state

by Protestant Prussia. Hence, there were no patron saints to celebrate in defiant demonstration of pre-Prussian nationalism, and no anniversaries that demanded public affirmation of either a parochial or an imperial German identity. Of the two German-American celebrations of note in Brooklyn, one was a parade that followed the German victory over the French in 1871. Nationalist to the core, the march was not repeated in subsequent years. The other was the annual celebration of *Pfingstmontag*, or Pentecost Monday, which consisted of a parade of German groups from Williamsburg to parks in Williamsburg, Bushwick, and Ridgewood, with some marchers peeling off at each park for an afternoon of picnicking. Though *Pfingstmontag* was nominally a religious celebration, Germans did not carry or display religious pageants or emblems (unlike traditional Whitsun and Whit Monday processions in England and elsewhere). *Pfingstmontag* had little to do with the German nation or with any form of pre-national, national, or imperial politics. The parade did not pass City Hall, the mayor was not asked to stand in review, and organizers did not attempt to fly the German flag from Brooklyn's public buildings.[29]

Even more than the Irish, Germans built and joined institutions. As with the parades, their institutions expressed German culture with little need for political nationalism. German immigrants flocked to *turnvereine* (the gymnastic clubs that also promoted German culture and liberal politics) and music societies of various kinds—brass bands, singing societies, groups devoted to Baroque or classical music or a specific German composer. They joined shooting clubs, militia units, fraternal lodges, benevolent societies, and labor unions in German-dominated trades. All through the 16th ward, and beyond to adjoining wards as Dutchtown expanded, meeting halls hosted hundreds of these groups—Turn Hall, Germania Hall, Union Saenger Hall, Humboldt Hall, Burger's Hall, Baumgartner's Military Hall, Teutonia Hall, to name a few.[30] The comings and goings of group members were part of the fabric of German-American Brooklyn. A few halls and organizations carried names suggestive of German political nationalism, but many expressed the German notion of the *volk*, a type of nationalism that transcended politics and national boundaries on behalf of a deeper unity based on common traditions and language. This sentiment was not absent from Irish-American nationalism, but it ran more deeply among the Germans and was not animated—or complicated—by political struggles in the homeland.

Language was central to German-American identity, not least because it established this immigrant group as an alien minority within an English-speaking country. An organizing principle of unification in the Old World, language brought into one nation nearly all the German-speaking states, principalities, and still-independent Hanseatic cities of central Europe.[31] So when immigrants brought the German language to America they brought a good deal of cultural baggage with it. Almost inevitably the most prominent issue arising from the settlement of Williamsburg's Dutchtown was whether German should be taught in Brooklyn's public schools. Raised first in 1870, and again in 1873, the issue became significant in 1876 when Mayor Schroeder proposed adding German to the curriculum.[32] Schroeder had practical reasons for doing so—Dutchtown's public schools were underutilized, as many German immigrants sent their children to German-language private schools. But the issue transcended practicality. Some of the Germans who appeared before the board of education spoke of the German language as offering "further culture" and a "moral influence," and Schroeder argued that better-off Germans would never send their children to a school that did not teach this central element of German identity.[33]

Perhaps the most telling contribution to the controversy came from James J. O'Donnell, a member of the St. Patrick's Society. The Irish, too, had a language, O'Donnell pointed out, and its introduction into the public school curriculum would be more efficient because its alphabet had ten fewer letters than either English or German. That said, "the Irish will waive all claims" if Germans agreed to allow their children to learn only the language of the United States Constitution.[34] Evidently, it took an Irishman to chastise the Germans. A Philo-Celtic Society emerged in Brooklyn a few years later to urge a boycott of Irish-American newspapers that did not include instruction in the Irish language, but it soon left the scene.[35] The battle over German in the schools, by contrast, raged on and was resolved temporarily when the board of education voted 23 to 16 against introducing it into the curriculum. It appeared again, not for the last time, in 1890, when a "monster meeting" of representatives of 166 German societies pressed the issue.[36] Brooklyn's Germans were clearly no more amused on the subject of language than its Irish were on the subjects of tenantry and British rule in Ireland. The difference was that the Irish battle had to be fought overseas, while the German one focused on life in America.

The concept of a German *volk* did not extend easily to the Jews among Brooklyn's German immigrants. Some Jewish immigrants, especially the wealthier and better educated, maintained a German identity that reflected their partial integration into nineteenth-century German society—an integration that, among other things, gave birth to a religious Reform movement emulating practices of their Christian neighbors. But the ethnic identity of German Jews, even within the Reform community, remained above all that of the Jewish diaspora, and the power of that identity was even stronger among Jews who had migrated to Germany from Russia and the Austro-Hungarian Empire before departing to the United States. That identity would manifest itself late in the century in relief efforts for Russian Jews.

It is difficult to estimate how many of Brooklyn's German immigrants were Jewish and still more difficult to know how many Jews brought with them important elements of German culture. Among the delegates to the large 1890 meeting protesting the absence of German from the public school curriculum was Rabbi Leopold Wintner, a Hungarian-born, German-educated leader of the Reform community.[37] He was almost certainly not alone, but evidence of cooperation among Christian and Jewish German immigrants is rare in the historical record. Although they may have shared a language and culture, these two communities appear to have remained largely distinct.

Before the Civil War few Jews lived in Brooklyn, which had only two places of Jewish worship, both in rented rooms. The first, a small Orthodox congregation, Kahal Kadosh Beth Elohim, was organized in Williamsburgh in 1848; the second, Baith (Beth) Israel, also Orthodox, met from 1856 in a room above a store in Atlantic Street before building Brooklyn's first synagogue on the corner of Boerum Place and State Street in 1862.[38] Several more congregations soon appeared, some as splinter groups from the first two. Within a decade of the end of the war, Brooklyn had six synagogues, and a newspaper account of the Rosh Hashanah services in 1877 estimated five thousand worshipers, a clear indication that the Jewish population of Brooklyn was growing significantly.[39] Later estimates confirm this perception: twelve thousand Jewish residents in 1886, twenty-five in 1891, and fifty-thousand at the end of the century.[40]

FIGURE 5.4. Congregation Baith Israel synagogue, Boerum Place (1862), the first Jewish house of worship built on Long Island (© Kane Street Synagogue).

These figures suggest that Brooklyn's Jewish community was large enough by the 1880s or 1890s to generate the kinds of institutions established by the Irish and the Christian Germans. The levels of organization among the Jews, however, did not match these other immigrant groups. Interestingly, even the most German of these immigrants did not form music societies or *turnvereine*, nor did they spend their Sunday afternoons in beer gardens. To be sure, they did establish Jewish benevolent societies, a YMHA of uncertain longevity, a number of fraternal lodges and men's clubs, and a Ladies' Sewing Circle that made garments and linens for the jewel in Jewish Brooklyn's institutional crown, the Hebrew Orphan Asylum.[41] Incorporated in 1878, the orphan asylum began modestly with four boys and girls in a small rented house on Stuyvesant Avenue in the suburban neighborhood later known as Stuyvesant Heights. Within five years, when four children became forty, a larger house was built on the adjacent property, and in 1892 the Orphan Asylum Society, now an organization with more than five hundred members, erected a still larger structure to house more than a hundred Jewish children. By far the most visible Jewish benevolent institution in nineteenth-century Brooklyn, the orphan asylum attracted Christian dignitaries such as Kinsella, Beecher, Father Sylvester Malone, and mayors Seth Low and David Boody to its fundraisers and dedications.[42] The attention it received points to both the tradition of Jewish benevolence and the limited organizational life of Brooklyn's Jews during those formative years.

The synagogues' role as centers of communal life was more limited than that of Protestant and Catholic churches. Orthodoxy was declining in Brooklyn, with many synagogues adopting or moving toward the less demanding—and less cathartic—practices of the Reform movement. The synagogues, too, did not have large memberships and generally attracted small groups of worshipers to their services. Some German Jewish immigrants were agnostics and atheists, and some professed believers were drawn more to secular than religious life. Equally important, many Jewish businessmen could not afford to close their stores on the Jewish Sabbath, their busiest day of the week. Some of them embraced the radical idea of shifting the Sabbath services to Sunday, an initiative Temple Israel adopted.[43] The deeper problem, though, was an apparently widespread indifference to religion and the communal life synagogues might have encouraged. Near the end of an article in 1886 about the city's Jews, the *Eagle* concluded that though Brooklyn "will soon have cause to be proud of its synagogues as it is now proud of its churches," the present state of Jewish worship was not encouraging: "There are many thousands of Hebrews in Brooklyn who pay no attention to the synagogues—not even on holidays. . . . In the synagogue and out of it there is much indifference."[44]

Related to the weak religiosity of Brooklyn's German Jewish immigrants was a similarly weak sense of Jewish exclusivity. Orthodoxy expressed that exclusivity in various ways, including the clothing and long beards of its men. Continuing traditions that made some Jews visibly alien stimulated no small amount of anti-Semitism in neighborhoods where Orthodox Jews and Gentiles lived in close proximity.[45] But Reform Jews did not set themselves apart in this way. Their clothing and personal grooming were indistinguishable from those of native Christians and the German secular education of the more affluent among them enhanced the possibilities of mutual discourse, even if the newcomers gave voice to their learning in accents strange to the native-born. And the relatively small footprint of Jewish religious institutions offered little challenge to the City of Churches, a phrase used without resentment or any sense of exclusion by two Jewish speakers at the cornerstone ceremony of the Hebrew Orphan Asylum.[46]

An example of positive discourse across the divides of religion and nationality was the friendship between Plymouth Church's Henry Ward Beecher and Rabbi Leopold Wintner of Temple Beth Elohim. By 1878, when Wintner arrived in Brooklyn to take the helm of this Reform congregation Beecher had already established himself as a friend of the Jews. A year earlier he delivered a sermon titled "Jew and Gentile" that responded to the denial of accommodations to Jewish banker Joseph Seligman by the Grand Union Hotel in Saratoga Springs. Seligman's wealth and prominence turned the incident into one of the first major anti-Semitic scandals in American history. Beecher pounced eleven days later with a forcible embrace not only of Seligman, a personal friend, but of the Jewish people as "the unrecognized benefactors of the human race" through long-ingrained "attributes of truth, of justice, of humanity, of morality, of gentleness, and of humility."[47]

Beecher had spoken before, earnestly and glowingly, of the Jewish people and of Judaism as the indispensable source of Christianity. In a letter to President Grover Cleveland, Beecher argued that Brooklynite Oscar Straus should be appointed US minister to Turkey because he was Jewish. "Christianity itself suckled at the bosom of Judaism," he explained. "We are Jews ourselves gone to blossom and fruit."[48] Beecher went far beyond metaphors of this sort in his praise of the current generation of Jews, including those who migrated to America. That the Jews of Brooklyn revered Beecher as a friend and bulwark against local anti-Semitism is not surprising. Nor is it surprising, given Rabbi Wintner's background and ideas, that the two should have developed a warm friendship. Both men were sons of clergy, and both saw themselves as modernizers of their faiths. Both had held pastorates in the American Midwest. Beecher no doubt admired Wintner's extensive German education (he studied at several universities and received a PhD from Tübingen), while Wintner could not have failed to be impressed by Beecher's cosmopolitanism and fame. That one was a Christian and the other a Jew might even have strengthened the bond between them. Beecher gave his first address to a synagogue at Temple Beth Elohim; when he died, Wintner spoke at Plymouth Church after having eulogized Beecher at Beth Elohim that morning.[49]

One friendship, of course, does not prove a wider accommodation between Reform Jews and Protestants, nor did it mean that anti-Semitism in Brooklyn was confined to harassment of Orthodox Jews on the streets of Williamsburg or East New York. The *Eagle* no doubt failed to capture many discriminatory incidents in the relations between Jews and Gentiles, but journals such as the *American Hebrew and Jewish Messenger* deepen the historical record with reports intended to sharpen the vigilance of local Jews. An example was its description of attacks by Shelter Island residents on a fruit store opened by a Jew. The attackers broke windows, smashed in doors, and "intimated that another raid will follow if the Jew does not pack up and leave town." Sitting between the North and South Forks of the eastern end of Long Island, Shelter Island is far from New York and Brooklyn, but the *American Hebrew* did not miss the opportunity to lampoon rubes who could not grasp the advantages a Jewish storekeeper could bring to a place "said to be good only for hoeing potatoes and burying the dead." "This is a country," it explained, "where, when a train is stalled in a snowdrift, it is allowed to stick there till the heat of the Fourth of July thaws it out." These jokes might have made the Shelter Island incident seem remote to city people, but the journal did not allow its readers to dismiss the danger on that account: "This is not a cablegram from Russia or Germany, or France or Algiers; nor yet is it a telegram from the wilds of Louisiana, where such things have been done before, nor from the southern states, where the lynch law prevails."[50]

And the *American Hebrew* provided examples much closer to home. In 1896 it reported some surprisingly inflammatory language from the "acknowledged liberal and fair-minded spiritual leader," Rev. Lyman Abbott, Beecher's successor at Plymouth Church. Abbott told his congregation that the Jews of Jesus' time "rose in wrath and would have mobbed him" because "in that age Jews hated Christians a little more than Christians hate the Jews today. And that is saying a great deal."[51] Abbott surely intended no harm, but the Jewish people of his city were now warned that dangerous language could come from a friend almost as easily as from an enemy.

Nearly ten years earlier, Jews in New York and Brooklyn had seen for themselves the effects of a decision by Austin Corbin, the president of Coney Island's Manhattan Beach Hotel, to exclude them from the hotel and its adjoining beach. In an interview with a reporter from the *New York Herald* in 1879 about this replay of the Seligman affair Corbin explained that since respectable Christians were being driven away by the presence of Jews, the exclusion was no more than a practical business decision. He then undermined this rationale by expressing his own anti-Semitic feelings: "Personally, I am opposed to Jews. . . . They are contemptible as a class, and I never knew but one 'white' Jew in my life."[52] Corbin's views were amplified by his standing as a Wall Street banker as well as the president of the hotel and its feeder railroad. The policy of the Manhattan Beach and the reasons for it, though, are not clear. Another of the hotel's proprietors spoke of excluding only ill-behaved lower-class Jews from Manhattan's East Side and claimed wealthy Jews continued to be welcome and even approved of the policy.

Perhaps the best thing that can be said about the incident at the Manhattan Beach Hotel is that it was controversial enough to require Corbin to explain at length why Jews, and no other group, were being singled out for exclusion. To be sure, many Christians appeared to accept as reasonable his description of Jews as "contemptible." One who did not was James H. Breslin, Corbin's competitor at the Brighton Beach Hotel. After calling Corbin "a devilish good fellow," he stood up for his own Jewish guests as "just as well behaved and respectable and as prompt to pay their bills as anybody else. There are several staying here now and we are glad to have them." Breslin seemed pleased with his contribution to the debate over the qualities of Jewish people. He asked the reporter: "Is that all you want of me? Well, let's go and have a drink on it."[53]

In the mid-1870s another group arrived in Brooklyn that was more alien to the City of Churches than Jews. "MONGOLS" was the *Eagle* front-page headline on September 1, 1876. Beneath it was "Brooklyn Invaded by the Celestials." The occasion for this dire warning was the opening of a laundry on Court Street by three Chinese men. These were not the first Chinese to move to Brooklyn; the 1870 US census recorded seven Chinese residents.[54] If it seems ludicrous to consider these newcomers invaders, racial mockery was the *Eagle*'s intent. The article on the Chinese laundry included reporting, real or imaginary, of a fearful reaction by the white and Black washerwomen of South Brooklyn, who created "a vigilance committee of indignant Amazons . . . who should in the dead of night seize the Chinamen by their pig tails," march them to the ferry landing, and warn them "never again

to disfigure the streets of the City of Churches with their ungainly shad-
ows." When this banishment did not happen, the paper concluded that wiser
heads had decided that "the almond-eyed gentlemen" would never find favor
among the people of Brooklyn, so no action would be necessary. The laundry succeeded, however, even though the "pagans" were not happy about the
crowds of small boys and indignant washerwomen who "continually crowd
the doorway and drive the poor fellows nigh crazy with their yells, impreca-
tions, and maledictions."[55]

This tiny Chinese presence in Brooklyn increased gradually over the ensu-
ing decades, reaching 1,206 "Celestial" souls by the end of the century (along
with 94 people from Japan). The Chinese-born were distributed evenly
through the city, a clear indication that their economic role in Brooklyn
continued to be in laundering and perhaps other neighborhood services.[56]
Even in the early stages of this population increase some native Christians in
Brooklyn saw the Chinese as a civic and missionary opportunity, and opened
Sunday schools to instruct them in English, "the duties of citizenship," and
"the truths of the Bible." The first school for the Chinese was hosted by the
YMCA in 1879. Within a year or two half a dozen more appeared in Baptist, Congregational, and Reformed churches, some of which also conducted
overseas missions to China.[57] In 1882 the students at the First Baptist Church
arranged a Chinese New Year public reception, which might well have been
the first (but not the last) occasion at which non-Asian Brooklynites tasted
Chinese food.[58] These efforts were underscored by Beecher, who, on a trip
to California, objected to the treatment of the Chinese on the West Coast
as "shameful and ridiculous" and announced his opposition to the recently
enacted Chinese Exclusion Act.[59] The Chinese in Brooklyn, Beecher implied,
were treated more tolerantly than those on the West Coast.

That relative tolerance continued through the latter decades of the century, but so did objections to the Chinese, on the grounds of race as well as
unfair competition with Irish and African American washerwomen. Sunday
school instruction in English, American public institutions, and Christian
doctrine were intended to benefit the Chinese, but at the core was the motive
of missionaries to convert them to Christianity.[60] And complaints on behalf
of the washerwomen easily slid into racial epithets. "But it is not with the
commercial aspect of John Chinaman's immigration that we have to deal,"
wrote the *Eagle* in 1886. "It is with his habits, his vices, his foibles. Wherever
the moon eyed stranger goes, there go his vices," including opium smoking,
illegal gambling, and "bestial habits." Like other articles on the Chinese, this
one included an alleged interview with a laundryman, which allowed the reporter to ridicule the latter's English and caricature his values and behavior.[61]

The *Eagle* and several of Brooklyn's Protestant notables rose in defense of the Chinese when a new national law extended the 1882 Exclusion Act and required the Chinese who were already in America to register and carry a resident permit.[62] But these high-profile protests against violations of minority rights did not erase the belief, no doubt more widely held, that the Chinese were an alien, inferior race.

Part of the problem in accepting the Chinese was their newness to and scarcity in the city. These challenges did not exist with respect to another minority, African Americans, some of whom could boast of Brooklyn roots as deep as those of the Dutch and sniff at Yankees as Johnnies-come-lately. But precedence made little difference in matters of race. The Brooklyn press headed stories with "Our Colored 'Bredren' " or "Rejoice ye Darkies All" as easily as "Brooklyn Invaded by the Celestials," and the stories themselves revealed a society deeply divided by race. The white and Black populations of Brooklyn were not entirely segregated, but they were largely so, and encounters in public spaces and on public facilities such as ferries and streetcars often led to conflict and questions about what rights Black people could assert within a largely unsympathetic white society.[63]

This question arose in explicit fashion when well-known African American leaders came to Brooklyn to address racially integrated audiences. The results of these public meetings were mixed. Harriet Tubman spoke to a large audience at the Bridge Street AME Church in October 1865, recounting her extraordinary experiences as an escaped slave, a Union spy, and a guide to freedom on the Underground Railroad (for which the Bridge Street Church was a stop). According to an *Eagle* reporter, who had little to say about the substance of the speech, the decrepit gallery of the church was on the verge of collapse, and Tubman's "negro phrases" provoked "shouts of laughter from the congregation," with whites, who apparently came to be entertained rather than enlightened, "entering most heartily into it."[64]

Less than a month later, when two members of the YMCA asked to use the Brooklyn Academy of Music for a speech by Frederick A. Douglass, several members of the academy's board of directors expressed the fear that an address by Douglass would set a precedent for other appearances by African Americans, "negroes would begin to crowd the audiences at the Academy," and white people would no longer be willing to attend productions there. A truer motive for this dissent may have been concern that this powerful orator would use the occasion to repeat his harsh critique of President Andrew Johnson's efforts to undo the gains in Black civil rights set in motion by President Lincoln and Congressional Republicans. How else to understand the claim that approval of the speech would set a dangerous precedent when Douglass had already spoken to a racially integrated academy audience of three thousand people, in May 1863, on the subject "What Shall be Done with the Negro," and was "received with loud applause"? In any case, persuaded in part by Theodore Tilton, then a close associate of Beecher, the board voted 11 to 6 to authorize the event. One dissenting member resigned in protest.[65]

Douglass appeared at a packed Academy of Music on January 29, 1866, eliciting "volley after volley of applause" from a mostly white audience as he excoriated Johnson and rebuked those who had opposed his visit: "The day is coming when Brooklyn will be quite ashamed that any subjection could have been made to a man appearing before it for the purpose of vindicating the cause of justice, of humanity, and of liberty." The *Eagle*, which had so recently mocked Tubman, printed a transcript of Douglass' two-hour speech in three prominently placed columns.[66]

The enthusiastic reception of Douglass at the Academy of Music did not translate into support by a majority of Brooklynites for equal rights for African Americans. In 1869, a referendum to retain New York State's property qualifications for Black suffrage passed by a relatively narrow margin. Offsetting upstate Republicans' support for repeal, substantial majorities in New York City and Brooklyn voted to retain the property qualifications (58.2 percent in Kings County, with Irish Catholics mostly likely to support retention, and Yankee Protestants most likely to support repeal). Shortly before the vote, the *Eagle* asked its readers: "Are you willing to declare by your vote that you are exactly and precisely the equivalent of a negro, neither more nor less?" Brooklyn answered this question with clarity.[67] African Americans did not achieve universal manhood suffrage in New York State until the ratification of the 15th Amendment to the US Constitution in 1870.

Support for Reconstruction, and for Black rights generally, soon waned in the North, and though Black activists continued to oppose discrimination in employment and public accommodation, white Brooklynites evinced little interest in these issues. The only sustained discussion of race in Brooklyn during these years concerned the public school system. State law did not mandate racial integration or segregation of the schools; it gave considerable latitude to local school boards, and in Brooklyn the board of education created and maintained an almost entirely segregated system. But local decisions led to local disputes. On at least two occasions, an African American father demanded that the board enroll his child in a white school closer to their home than that district's school for Black children. In both instances the demand was fueled not merely by questions of convenience but also by new

Constitutional amendments and civil rights laws that seemed to guarantee the rights of African Americans to equal treatment under the law.[68]

This mixture of motives appeared in other disputes. In 1869, while deciding whether a white teacher should be continued at Colored School No. 2 in Weeksville, a special committee of the Brooklyn Board of Education (chaired by Thomas Kinsella) reinforced the principle and practical necessity of school segregation: "The healthy public sentiment which aids in preventing a more intimate relationship between blacks and whites, your Committee believe ought not be impaired. . . . The welfare and perpetuity of our Public school system demand separate schools for the two races." After discovering that forty white children were enrolled in this school intended for African Americans, the committee recommended that both the teacher and these children be relocated to white schools.[69]

The "healthy public sentiment" in favor of racial segregation was repeated often in the *Brooklyn Daily Eagle*. But the assumption that the separation of the races was the natural order of things occasionally coincided with advocacy for improved conditions for Brooklyn's African Americans. "The Brooklyn Board of Education maintains separate schools for the accommodation of the children of the colored people of Brooklyn," it wrote in June of 1880, and "this arrangement is desirable and satisfactory." But the *Eagle* also argued for better schools for Black children and for adding an African American to the board of education.[70] This last reform was achieved in 1882 with the appointment of Philip A. White, a Brooklyn-dwelling New York City druggist. White's appointment was appropriate, the *Eagle* opined, because he provided leadership and oversight for the city's colored schools, not because he was an advocate for integration. "The reasons for maintaining separated colored schools are obvious enough, but they can only be deemed valid if it also appears that they work no disadvantage to the colored child."[71] The *Eagle* got more than it bargained for. The year after he joined the board, White offered a motion to permit Black children to enroll in any school in the city. It was adopted, and though a second motion (not offered by White) to abolish the Black schools altogether was postponed, Brooklyn was on its way to a single and racially integrated school system.[72]

Although White's initiative ultimately produced de facto integration of Brooklyn's schools, the distinction between colored and white schools was not removed for another decade. White died in 1891 and was replaced on the board by another influential African American, the lawyer and sometime Methodist Episcopal minister, T. McCants Stewart. Responding to the plan for a new school in Weeksville, Stewart insisted on the elimination of the designation "colored" from the existing school before moving on to proposals for the racial integration of both. The battle was long and complicated, resulting for a time in an African American school on the first floor and a school for white students on the second floor of the same building. Stewart and his allies on the board of education ultimately achieved the full integration of the student body and the faculty in P.S. 83. Brooklyn had been slow among northern cities in integrating its schools, but this school may have been the first to have African Americans teaching white children on a regular basis. Within a short time, all formal racial distinctions were removed from the Brooklyn school system, even as racism remained a fact of life in the County of Kings.[73]

An important context for this history of race in the Brooklyn school system, and in particular the resistance of white leaders to integration, was the small size of the city's African American population. In 1870 fewer than five thousand Black people resided in Brooklyn, a little more than 1 percent of the total population and an increase of only six hundred or so from the year before the Civil War. Only five hundred African American children attended

FIGURE 5.5. Thomas McCants Stewart (Schomburg Center for Research in Black Culture, New York Public Library).

Brooklyn schools in 1870, compared to more than sixty-five thousand whites. Since well over half of the Black population was concentrated in only four wards (about 20 percent in the 9th ward, where Weeksville and Carrsville were located), most areas of the city would have seen no more than a handful of Black students in their neighborhood schools, and some none at all, if the system had been racially integrated.[74] African American school enrollments doubled during the next decade while the overall African American population increased by about two-thirds, but there were still very few Black school children in Brooklyn when the issue of integration was resolved.[75] Had they had a mind to, the *Eagle* editors could have likened the resistance to school integration to "employing dynamite to kill flies or a sledge hammer to repair a watch."

The small size of the Black population (still less than 2 percent of Brooklyn's overall population at the end of the century) was relevant as well to organized community life among adult African Americans, as were the limited means available to people still largely confined to the lower rungs of the economic ladder.[76] In addition to several wealthy Black Brooklynites (led by Elizabeth Gloucester, who ran an elegant Brooklyn Heights boarding house and owned several rental properties) there was a small class of well-off professionals and businessmen.[77] But about two-thirds of Brooklyn's African American workers were concentrated in a small number of low-paying jobs—laborers, laundresses, seamen, porters, and whitewashers; many of the rest were gardeners, carmen, drivers, hairdressers, cooks, waiters, coachmen, and stewards. African American men were underrepresented in the skilled trades and small proprietorships. They were greatly disadvantaged in municipal employment, a significant channel of upward mobility that belonged largely to the Irish, through the patronage belonging to the Democratic Party.[78]

The controller of that channel was Brooklyn's political boss, Hugh McLaughlin, who was born and raised near the docks of South Brooklyn and rose through the party, based on fast fists and firm leadership, to exercise complete authority for decades over municipal employment. Whether McLaughlin was interested in Ireland's struggles is unknown, but many Irish immigrants and second-generation Irish-Americans wound up in City Hall offices, on the streets as policemen, and in other public positions. What the Irish got African Americans did not.[79] Only two Black men served on the Brooklyn police department during these decades. Their appointments were newsworthy enough to earn long biographical articles in the *Eagle*.[80] A few patronage positions did go to Brooklyn's African Americans, but they were with the federal Custom House in New York, which was usually under the control of the Republican Party. Nearly all of these appointees were porters and messengers.[81]

Black Brooklynites, then, had neither the numbers nor the resources to bring to life the hundreds of organizations created by white native Protestants and Irish and German immigrants. Nonetheless, they developed an organized communal life. Brooklyn's fourteen Black churches were powerful neighborhood centers, some of which formed literary societies and lyceums. In 1892 the *Eagle* profiled several of them, commenting that "there is no class of Brooklyn's citizens that is fonder of literary pursuits than the Afro American," and "there is no other city in the Union that possesses as intelligent a community of young people as the City of Churches." Bringing African American organizations under Brooklyn's City of Churches umbrella was notable for the *Eagle*, and the profiles that followed were devoid of racist satire.[82] African American men also formed fraternal lodges that functioned not only for fellowship but as much needed mutual benefit societies. There were Masons, Good Samaritans, Knights of Pythias, Knights Templar, a United Order of St. Luke, an Order of Love and Charity, and no doubt others.[83] A Williamsburgh Colored Coachmen's Club and a Saloonsmen's Protective Union were closer in form and purpose to these mutual benefit lodges than they were to labor unions.[84] There were at least two women's benevolent societies, the Abyssinian Benevolent Daughters of Esther Association and a local branch of the New York-based interracial society, King's Daughters. Organizations beyond this axis of mutual benevolence included a militia unit named the Weeksville Guard and a baseball club, the Weeksville Unknowns.[85]

For several years near to and after the end of the Civil War the most powerful secular organization in Brooklyn's African American community was the African Civilization Society. Founded in New York in 1858 to promote emigration to Africa, the society relocated to Weeksville in 1864 after redefining its goal to address the interests, and in particular the education, of freed people in the American South. By 1868 it operated multiple schools in nine southern states and published a newspaper, the *Freedman's Torchlight*.[86] Similarly, a Kings County Colored Men's Association, which may have been a 9th ward appendage of the Republican Party, met in 1866 to petition Congress "to restore the freedmen to their homes and give them all necessary protection."[87]

For the small number of Blacks who had migrated to Brooklyn from the South, efforts for the relief of racial brethren "back home" were something like the Land League and Home Rule contributions of Irish immigrants; for home-grown Black Brooklynites they more closely resembled the stateless,

ethnic-based responsibilities of Jews. Philanthropic and political efforts ranging beyond the local community, in any case, reflected the political moment
of emancipation and the reintegration of the Union.

That moment did not last. The African Civilization Society did not survive
into the next decade, in large part because of controversies over its management of the Black orphan asylum in Weeksville.[88] The Kings County
Colored Men's Association seems to have folded as well, although a Kings
County Colored Club and a Kings County Colored Citizens Republican
League were actively promoting local African American interests within the
Republican Party in the 1880s.[89] The fraternal and benevolent societies that
had emerged by that time focused mainly on their own members and on the
well-being of Brooklyn's Black community. In 1891 a new Afro American
League preserved something of the wider vision of the early post–Civil War
organizations, while attending as well to local affairs. Its constitution referred
to school funding and (mostly local) taxation, but also to lynching, racial
discrimination on railroads and steamboats, penal reform, and assistance to
"healthy immigration from terror ridden sections to other and more law
abiding sections."[90]

Brooklyn's African Americans held an annual celebration, but unlike the
Irish on St. Patrick's Day, or the Germans on *Pfingstmontag*, they did not do
so by commandeering public space. Instead of parading in public streets or
meeting in a public park, celebrants gathered in one or two private pleasure
grounds. No community organization or committee seems to have been
involved; the celebration appears to have been organized as a commercial
event. Attendees enjoyed music, dancing, games, food, drink (not including
"spirituous liquors"), and other attractions. Many of those who paid the price
of admission may have looked forward to no more than a rollicking good
time. But there was also content of considerable meaning to the African
American community. The celebration was held each August 1st, beginning
apparently during the 1850s, to commemorate at first the freeing of slaves
in the British West Indies and then, after the Civil War, both the British and
American emancipations. Along with dancing and games were speeches by
local and national African American leaders (Frederick Douglass addressed at
least one of these events), readings of both proclamations of emancipation,
and cheers for Douglass, Lincoln, and other heroes of American emancipation. The celebration was staged each year through 1877 and during at least
some of the years that followed. The *Eagle* took note of an 1884 celebration
as "never more enthusiastically observed in twenty-eight years."[91] Some of
those who listened to the speeches and readings—and some who just danced
and had a good time—came to the pleasure ground to celebrate their own

emancipation from slavery. Others expressed their identification with the liberation and continuing struggles of a people.

If the African Americans of Brooklyn were unwilling or unable as a group to utilize public space to protest continuing struggles, others did, and not always peacefully. The first stages of American industrialization were also the first stages of the American labor movement. In the take-off years preceding the Civil War critical changes in key industries often violated traditional understandings between the workers and employers of a preindustrial craft economy. As industrial development accelerated in the post–Civil War period, producing more and more factories and mills the size of Rhenish castles, these divergences between what was now called capital and labor deepened. Worrisome enough during the relatively prosperous years following the war, they became calamitous during and after the depression of the mid-1870s, setting off a period of the deepest conflicts between capital and labor in American history. The City of Churches and Homes, and also of factories, docks, tenements, and a mostly immigrant working class, Brooklyn had its share of this conflict and of workers' institution building that helped carry it into the streets of the city.

The formation of unions and other workers' associations during this period was a significant phenomenon. A good sampling of an admittedly incomplete record is provided by the local press, which often reported on meetings of labor unions and generally identified the organization behind a strike or strike threat. At the beginning of the depression in 1873, for example, a Brooklyn carpenters' union threatened a strike for a raise and an eight-hour day. The following year a meeting of the Plumbers' and Fitters' Protective and Benevolent Society, once a traditional trade association open to masters and journeymen, revealed that it had evolved into a workers' union from which "bosses" were excluded. A strike by brewery workers against three large New York companies in 1881 resulted in a workers' boycott of their beer that extended to Brooklyn. Unions representing, among others, piano makers, cigar makers, wood carvers, clothing cutters, silk weavers, and bakers organized the boycott.[92] Stories touching upon specific episodes of unionization or union activity in Brooklyn multiplied over the years. They reached another level in 1891 when the *Eagle* reported on the seven-year expansion of Brooklyn's Central Labor Union, founded in 1884 and now representative of more than 125 local workingmen's organizations.[93]

As they read about unionization in the newspapers, Brooklyn's white-collar suburbanites also saw union men take to the streets. Brooklyn witnessed numerous strikes, many of them small and often quickly broken by the hiring of replacement workers, or scabs, who were easy to recruit among recent immigrants eager to work and not yet integrated into Brooklyn's working-class organizations. Often, as in a coopers' strike in 1882 involving eighty men, much of the strikers' energy was directed toward the scabs, beginning on occasion with friendly pleas to stay home but often escalating into violence.[94] These strikes were usually futile. Laws did not yet compel employers to negotiate with duly constituted unions. Business owners could usually count on more than a little help from their friends in the courts, City Hall, and the state Capitol. And they invariably had the resources to outlast the workers in lengthy work stoppages.

Although smaller strikes were hardly noticed outside their immediate neighborhood, the walkout of some 2,500 sugar refinery workers in the spring of 1886 was too big to ignore. The grievances that led to the strike were low wages, long hours, and Sunday work, but other forms of exploitation lay in the background of the dispute, such as the installation in each refinery of a beer saloon open to the workers after their long hours of work in stifling heat. The workers could drink as much as they liked, and the tab would be deducted from their monthly pay. Many workers went home to their families on payday with less than half of what they had earned. The refinery workers were mostly German and Polish immigrants, many of them non-English speaking, and their Sugar House Workingmen's Union was less than a month old. Although the Central Labor Union helped and the refinery's drivers and longshoremen vowed to stay out for the duration, the asymmetry of resources between the sugar companies and the strikers was as great as it usually was in smaller strikes. The *Eagle* called it "the most extensive and probably the most desperate labor strike that Brooklyn has ever known," and covered it daily until the strikers, running out of money, applied to return to work at the old rates of pay.[95]

The sugar strike of 1886 was not especially violent, largely because the refineries shut most of their operations instead of hiring replacement workers. A more violent strike that affected Brooklynites living far from the waterfront sugar refineries occurred nine years later. A massive turnout of transit workers had a devastating impact on late-nineteenth-century Brooklyn, with its many miles of lines connecting commuter suburbs to downtown Brooklyn and New York City. It began on January 14, 1895, with some five thousand motormen and conductors on all but two of Brooklyn's trolley lines refusing to work until they received a twenty-five-cent raise. The strike started out peacefully, with the *Eagle* observing that "of all the strikes which have ever taken place in this city this is by far the quietest." The next day's headline was VIOLENCE, although very little violence was reported. A fully justified headline, BAYONETED, appeared after several days of escalating attacks on cars operated by replacement motormen resulted in intervention by the state militia. In response to the taunts of a large crowd that had gathered near the East New York trolley barn, militiamen charged with bayonets fixed and wounded one man. The crowd responded with more than taunts. Before the day was done several more militia charges resulted in fifteen ambulance calls to cart away wounded civilians. Later in the evening club-wielding mounted police joined the militia. The crowd was finally dispersed by one o'clock in the morning. The violence waxed and waned over the next three weeks as trolley service was restored, and the battle moved into the courts and the chambers of the Common Council. Defeated on all fronts, the strikers offered a peace proposal. The strike had lasted a month and gained the strikers almost nothing.[96]

Brooklyn's workingmen had found a happier way of taking to the streets in 1887 when the state legislature, acting on a proposal from New York's Central Labor Union, established Labor Day as a legal holiday. On September 5 of that year the first Labor Day parade assembled in Williamsburg for a long march to Ridgewood Park to meet "sweethearts and wives and dance and eat and drink and be merry from 2 o'clock in the afternoon till slumbrous midnight." Alongside fifty bands an estimated twelve thousand

FIGURE 5.6. Violent protest during the Brooklyn transit strike of 1895 (Wallach Division Picture Collection, New York Public Library).

workers representing fifty of Brooklyn's two hundred labor unions, plus as-
sorted socialists, anarchists, prohibitionists, Republicans, and Democrats,
participated in an event intended to be entirely free of politics. The police
were not mobilized, and the *Eagle* wondered whether Ridgewood Park would
be "rent asunder" when the union men of Vinegar Hill and South Brooklyn
came in contact with the socialists of the 16th and 18th wards (i.e., radical
Germans), "to say nothing of the old standing prejudices of Hibernians and
Teutons." It was not and the day was considered a big success, except perhaps
by the socialists, who were prevented from adding red flags to the procession
or radical speeches to the festivities in the park.

In this and following years the Labor Day parade showcased Brooklyn's
unions, including those of nonindustrial trades and occupational groups,
such as transit workers, longshoremen, laborers, and, in their considerable
variety, the construction trades. (Among the latter were two unions that
spoke to Brooklyn's suburban character: the Brown Stone Cutters Association and the Brown Stone Rubbers Association.) The parade also revealed
divisions between socialists and practical unionists that was at the same time
an ethnic division between Germans and nearly everyone else. Another division was even more significant: This was a specifically working-class event,
organized by unions and lacking any representation by Brooklyn's religious
and political leadership. Clergymen did not offer opening prayers or bene-
dictions; political leaders did not stand in review. Significantly, the parade
moved eastward through the city's Eastern District, and was reviewed at Williamsburg's Labor Lyceum by the marshals and other officers of the Central
Labor Union, and not by the mayor at City Hall.[97]

The unions on display at the Labor Day parade were formed by workingmen interested primarily in higher wages, shorter hours, and better working
conditions. Some of Brooklyn's working women were organized too, but
into clubs rather than unions, and for far different purposes. The clubs offered sociability among "working girls," classes in cooking, sewing, hygiene,
English, and other useful subjects, and amusements free from "all taint of fri-
volity and immorality." They were formed by middle- and upper-class Protestant women who were not interested in challenging the very low wages
paid to seamstresses, milliners, and female factory workers. As Mrs. Barnard,
a founding matron of one of the Brooklyn clubs explained, "we do not seek
to inspire them with ideas above their position in life. We simply wish to
develop their intellects; to help them in the performance of their duties."
So explicit a rejection of labor militancy and so clear a dedication to moral
amusement and sociability accords well with the tradition of religion-based
intervention in working-class affairs. The philanthropists, it is worth noting,

kept explicit religious exercises and instruction at arm's length from these working girls' clubs. In part a strategy to bridge religious differences among the members, their approach also reflected impatience with the results of overtly religious intervention in the clubs' affairs. When Mrs. Barnard told her minister, "Keep away from us," she added, "we shall do better if left to our own devices."[98] Those devices were moral influences steeped in Protestantism. Still, the working girls' clubs established an explicitly religion-free zone for their activities, and this made them similar, outwardly at least, to the much larger number of men's labor unions, which were entirely secular in their purpose and organization.

The changes we have identified in the last two chapters require an assessment of Brooklyn's long-established Protestant hegemony. What was the power and reach of Yankee Protestantism at the end of the nineteenth century, when so many Brooklynites were neither Yankee nor Protestant? Clearly, the reach of the old order across the newly settled eighty-one square miles was more limited than it had been when Brooklyn was a much smaller city. It did not extend easily to the immigrant-dominated neighborhoods of the waterfront and an expanding industrial zone. Samuel Lane Loomis, minister of Brooklyn's Tompkins Avenue Congregational Church, no doubt spoke for many members of the Protestant establishment when he sounded the alarm about the threat urban laborers posed to traditional religious practices and values. At a time of social and political upheaval, Loomis wrote in 1887, when civilization "depends upon the purity of its faith," Protestant churches in the nation's cities, "as a rule, have no following among working men."[99]

Nor did the old order fully control the gaiety of Coney Island, or the city's half-dozen theaters, or episodic outbreaks of Sunday baseball in places like Red Hook. The mayors of Brooklyn during this period were likely to be immigrants who did not enforce Yankee-driven blue laws with the rigor of a George Hall or an Edward A. Lambert. Seth Low was there to hold the fort for several years as mayor during the 1880s, but he was more intent on promoting secular progressivism than preserving Yankee Protestant culture. Beecher and Talmage, the great Protestant magnets (and magnates), were gone, and Richard Salter Storrs would die in 1900. Even some of Brooklyn's famed suburbs were now ethnically diverse, places where the neighborhood church was as likely to be Roman Catholic as Protestant.

Looking back on these years in 1915, *Brooklyn Life* wrote of the diminishing power of the "New England element." Gertrude Lefferts Vanderbilt had written in a similar vein in 1881 of the passing of the era of Dutch dominance in Flatbush. Noting that the "first ripple of the rising tide has touched our borders," Mrs. Vanderbilt predicted that "before long the sudden rush of some great wave will sweep away every trace of village life," leaving in its wake only "reminiscences and traditions, while the old family names mark the localities still, as the projecting peaks mark the submerged rock. All that relates to home and kindred has its interest, especially when we know that the home is soon to be broken up and the ties of kindred sundered." Echoing Vanderbilt, another old-timer wrote with resignation from the heart of Yankee Brooklyn that "strangers from apartment houses sit in the ancient family pews of Samuel Harrison Cox's First Presbyterian Church and Henry Ward Beecher's Plymouth Church. The old home of the Church of the Pilgrims, where Richard Salter Storrs once held forth, is now the Maronite rite Catholic Church of Our Lady of Lebanon."[100]

But if Yankee (and in Flatbush, Dutch) Protestantism was no longer hegemonic, it was by no means dissolved and without force. Large numbers of Brooklynites and large areas of this "moral suburb" were still attentive to its strictures and responsive to its values. Outnumbered, and even surrounded, Protestant leaders of the old order were not outgunned. Native white Protestants continued to control Brooklyn's (and in some cases New York City's) largest manufacturing, mercantile, banking, transportation, and real estate industries. Massachusetts-born Horace B. Claflin, who owned one of the world's largest dry goods establishments, cofounded the Continental Bank of New York, lived on Pierrepont Street in Brooklyn Heights, and was a founding trustee of Beecher's Plymouth Church, was an exemplar (if a particularly wealthy one) of the continuing status and power of those who constituted the old order.[101] At the same time, the Irish, Christian and Jewish Germans, and African Americans were establishing their own social, cultural, and religious institutions, and within their own communities were less subject to the direction and dictation of wealthy, white, native-born Protestants. Some had acquired the wealth that led to power. In the waning decades of the nineteenth-century, then, the New England element and its allies ruled but did not reign. And in the new century they would retreat further before a much larger army of Others who would create in Brooklyn a place like no other, not even its former self.

CHAPTER 6

Transformation

Combining New York and Brooklyn into a single city was an old idea. Sometimes, as with Alden Spooner's disgusted reaction in 1833 to a Brooklyn city charter that did not address the issue of ferry and riverfront rights, it took the form of incorporating Brooklyn into New York as just another couple of wards of the larger city. Sometimes it went the other way, as with the *Brooklyn Eagle*'s proposal—tongue firmly planted in cheek—to annex New York to Brooklyn. However it was expressed, the notion of combining the two cities recurred often enough to give it the aura of inevitability to many who lived on both sides of the East River. Yet to turn this seemingly simple idea into a real project needed more than the passage of time; it needed the efforts of a powerful, clearheaded, and determined proponent to start the process and a set of equally powerful proponents to see it through.

The proponent who finally mattered was Andrew Haswell Green, the tight-fisted but visionary comptroller of both the Central Park Commission and the City of New York, who was active in many projects for the betterment of the city, from the New York Public Library to the Metropolitan Museum of Art and the American Museum of Natural History, the street plan and parks of the northern end of Manhattan, the bridging of the Harlem River, and the Bronx Zoo. Green broached the subject of the consolidation of Manhattan and its surrounding New York counties into a vast and politically integrated metropolis as early as 1868. He does not appear to have been involved when serious discussions arose in 1873, nor was he the force behind a consolidation proposal by the New York State Chamber of Commerce in 1887. But he became the principal advocate of this proposal, and in 1890 convinced the state legislature to create a Greater New York Commission. The commission elected Green as its president and for vice president turned to James S. T. Stranahan, Brooklyn's most powerful consolidation supporter.

Green's commission did not agree on a specific plan for consolidation but kept the promised benefits before the public eye. Consolidation assured that Chicago, which was steadily absorbing the smaller towns around it, would not grow larger than New York and usurp its role as the national center of finance and trade. It promised greater coordination and economies in the expansion of municipal services, which in turn would spur more rapid development in the less-settled parts of northern Manhattan and the annexed counties. To Brooklyn it promised a lower rate of taxation to homeowners (Brooklyn's rate was twice as high as Manhattan's because it had fewer large commercial buildings to absorb the costs of municipal government); escape from a rapidly approaching, state-mandated limit to the city's borrowing capacity; and perhaps above all, water. Brooklyn's water system was approaching capacity as the city continued to grow, and the expansion of its Long Island supply was opposed by the growing towns of Suffolk County. New York City's Croton system could provide all the water Brooklyn would require for years to come. These were compelling reasons, but Green knew there was opposition in Brooklyn, and he searched for additional allies. In 1892 some of the wealthiest business leaders formed the Brooklyn Consolidation League. This group had yet another motive for approving consolidation. Most were "Swallowtail" Democrats opposed to Hugh McLaughlin's control of Brooklyn's Democratic Party. Consolidation would at a stroke remove the foundation of McLaughlin's power.

Armed with support in Brooklyn and Manhattan, Green's commission approached the legislature for a bill authorizing a referendum on consolidation to be held in all the affected counties. The referendum was held in 1894, and the result was a large majority in favor—everywhere except Brooklyn, where consolidation was approved by 277 votes out of the 129,211 cast. Not easily interpreted, this slim margin may well have reflected concerns that the devil would reside in details concocted only after the voters had spoken, for this vote was on the idea of consolidation rather than a fully articulated plan. A recent report on police corruption in New York City no doubt increased the wariness of many Brooklyn voters. The opposition, in any case, did not rest. Within a week a League of Loyal Citizens was formed to argue for a new referendum.

This new league did not get its referendum, but it thrived on the uncertainties that lay ahead. At the moment of triumph for Andrew Green's commission, the political landscape changed with a statewide electoral victory by the Republican Party. When Green, a Swallowtail Democrat, arrived in Albany early in 1895 to seek authorization to draft a consolidation charter, he was rebuffed in favor of a proposal for a new commission by the new Republican governor, Levi P. Morton. Thomas C. Platt, the real power in New York's Republican Party, guided a new bill through the legislature in 1896 and engineered approval of the new commission's proposed city charter the following year. Green was a member of that commission, but illness prevented him from having much impact on its deliberations. He was happy to acknowledge Platt as "the Father of Greater New York." Platt, in return, named Green its "Grandfather."[1] The date set for consolidation was January 1, 1898.

Celebrations were held in Manhattan and Brooklyn on a rainy and cold New Year's Eve to greet the midnight advent of the new metropolis. The City of Brooklyn passed into history at that moment, but Brooklyn did not, for as a concession to Brooklyn's deep sense of identity, the commission created a form of government in which each of the consolidating cities and counties would be known as boroughs within the new City of New York. Each borough would have a president, a borough hall, a degree of local autonomy, and a name. On that New Year's Eve Brooklyn's political leaders gathered in the Common Council chamber of what was about to become Brooklyn Borough Hall. Among the speakers was *Eagle* editor St. Clair McKelway, who concluded: "And, therefore, not farewell to Brooklyn, for borough it may be, Brooklyn it is, Brooklyn it remains, and Brooklynites we are."[2]

McKelway had opposed consolidation. His refusal to eulogize Brooklyn—his creation, rather, of an apt motto for many generations of Brooklynites—calls attention to an opposition focused primarily on Brooklyn's long-cherished identity as the City of Churches, whose most outspoken leaders included Protestant clergy and laymen who maintained a strong Yankee identity: Richard Salter Storrs of the Church of the Pilgrims, Lyman Abbott of Plymouth Church, Theodore L. Cuyler of the Lafayette Avenue Presbyterian Church, Charles H. Hall of Holy Trinity Church, Bishop Abram N. Littlejohn of the Episcopal Diocese of Long Island, and Robert D. Benedict of the New England Society of Brooklyn. A. A. Low and Henry E. Pierrepont represented two of Brooklyn's oldest and wealthiest Yankee families. "What distinguished the Loyal Leaguers . . . was their vision of Brooklyn," writes one historian of this era. "All of them were deeply devoted to Brooklyn's Anglo-American Protestant institutions and to the way of life those institutions symbolized and encouraged."[3] Theirs was a world, writes another, of "New England virtues, seasoned, mildly, with a dash of Dutch character."[4]

These men feared the changes consolidation would bring to that way of life and their authority over it. The simple fact of unification with sinful New York was troubling enough, but the transfer of most aspects of municipal authority to a mayor who might care little about Brooklyn's laws and traditions, and to a city council on which Brooklyn's representatives would always be outnumbered, raised more specific concerns. Would the new city government threaten the sanctity of Brooklyn's Sabbath even more than Coney Island and the unlocked side doors of Red Hook saloons? How free with licensing would this government be and how tough on houses of ill repute? What influence could the old Yankee leaders exert over a City Hall on the wrong side of the river? Beyond these concerns were even deeper ones based on demographics. To New Yorkers consolidation promised a transportation system that could begin to relieve the overcrowding of Manhattan's immigrant East Side, reputedly the most congested acreage on the planet. Brooklynites of the League of Loyal Citizens saw this as more threat than opportunity. When Richard Storrs looked across the river, he saw the tenements of the East Side "into which the political sewage of Europe is being dumped every week."[5] With consolidation, he feared, this "sewage" would seep into Brooklyn, altering the balance between suburban homes and tenements and between its comparatively homogeneous population and a most un-Yankee-like population of Jews and Catholics from Eastern and Southern Europe.

In 1896, as the consolidation bill worked its way through the state legislature, Brooklyn's final mayor, the German-American Frederick W. Wurster, wrote with equanimity about the changes to come: "Brooklyn is largely a New England and American city. That element is large enough to assimilate any foreign element in or coming to Brooklyn."[6] But Storrs's fears, expressed with an exaggerated notion of Brooklyn's existing homogeneity, were well grounded. Storrs did not live to see it, but the twentieth-century Borough of Brooklyn would be transformed by the migration of Eastern and Southern Europeans from Manhattan's East Side. Consolidation, through the promotion of inter-borough transportation, facilitated this mass movement of people.

During the first fifteen years of the twentieth century more than thirteen million immigrants arrived at American ports, a number far exceeding any comparable period in the nation's history. Nearly six million, many of them Jewish, arrived from Russia, the Baltics, the Austro-Hungarian Empire, and other areas of Eastern Europe. Three million came from Italy. British, Irish, German, and Scandinavian migrants arrived as well, but their numbers were dwarfed by the so-called New Immigrants from the east and south.[7] The majority of these immigrants entered the country through New York, and some found their first American homes in the tenements of Manhattan's East Side, which were already crowded with immigrant families. The two square miles of this district housed more than four hundred fifty thousand people at the turn of the century and added another one hundred thousand by 1910, even as some began the flow across the East River.[8]

As Storrs spoke of the dangers to Brooklyn's character, plans were underway to improve the physical connections between the two great cities. The Brooklyn Bridge had become increasingly crowded over the years and it did not take long for proposals to emerge for a second bridge over the East River. Construction began in 1896 and was completed in half the time it took to build the Brooklyn Bridge, opening to traffic on December 19, 1903. Built almost entirely of steel, it eclipsed the Brooklyn Bridge as the world's longest suspension bridge by four and a half feet. Most notable, though, was its route. Its Brooklyn terminus was Williamsburg, near Broadway, the long thoroughfare forming the boundary between Bushwick and Bedford and ending a stone's throw from Brownsville and East New York. The bridge's Manhattan terminus, as Storrs knew when he spoke of Europe's sewage, was Delancey Street in the heart of the predominantly Jewish East Side. Almost immediately, the Williamsburg Bridge began carrying thousands of East Side tenement dwellers, many of them displaced by the bridge itself, to new homes in Williamsburg's Dutchtown, in Bushwick and Bedford, and in Brownsville and East New York. The bridge quickly acquired two nicknames: the Jews' Highway and the Passover Bridge.

Even before the Williamsburg Bridge was completed, construction began on a third bridge between Manhattan and Brooklyn. Built between 1901 and 1909, the Manhattan Bridge linked Canal Street in Manhattan to Brooklyn's Flatbush Avenue. Because its location was so close to the Brooklyn Bridge, and particularly its downtown Brooklyn terminus, the Manhattan Bridge at first played a somewhat smaller role in transferring immigrant homes to Brooklyn. It became more important after 1915 when it began to carry a Brooklyn Rapid Transit (BRT) subway line across the river and down Brooklyn's Fourth Avenue, rejuvenating suburban growth in the southwestern quadrant of the borough as far as Bay Ridge. New York's new subway system, which fed more lines to Brooklyn through tunnels under the river, was an enormous stimulus to Brooklyn's expansion. The first to link Manhattan

FIGURE 6.1. The Williamsburg Bridge (Library of Congress Prints & Photographs Division).

to Brooklyn, an Interborough Rapid Transit (IRT) line, tunneled from Manhattan's South Ferry under the East River and Brooklyn Heights (the Joralemon Street Tunnel) to Borough Hall and a terminus at Flatbush and Atlantic Avenues, where there was also a terminal of the Long Island Railroad. This subway allowed Brooklynites access to Manhattan from many neighborhoods, old and new. It opened in 1908, more than a year before the Manhattan Bridge, and seven years before the bridge began to carry the BRT's Fourth Avenue subway. Three more subway tunnels linked the two boroughs by 1924, the last carrying a BRT line from 14th Street in Manhattan into Williamsburg and, within a few years, all the way to Canarsie in the southeast corner of Brooklyn.

Three bridges and four subway tunnels bound Brooklyn to Manhattan more closely than the ferries had ever done. They also put these old watercraft out of business. The Fulton Ferry, which operated from a slip only a few yards from the eastern tower of the Brooklyn Bridge, sent out its last boat in January of 1924, nearly three centuries after ferry service began on the East River, 110 years after Robert Fulton's steam ferries began to ply the river, and forty years after the great bridge was supposed to make ferry service obsolete. Brooklyn's South Ferry held on until 1933. Whatever mourning there may have been for the loss of these ancient services (and for the magic Walt Whitman described in the river crossing) was overshadowed, in the local press at least, by dozens of favorable descriptions of the various new transit facilities, and by predictions of booming real estate markets. The League of Loyal Citizens had predicted that these improvements would destroy Brooklyn's unique character. But once the bridges and subways were built they were greeted, even by consolidation opponents such as St. Clair McKelway's *Brooklyn Daily Eagle*, as routes to a brighter future.

The numbers confirmed both Yankee anxieties and promoters' dreams. Between 1900 and 1910 Brooklyn added some six hundred thousand new residents; in the next decade it added four hundred thousand more. These new Brooklynites put the old "town across the river" on the cusp of passing Manhattan in size. During the 1920s it became New York's most populous borough, its nearly 2.6 million inhabitants easily surpassing Manhattan's 1.9 million. Manhattan lost nearly half a million people between 1910 and 1930 to Brooklyn, the other outer boroughs, and more distant suburbs. Much of that outward migration originated from the East Side, which accounted for more than half of Manhattan's population loss.[9] Brooklyn grew from other sources as well, but its population mix in 1930 reveals the importance of the borough as an area of second settlement for the New Immigrants. In that year immigrants and their children amounted to fully 78 percent of Brooklyn's population. African Americans contributed another 3 percent (growing, but still small), which means that native-born white Brooklynites with native-born parents constituted only 19 percent of the total population.[10] Since a large if unknowable number within this 19 percent were third-generation Irish Catholics and German Protestants, Catholics, and Jews, the proportion of Anglo-Dutch Protestants in the City of Churches must have been very small. Already an important feature of the nineteenth-century city, Brooklyn's ethnic and religious diversity was the defining fact of the early twentieth-century borough. Although Yankee Protestants retained elements of their former influence in this new urban mosaic, the extent of that influence was contained as never before by the massive influx of immigrants that so worried the Rev. Richard Salter Storrs.

Nearly eight hundred thousand of Brooklyn's population in 1930, a little more than 30 percent of the total, were Eastern Europeans and their children. This group included Russian Orthodox Christians as well as Jews and Catholics from the Baltics and the Austro-Hungarian Empire. Many were

Jews fleeing the pogroms and restrictive laws of Russia and attracted by the economic opportunities of the United States. The Jewish presence among this diverse population is difficult to calculate. The 1930 census reported 317,485 immigrants in Brooklyn whose mother tongue was Yiddish.[11] If we assume all these Yiddish speakers were from Eastern Europe (a few might have emigrated from Central and Western European countries) and that all the Eastern European Jewish immigrants in Brooklyn reported Yiddish, rather than Russian, Polish, or Hungarian, as their mother tongue, we can conclude that 85 percent of Brooklyn's Eastern European immigrants were Jews, and that, counting their American-born children (who were not asked the language question), about 675,000 Eastern European Jews lived in Brooklyn in 1930.[12] This calculation does not, however, account for German-speaking Jews among 265,000 German and Austrian immigrants and their American-born children, a sprinkling of Spanish and Portuguese speakers from South America, and a number of third-generation Jews whose parents and grandparents (mostly German in background) had formed the Jewish communities of Brooklyn and New York City in the nineteenth century. We estimate the actual number of Brooklyn's Jews in 1930 as within the range of 750,000 and 850,000, at least fifteen times the 50,000 or so who lived in the new borough at the turn of the century. From the small if visible community of the 1890s they had become Brooklyn's largest population cohort.[13]

A significant portion of Brooklyn's Eastern European Jews arrived in the borough during the dozen or so years between the opening of the Williamsburg Bridge and World War I. According to contemporary estimates, the Jewish population of Brooklyn grew to approximately three hundred thousand by 1910 and to five hundred thousand or more by 1916, the year before the United States entered the war.[14] The bulk of this new population settled in two areas—the old Dutchtown district of Williamsburg and the more distant former New Lots village of Brownsville—both in the path of transit lines leading away from the Williamsburg Bridge. Both offered inducements beyond easy transportation for would-be commuters to East Side jobs, including existing synagogues and kosher butcher shops. Williamsburg's 16th ward (extending eastward into the 18th) was a settled urban neighborhood that conformed to no one's image of a suburb. Even before the bridge, the *Eagle* portrayed it as Brooklyn's equivalent to Manhattan's East Side.[15] But it was not as crowded as the East Side and cost became a significant attraction when, in 1904 and 1905, East Side landlords increased rents that many families already struggled to afford.[16] Some East Side Jews thought of Williamsburg as a step up in the world; for others it was merely an affordable place to live.

FIGURE 6.2. Jewish women and girls recite Rosh Hashanah prayers on the Williamsburg Bridge (Library of Congress Prints & Photographs Division).

Brownsville was different. It was a suburb in the older meaning of a hybrid urban periphery, more affordable than lovely, where stores, taverns, workshops, a few factories, and a surviving farm or two shared space with the small frame houses and shanties of a semi-rural working population that included a number of immigrants from Scotland. The rustic and ethnic character of Brownsville began to change during the 1880s, when a Russian Jewish clothing contractor named Elias Kaplan transferred his large East Side shop there and arranged to have two-family houses built for his workers. Businesses in clothing and other trades followed, and Brownsville was gradually transformed into a Jewish community that attracted much larger numbers after the Williamsburg Bridge was opened.

As it grew, Brownsville was transformed from a small village of unpaved and unlighted streets into a more imposing if distant urban section of Brooklyn, with a full range of municipal services and a growing commercial center (its main artery, Pitkin Avenue, named after the region's visionary pioneer) surrounded by streets lined with one- and two-family homes. In the years following the opening of the bridge, Brownsville attracted more East Siders than Williamsburg, and as the local population climbed past one hundred thousand, tenements, not houses, dominated the townscape. As it pushed upward and outward into still-empty fields, Brownsville gave the impression of a walled town.[17]

The two core Eastern European Jewish communities of pre–World War I Brooklyn soon became as densely populated as Manhattan's East Side. Rising density brought higher rents, as it had done on the East Side. Not surprisingly, these led to a leveling of the growth of Williamsburg and Brownsville, which was also affected by the slowing of foreign immigration during and after the war, and by an exodus from both places to other, more suburban neighborhoods in and beyond Brooklyn. Some of those who moved sought cheaper rents, while others who had prospered looked for better homes in more prestigious neighborhoods. Williamsburg's better-off Jews, for example, moved slightly southward into brownstone neighborhoods near downtown Brooklyn and in South Brooklyn, where, as it happens, nineteenth-century German Jews had lived without creating a distinct Jewish quarter. Others went further south, to Borough Park, Dyker Heights, Bensonhurst, and Bath Beach, where land was cheap and brand-new suburban homes could be purchased on easy terms. Brownsville's out-migrants found similar

FIGURE 6.3. Apartments above stores, Pitkin and Saratoga Avenues, Brownsville (Milstein Division, New York Public Library).

conditions in nearby Flatbush and Canarsie.[18] A detailed postwar study of the expansion of Brooklyn's Jewish population indicated a typical sequence in each: initial single-family homes, followed by duplex homes, and then by apartment houses, the latter making possible a still larger local migration.[19]

This pattern of resettlement from Manhattan's East Side to Williamsburg, Brownsville, and then more suburban areas fits well with an often-repeated story of immigrant upward mobility in the United States—the realization of the American Dream for millions, Jews and others, who came in search of a better life for themselves and their families. The house in the suburbs was and still is an expression of that success. But the outward migration from neighborhoods of initial immigrant settlement was a more complicated phenomenon, even among immigrants who were not just looking for cheaper housing.

An episode in Michael Gold's 1930 novel *Jews without Money*—a fictionalized memoir of growing up on Manhattan's East Side before and after the turn of the century—captures the most significant of these complications. Mikey, the narrator, describes his father Herman as a man of fierce if

FIGURE 6.4. Newly built townhouses in Dyker Heights, 77th Street and 12th Avenue, offered for sale by a Jewish firm, 1928 (Milstein Division, New York Public Library).

often-thwarted ambition who seems finally to have found an avenue to success as a foreman for Zachariah Cohen, a painting contractor who is dabbling in home construction in the embryonic suburb of Brooklyn's Borough Park:

> "We are going to move from the East Side," my father announced one night. "My Boss advised me to move out to Borough Park, where he himself lives. He is willing to sell me a house and lot on the installment plan. He says a man with a future should not live on the East Side."
>
> "But all my friends live here," my mother said. "I would miss them. It is only people with money who live in Borough Park."
>
> "What of it?" said my father. "I also will soon be rich."

The family journeys one Sunday to Borough Park, where they visit Cohen's gaudy house, and then "through slushy weeds under the damp sky" the row of eight wooden houses within which stands the one Herman hopes to buy. On the way home Herman asks his wife what she thought of it:

> "I don't like it," said my mother.
>
> "And why not?" my father said indignantly. "Are you so much in love with that sewer of an East Side?"
>
> "No," said my mother. "But I will be lonesome here. I am used only to plain people; I will miss the neighbors on Chrystie Street."
>
> "But there will be neighbors here," said my father.
>
> "Herman, don't make me do it," my mother pleaded. "I can't do it, Herman. My heart is heavy thinking about it."
>
> "Foolishness!" my father exclaimed, biting his cigar. "We will move here, I say! You must not hold me down! I refuse to be an East Side beggar all my life! Do you hear?"
>
> My mother turned her face from him, and stared at the weeds, the slush, the exultant signboards of Borough Park.[20]

Mikey's family never makes that move. Two months after the visit to Borough Park Herman falls from a scaffold, breaking both of his feet and ending his dreams of wealth and suburban living. After a year of convalescing he finds work peddling bananas on the East Side. Mikey's mother continues to experience the hardships and satisfactions of a poor ghetto family in a familiar and mutually supportive community.

In this episode Gold conveys the opposing values that made departure from the ghetto, in proletarian novels and in real life, more complicated than escape to a better life. Gold's sympathy with Mikey's mother reflects his left-wing ideology—he was editor of *The New Masses* and a columnist for the Communist Party's *Daily Worker*—but his book is more than a political

polemic. His portrayals of the crowded Jewish quarter of New York illumi-
nate the lives that could be lived there, with synagogues, shops, cafes, and
Yiddish theater giving them shape and meaning.[21] Most of the Jewish immigrants in this community did leave, and many were glad to go. Real-life
Zacharias Cohens had little trouble selling their rows of wood-frame houses
in Borough Park. But dense social worlds do not surrender their children or
their communal identities easily.

Among the ligaments of these Jewish communities—the East Side, Williamsburg, Brownsville, and beyond—were the institutions that were built
there. Unlike the German Jews, who in Brooklyn built a small number of
poorly attended (mostly Reform) synagogues, Russian and other Eastern European Jews founded many active and well-attended traditional synagogues
that in turn spawned social and mutual benefit societies intended to provide
a physically mobile and generally needy community with sociability, health
care, loans, life insurance, and places to be buried. They also established numerous charities independent of the synagogues, along with a (mostly German) Brooklyn Federation of Jewish Charities to coordinate their efforts. To
serve the five hundred thousand Jews in Brooklyn, the *Eagle* noted in 1916,
"it would seem as if there were nearly 500,000 charitable organizations."[22]

Clubs, a revived YMHA, labor unions, and Zionist and other political organizations attracted more secular and radical members of the community.[23]
For the religious, though, synagogues were the vital centers of community
life. Synagogue membership and attendant benefits were sometimes tied to
the immigrants' communities of origin, which echoed the immigration process itself. Many Jewish immigrants arrived with the promise of employment
from family members or former neighbors who had preceded them to the
United States (Mikey's father had a job waiting for him in the suspender-
end factory of a neighbor from his Rumanian village), which could lead to
synagogue and other memberships, a process that personalized these institutional and contractual relations in the American *shtetl*.[24]

Secular Jews did not need the synagogue to find their way into mutual
benefit societies, some of which were formed among residents from the
same village or *shtetl* without reference to religion, nor did they lack other
forms of organized sociability. The unionists and political radicals among
them enjoyed a particularly extensive associational life in union halls, political
meeting rooms, cafes, and the Labor Lyceum. These two poles of the Jewish
community (call them the Orthodox and the Radicals) account for some of
the organizational density within the community, for each pole insisted on its
own institutions. The separation was not absolute—religious garment workers belonged to unions, and both groups promoted Zionism and expressed

support for Jews who remained in the Old World—but numerous organizations catered to one or the other of these poles of Jewish society. What the Orthodox and the Radicals shared, beyond some overlap of membership and purpose, was the inclination and the ability to form institutions from their own resources, within the narrow spaces of Siegel Street and Pitkin Avenue.

They also shared the benefits that came from resources beyond the East European Jewish community. A number of German Jews of Manhattan and Brooklyn had become quite wealthy. Despite the rise of elite anti-Semitism signaled by the Seligman affair, these Jews—uptown Jews in common parlance—had carved out a significant if largely separate space for themselves in the upper strata of American society. The arrival in America of massive numbers of poor Eastern European Jews and the settlement of many of them in New York presented wealthy Jews with a philanthropic opportunity that grew from two different motives. They desired to help coreligionists in their adaptation to new surroundings; and they feared that these easily reviled, Yiddish-speaking aliens, Orthodox and Radicals alike, threatened their own standing in American society. Both motives led to the dual strategy of uplifting and Americanizing the refugees through institutions that lay beyond the financial reach of the immigrants themselves.[25] In Brooklyn a large Jewish Hospital, which opened in 1906, was one such institution. But a somewhat earlier one, the Hebrew Educational Society of Brooklyn, was perhaps the most important.

In 1898 Adolphus S. Solomon, acting as the American general agent of the Europe-based Baron de Hirsch Fund, financed a small vacation school for Brownsville's Jewish children that also offered English-language instruction for adults. A year later, he and another de Hirsch Fund trustee, Abraham Abraham, proposed the enlargement of this school into a multi-purpose community center. Abraham's leadership was especially important. Born in Manhattan to Bavarian immigrants, Abraham made his fortune as the principal owner of Brooklyn's largest department store and became the city's most important leader of local Jewish institutions. He was a long-term president of Brooklyn's (Reform) Temple Israel and the Hebrew Orphan Asylum, as well as president of the new Jewish Hospital, and an influential member of the Brooklyn Federation of Jewish Charities and other Jewish philanthropies. He was not the founding president of the Hebrew Educational Society; that distinction fell to his son-in-law, Simon F. Rothschild, an appointment that underscored the role of this family, and of wealthy German Jews more generally, in the founding of vital new Brownsville institutions.[26]

From its new home on Pitkin Avenue, the Hebrew Educational Society (HES) offered schooling from kindergarten to adult night school, a library, a gym, public baths, lectures, youth clubs and dances, English and Yiddish theater (they did not ask Yankee Protestants or German Jews if this was suitable), even a branch bank. In its varied educational program, the HES revealed an important motivational distinction between the German Jewish founders and local leaders from the Russian Jewish community. The former stressed classes in English and citizenship training as a route to a rapid and thorough Americanization, while the latter insisted on a weekday afternoon school in Hebrew and Judaism intended to preserve Jewish identity even as Brownsville's residents sought American citizenship. The Abrahams and Rothschilds who supported the HES may have wished for a more complete washing of Jewishness from Brownsville's growing Eastern European population. The Brownsvillians themselves, whether they gravitated to the Orthodox or Radical poles of Jewish society, were interested in becoming Americans without surrendering their notion—however different that may have been from Abraham Abraham's—of what it meant to be Jewish.[27]

The Hebrew Educational Society did not seek to replace Brooklyn's public schools. Some of Brownsville's Jewish children attended the afternoon Hebrew schools of local synagogues or the HES, but nearly all of them attended public schools, which have long been recognized as the great assimilators of immigrant children. Perhaps this Americanizing effect was modified in homogeneous neighborhoods such as Brownsville, where nearly all the students were Jewish. Significantly, however, when the parents of these students protested against the singing of Christmas carols and other forms of Christian celebration and worship in the public schools, as they did regularly throughout this period and beyond, their objections were directed to the entire school system of Brooklyn, not only to schools in their own neighborhoods. And they made it clear that they were speaking as American citizens in defense of the Constitutional principle of secular governance, not as a religious minority who lacked the power to insert their own celebrations and sacred texts into the curriculum.[28] By speaking up, frequently and forcefully, Jews asserted that they were not strangers in a strange land but Americans with the same rights as the Yankee Protestants who put Christian celebration in the schools in the first place. They made the same claim, more implicitly and not without irony, in their support of Jews who remained in Russia and of the Zionist idea of establishing a Middle Eastern Jewish homeland. Expressions of this support contain no hint of an intention to leave the United States, either to a reformed, less anti-Semitic Russia, or a restored Jewish homeland. The Jews of Brooklyn, Orthodox and Radical, rich and poor, Brownsvillian and Borough Parker, were here to stay, as Americans and as Jews.

Reconciling these dual identities constitutes a central theme in Jewish-American literature from Abraham Cahan to Philip Roth. It is beautifully conveyed, too, in the memoir of a Brownsville native, Alfred Kazin. As a teen, Kazin took long, solitary walks during which he reflected on the limits Brownsville placed on him. "We were of the city," he writes, "but somehow not in it." His favorite route took him up a hill to the old Ridgewood reservoir, where he looked across Brooklyn to the skyscrapers of Manhattan. "I saw New York as a foreign city. . . . I would come back to Brownsville along Liberty Avenue, and, as soon as I could see blocks ahead of me the Labor Lyceum, the malted milk and Fatima signs over the candy stores, the old women in their housedresses sitting in front of the tenements like priestesses of an ancient cult, knew I was home." "We were at the end of the line," Kazin continues. "We were the children of the immigrants who had camped at the city's back door, in New York's rawest, remotest, cheapest ghetto." Finally: "*They* were New York, the Gentiles, America; we were Brownsville— *Brunzvil*, as the old folks said—the dust of the earth to all Jews with money, and notoriously a place that measured all success by our skill in getting away from it."[29]

Kazin may have feared a stunted life in Brunzvil, but he got away from it by becoming a master of American literature, one of the most respected literary scholars and critics of his time. In another memoir he proclaimed himself a *New York Jew*, but this identity (larger than Brownsville) comported well with his comfort in the works of Emerson, Faulkner, and Fitzgerald. For all his insight he might not have fully appreciated the extent to which Brooklyn's "rawest, cheapest ghetto" launched him to his larger American life.

Jewish New Yorkers such as Kazin were acutely aware of how they differed from Anglo and Dutch Protestants who seemed to own the city, as well as Irish-Americans and German-Americans who had long since claimed their share of comfort and influence. But they differed, too, from other recent immigrant groups, such as Italians, who arrived in Manhattan and Brooklyn around the same time. Italian immigration to the United States increased gradually during the last two decades of the nineteenth century, and dramatically between 1900 and the beginning of World War I. In Brooklyn, an Italian immigrant population of barely more than a thousand in 1880 increased to thirty-seven thousand in 1900, and more than one hundred thousand by 1910. There were also American-born children in Brooklyn's growing Italian community, but fewer than in other immigrant groups, mainly because many Italian men came to Brooklyn to work and save rather than form families. Some were "birds of passage," keeping alive an old southern Italian tradition of repeat migration between Italian homes and work in distant lands. The *Eagle* estimated in 1902 that there were three times as many men as women among the Italians of Brooklyn, suggesting the presence of men who did not see America as their permanent home.[30] Almost surely an exaggeration, this ratio moderated over the years. The 1920 US census recorded 122 Italian males to 100 females in Brooklyn, still a larger gender imbalance than among Eastern Europeans, but an indication that this characteristic of the Italian community was disappearing. In 1930 the ratio of second-generation to immigrant Italians was only slightly lower than it was among Eastern Europeans. The Italian population of Brooklyn was just under four hundred thousand in that year, and nearly all of these people—a community about half the size of the Jews—apparently had no intention of returning to Italy.[31]

Another difference was the greater dispersal of the new Italian communities across the Brooklyn townscape. Like Jews who lived in Brownsville and Williamsburg's Dutchtown, most Italians settled first in Manhattan, mainly in a Little Italy just to the west of the Jewish East Side and came to Brooklyn

FIGURE 6.5.   Lewis Hine photo of Italian immigrants on Ellis Island (Photography Collection, New York Public Library).

during the same time Jews were pouring over the "Passover Bridge." But while Brooklyn's new Jews settled mostly in two communities, the Italians created at least nine or ten. The larger Italian settlements were nearer to the old ferry landings than to the Williamsburg Bridge (for which there was no Italian nickname), and the ferries, not the new transportation links between the boroughs, played the larger role in carrying Italians to Brooklyn. One Italian neighborhood was along the South Brooklyn waterfront still served by the South and Hamilton ferries. Another was in Vinegar Hill and the old downtown near the Catherine and Fulton ferries. A third, in Williamsburg's 14th ward, was near but not centered on the river, not especially close to a ferry, and significantly north of the bridge's Brooklyn terminus. Smaller settlements were in Gowanus, near Green-Wood Cemetery, a slice of the northern end of Brownsville (soon to be known as Ocean Hill), East New York, and a few other distant locations, including Flatbush, Coney Island, Bensonhurst, and Bay Ridge.[32]

The best explanation for the location of Italian settlements, especially the bigger ones, is that the Irish had preceded them there. Both groups, especially in the earlier years of their American residence, contained large numbers of men whose experience as small farmers and farm laborers in their home country gave them little access to the better paying jobs of the American urban economy. Many of them gravitated to areas on and near the East River waterfront, where they found jobs as day laborers on the docks and ditch diggers in nearby city streets. The Irish were the first to take these jobs and create neighborhoods in the old downtown, near the South Brooklyn and Williamsburg waterfronts and in Gowanus. Italians followed them, but only in part because of employment near the river and the Gowanus Canal. Roman Catholic churches, built for the Irish but available to Italians, were already numerous in these neighborhoods, as were parochial schools and other institutions maintained by each church. Irish parishioners often spurned Italians, and several new parishes were formed specifically for the newcomers. There would have been more of these, but the communities themselves were in transition as the Irish left for suburban neighborhoods, abandoning their old parishes to Italians. To the latter this was a significant housewarming gift, a set of crucial institutions they did not have to build for themselves.

Partly for this reason, and partly because a smaller population was spread over a larger number of settlements, Italians created and sustained fewer institutions than did Jews. Institution building may have been delayed somewhat, too, by the presence of those birds of passage who saw a village in southern Italy rather than a neighborhood in Brooklyn as their home. But the existing parish institutions did provide vital services to Italian neighborhoods, even when Irish clergy and laity did the heavy lifting. The Immaculate Conception Day Nursery on Sands Street served the downtown Irish for many years before opening an Italian branch on Front Street, in the heart of one of the largest Italian neighborhoods. The supervising clergy were the Right Rev. C. E. McDonnell (bishop of the Diocese of Brooklyn) and the Very Rev. P. J. McNamara, and the lay officers consisted mostly of Irish women. No woman with an Italian surname was listed among them, but 150 Italian children attended the nursery, others enrolled in after-school programs for older children, and some parents made use of the nursery's employment agency.[33] The charitable Women's Auxiliary of the St. Vincent de Paul Society of Brooklyn, another Irish-run organization, reached across the entire diocese, including places Italians had settled.[34] Well-to-do Protestants also got involved: "some of the best of Brooklyn's citizens," all from Brooklyn Heights, opened the Little Italy Neighborhood House in 1904 on Sackett Street near the South Brooklyn waterfront.[35]

Italians, though, were not simply passive receivers of other people's efforts. They formed their own benevolent societies, often based on their villages, cities, or districts of origin. La Lega Mutua Marsalese was organized by immigrants from the city of Marsala on the west coast of Sicily. La Societa Gragnanesi di Brooklyn assisted *campagnoli* from the Neapolitan district of Gragnano. La Societa Cittadini Giffonesi di Brooklyn did the same for migrants from the small city of Giffone in the heart of Calabria. There was also a Societa Nazionale Italiana, but whether this organization coordinated the work of the more parochial ones is difficult to say.[36]

The smaller mutual aid societies also functioned as social clubs, sponsoring dances, banquets, and summer picnics. They became visible to the outside world during parades and feasts celebrating a local patron saint.[37] Italians took to the streets more often than other ethnic groups, celebrating saints and Catholic holy days such as the Feast of the Assumption.[38] As expressions of the continuing tug of Italian nationalism they paraded everywhere on the birthday of Christopher Columbus and the anniversary of the 1861 unification of Italy, insisting, usually with success, that the Italian flag be flown on public buildings along with the Stars and Stripes.[39] They turned out in great numbers to mourn the assassination of King Umberto I on July 29, 1900, driven to the streets in part by the embarrassment that his assassin was an Italian-American anarchist, Gaetano Bresci, who lived not far from Brooklyn in Paterson, New Jersey. Bresci, alas, underscored for some Americans a stereotype of the Italian male as violent, lawless, and resistant to assimilation. To counter that stereotype and prove their American patriotism, Italians paraded with gusto on the Fourth of July ("il Quattro glorioso"), carrying American and Italian flags.[40] The surrender of Austria at the end of World War I brought a fresh and somewhat raucous expression of Italian nationalism into the streets, but the *Eagle* assured its readers that "our naturalized Italians are as good Americans as we have. There are no better citizens."[41]

Brooklyn's Italian men received some favorable coverage in the local press, which frequently described them as hard-working, thrifty, devoted to family, vivacious, picturesque, and moderate in their drinking.[42] But less generous or more apprehensive Americans distilled darker elements into the stereotype of the dangerous and resolutely alien Sicilian or southern Italian male, skilled in the use of a stiletto or gun, and possibly the member of a secret criminal society.[43] A somewhat less threatening stereotype could be the occasion for attempted humor, as in an *Eagle* profile of South Brooklyn's "Little Italy," which claimed "the first business of the Italian child of the laboring class is to get dirty, and during the rest of his life he exercises proper care that he does not become clean. . . . After he matures he still loves dirt, as evidenced by the fact that he usually shovels it at $1.25 per diem."[44] Italian workingmen, of course, did not love either dirt or low pay, but the number of Italian ditch and cellar diggers provided visible verification of this stereotype to Brooklynites who passed by in the streets—in contrast to poorly paid Jewish garment workers who worked indoors, out of sight to those willing to make simplistic judgments about immigrant workers' lives. Somehow, the cleanliness of the small businessmen in the Italian quarters did not register as forcefully as the dirt that covered men who toiled with shovels.

The dirt was real, as were episodes of violence that occurred when Italian men worked alongside Irish workers. A fistfight, or a general brawl, could be provoked by even a small ethnic insult; on one occasion it was an Italian worker's effrontery of humming an Irish tune, on another an Irishman's making fun of an Italian's clothes.[45] Again, ethnic conflict often played itself out in outdoor spaces, reinforcing negative perceptions about the larger communities to which they belonged.

Stereotypes arising from fistfights and dirty outdoor work were not as serious as those that branded Italian men as murderously criminal. The press often attributed reports of extortion under the threat of murder, kidnapping, or the bombing of businesses to the Black Hand, a frightening term suggestive (rightly or wrongly) of a single and secretive criminal organization alien to the American experience.[46] That the Black Hand was real, and responsible for all or most of the crimes attributed to it, was attested to by frequent reports on it in *Il Progresso*, New York's principal Italian-language newspaper. *Il Progresso* feared the damage the Black Hand and its imitators were doing not only to their individual victims, most or all of whom were Italian, but to the reputation of the entire Italian community. Editors stressed that secretive crime syndicates violated Italian values, posing a serious problem to law-abiding Italians whose fears and outrage were as great or greater than that of Americans who read about organized Italian crime in English-language newspapers.[47] The damage the Black Hand inflicted on the reputation of the Italian community persisted for decades, perpetuated by the infamy attached to the name Mafia.[48] Brooklyn's Jews grappled with anti-Semitism, a problem that came from outside the Jewish community and helped strengthen solidarity within it. Organized crime, in image and reality, was an internal problem for Italian-Americans who wished to prove themselves valuable and law-abiding citizens of their adopted country.

Jewish and Italian migrations do not complete the story of Brooklyn's growing diversity, though these two groups amounted to nearly half of the borough's population by the end of the 1920s. Catholics from Eastern Europe

FIGURE 6.6. "Business Is Booming" (cartoon by Nelson Harding, *Brooklyn Daily Eagle*, September 7, 1911).

were decidedly different from Jews and did not mix with them any more in the United States than they did in Europe. Polish Catholics settled in Greenpoint in the far northwestern corner of Brooklyn, in the northern part of Sunset Park, and in other areas far from Jewish neighborhoods. They found jobs in the sugar refineries, iron foundries, and other heavy industries (and as grave-diggers in Green-Wood Cemetery), places where Jews did not work.[49] By 1930 there were half a dozen Polish parishes and five that served Lithuanians, Slovaks, and Ukrainians. Another three were created for Catholics from the Middle East.[50] Greek and Russian Orthodox were also present, though not yet in large numbers. About ten thousand Greeks lived in Brooklyn in 1930, and the Russian Orthodox community might not have been much larger, but the churches of both groups added something new to Brooklyn's Christian world. A larger addition, at once familiar and foreign, were Norwegians and other Scandinavians who settled first in Red Hook, then moved southward to Sunset Park and, finally, to Bay Ridge. In 1930, about fifty thousand Scandinavian immigrants and their thirty-four thousand American-born children lived in Brooklyn. All these groups, and others, brought new languages, folkways, and institutions to Brooklyn's social mosaic. Older immigrant sources, meanwhile, were by no means outpaced. Next to Eastern Europeans and Italians, Irish and Germans constituted the largest immigrant groups in the borough, new Irish and their American-born children amounting to more than 150,000, and Germans more than 265,000. The most familiar of ethnic groups in early twentieth-century Brooklyn, they still bore the newcomers' hyphen. They were not to be confused with Yankees.[51]

The dozen or so years before the war saw the most explosive growth of Brooklyn's immigrant communities. This growth heightened concerns of Anglo and Dutch Protestants about the prevalence of hyphenated Americans, concerns that deepened during the war itself, even as the pace of immigration slowed dramatically. Once the war began (and especially after the United States became involved), the issue was not only numbers but the loyalty of immigrants and their children to the United States.

Interestingly, it took some time for that issue to be focused on Brooklyn's German population, even after popular sentiment toward the combatants had taken a decided turn in favor of the English and French. Apart from their resistance to boring Yankee Sundays and their dogged demand that German be taught in the public schools, Germans had long since established themselves as the most favored of Brooklyn's hyphenated Americans. Not many of them were poor or prone to crime or violence. They brought with them the gifts of lager beer and the beer garden, which even Yankees found difficult to criticize. Some were well educated, most were Protestant, and their attachments to the past were more cultural than political. They provided Brooklyn with three mayors (one of them American-born) during the latter years of the preconsolidation era.

In 1910 the *Eagle* published a series of long, favorable articles on "Our German-American Neighbors," and even as tensions mounted in Europe the tenor of reporting on the German community in Brooklyn remained mostly positive. The paper lauded a German Day festival in 1913 that included German, not American, patriotic music. In 1916, with the war well underway, an article on the contributions of "Germanic Citizens" to Brooklyn's progress was subheaded: "Local Institutions Exhibit Finest Traditions and Traits Making for The Development of Advanced Civic Life—What the Singing and the Turner Societies Have Done for Co-operation in the Community." Making no mention of the war, the article featured an illustration of a monument to Brooklyn's Germans who had died in the American Civil War. Even in 1918, just over five months before the end of a war in which American soldiers were dying from German bullets and mustard gas, the *Eagle*'s report on a Loyalty Parade of immigrant groups noted that the "most significant was the division of 'Americans of German origin'—no longer German-Americans, observe—marching with mottoes: 'Born in Germany—Made in America,' and 'We are loyal to the country of our children.'"[52]

Positive assessments of Brooklyn's Germans by the *Eagle* were offset by concerns rising within the larger community. Late in 1917, for example, with the outcome of the war in doubt, the Rev. Newell Dwight Hillis railed from the pulpit of Plymouth Church against a series of concerts by the Austrian violinist Fritz Kreisler (born Jewish, baptized as a child), pointing out that his nightly thousand-dollar fee could buy fifty rifles to use against American soldiers. Hillis could not prove that Kreisler subsidized the enemy arsenal, but he did succeed in getting this renowned violinist to cancel his concerts. A month later three German high school teachers were convicted of disloyalty, and in May of 1918 the Brooklyn Board of Education eliminated German from the school curriculum. "Our nation is aligned against German kultur," the board argued. "We have had too much of it. We need no more of it." In the same month the Riding and Driving Club of Brooklyn, following the actions of other clubs, forbade the use of German in its clubhouse during the duration of the war. In July, police charged a man named Edward Hall with snatching a German-language paper out of the hands of a passenger on a Brooklyn trolley car. "Five dollar fine," ruled Magistrate Dooley. "It was worth $10," Hall responded. "'Well, I'll make it $10,' decided the magistrate, agreeably." And in an *Eagle* column written less than two months before the armistice, Julius Chambers argued that the naturalization of Germans should be halted. The upsurge of applications for American citizenship, Chambers noted, came from Germans who "had no misgivings about remaining enemy aliens" as long as Germany stood a chance of winning the war. "These last hour applicants ought to be rejected and never accepted as American citizens."[53]

Anti-German sentiment continued after the end of the war. A curious expression of it, less than a week after the armistice, was the refusal by a Brooklyn judge to allow Dr. Charles Isador Weinsweig to change his last name to Warner. "I will not grant such leave," the judge explained, "where the effect of doing so is to enable persons of German extraction to conceal their origin. . . . Neither will I permit the adoption of the names of American families by foreigners." This was a negative way of eliminating the German-American's hyphen—he was simply a German and clearly not an American. Two weeks later the Board of Aldermen, acting at the urging of Brooklyn Borough president Edward Reigelmann (himself a German-American), voted to remove German names from Brooklyn's streets. In May 1919, an increasingly active American Defense Society criticized Brooklyn's Germania Club for a planned fundraising drive to benefit interned German soldiers and sailors. The club's president announced the cancelation of the drive, while insisting "we are Americans, first, last, and all the time." Concerts by German orchestras and singers were also canceled, and one *Eagle* correspondent objected to German-language preaching and instruction at the First German Presbyterian Church of Williamsburg. That July, one Frank Savolksi was convicted of disloyalty and sentenced to thirty days in the workhouse for flying a small German flag alongside the American flag. The sentencing magistrate added his personal opinion that the offender should be deported, inventing as he did so the category of "undesirable citizen."[54]

Even before anti-German sentiment heated up, native Brooklynites, like their counterparts throughout the United States, worried about the loyalties and prospects of assimilation of hyphenated Americans. Early in the war Brooklynites took steps to ensure all immigrants respected America's neutrality and evinced no loyalty other than to the United States. Only days after the war began a correspondent to the *Eagle* cautioned "the naturalized American citizen" to be "mindful of his renunciation of allegiance to his native country and his assumption of obligations and fealty to the United States of America."[55] Made long before American policy hardened against Germany, the warning applied as much to Russian, Italian, and even English immigrants as it did to those from Germany or Austria. Within a few months a new National Americanization Committee began a multifaceted effort to eliminate Old World loyalties within American ethnic communities, focusing on the New Immigrants from Eastern and Southern Europe. A poster distributed nationally by this committee in conjunction with the US Bureau of Education encouraged immigrants to study English and become citizens, offering this advice in English, Hebrew, Italian, and four Slavic languages, but, oddly, not in German. A swarthy Uncle Sam pictured in the poster shakes the hand of a young workingman devoid of stereotypical ethnic features. The large heading reads: "America First."[56]

The National Americanization Committee was one of many groups, formed mainly by upper- and middle-class white Protestants, that addressed the issue of hyphenated Americans. Another organization, New York's Colonial Daughters of the Seventeenth Century was addressed in March of 1916 by Mrs. A. H. Hildreth, president of the New York State Federation of Women's Clubs. A month later the better-known Daughters of the American Revolution formed a Brooklyn branch of its Loyal League under the leadership of Mrs. George Chapin Taft of Stuyvesant Heights. The league promoted patriotism among public school children with a variety of exercises, including patriotic essays and the signing of a now familiar pledge to the American flag ("and to the Republic for which it stands"). Although the DAR did not refer specifically to immigrant children as targets of these efforts, the organization's leaders understood that most of them, save for the Catholics, attended the public schools, and there can be little doubt that the Loyal League's patriotism program was aimed at them.[57] The Americanization initiative also targeted factories. In February 1917, a Brooklyn Community Chorus was organized to lead workers in singing "patriotic and other well-known songs" on their lunch break. Before the year was out smaller groups in Greenpoint and other neighborhoods were using the same approach.[58]

Americanizers applied their programs to all hyphenates well into the postwar period; indeed, this strategy received fresh impetus from a decided turn of fear and animosity away from Germans and toward Russians and other immigrants suspected of sympathy with or complicity in the Bolshevik Revolution and the international Communist movement. This first Red Scare was fueled not only by the revolution in Russia but by an escalation of labor conflict in the United States. Strikes increased dramatically in 1919, many of them led by the most radical of American labor organizations, the International Workers of the World (IWW), or Wobblies.

Brooklyn experienced few strikes in 1919, but there were many political radicals in and outside of the borough's labor movement, nearly all of them drawn from immigrant communities. Voices were raised against them from editorial and legislative desks, the pulpit, and judicial benches. In January a young "Bolshevist-dentist" named Morris Zucker was sentenced to fifteen years in prison and denied bail pending an appeal, for giving a "Red" speech at Brownsville's Labor Lyceum in violation of the Espionage Act. "Today there is nothing more important to the country than that its citizens be loyal," declared the judge, "and disloyalty to the United States will not be tolerated."[59] In February, the Rev. G. A. Simons, a former head of the Methodist Episcopal Church in Russia, declared before a Senate subcommittee that "the predominating influence on Bolshevist propaganda was the Yiddish element of the East Side."[60] Had he known New York better or waited two months he would have added Brownsville, where a meeting of prominent Bolsheviks took place in April. At least 1,100 of the 1,200 people in the audience, the *Eagle* reporter estimated, were immigrants or the children of immigrants, and most of them spoke Yiddish.[61] Yiddish was also the native tongue of a socialist hired in October by a private school in Brownsville to teach, of all things, English.[62]

US Attorney General A. Mitchell Palmer launched his (now infamous) raids in Brooklyn on November 8. Federal Secret Service agents and local police rounded up more than two hundred Reds in Brooklyn and more than five hundred throughout the city in raids on thirty district headquarters of the Communist Party. In Brownsville they raided Russian, Lithuanian, Ukrainian, Italian, and Jewish branches of the party and discovered a Communist Party dance underway in a hall on Pitkin Avenue. After allowing the women to leave they arrested fifty-two men. The largest haul in Brooklyn, though, was of members of the Finnish Socialist Society, which was staging a play that evening titled *The War*. More than one hundred Finns were arrested, again after women (and children) were allowed to go home.[63] The widely shared conviction that communism was an alien force was emphasized in Brooklyn six days after the raids when the *Eagle* published a political cartoon (drawn by Nelson Harding) showing a stereotypical Italian man, mean-looking, stiletto-armed, and labeled "Alien Red," about to be clubbed on the head by the star-studded arm of Uncle Sam.[64]

The Palmer raids resulted in the arrest of more than three thousand suspected radicals nationwide and the deportation of more than five hundred of them. Support for this draconian policy quickly waned, however, and fears of an American communist revolution gradually abated, temporarily at least, with the return of prosperity in the early 1920s. But the popular association between subversion and hyphenated Americans remained. The 1921 murder trial in Massachusetts of two Italian immigrant anarchists, Nicola Sacco and Bartolomeo Vanzetti, helped solidify the connection. Later assertions of their innocence were at once a landmark outcry against unjust treatment of the dispossessed and a reminder of the political radicalism of two immigrant men.

Attempts to deal with hyphenated Americans were three-pronged and occurred in overlapping phases: first, hastening Americanization through instruction of immigrant adults and their children in American civic values and the English language; then, arresting and deporting Communists and other political radicals deemed dangerous and incapable of assimilation; and, finally, pressing to restrict further immigration. At almost the same moment as the Sacco-Vanzetti trial the United States Congress enacted the Emergency Quota Act, limiting immigration from countries outside the Western hemisphere to 3 percent of the population from those countries residing in the United States in 1910. This draconian restriction, aimed at would-be immigrants from Eastern and Southern Europe, was significantly reinforced by the Immigration Act of 1924, which reduced the quota to 2 percent and changed the base year to 1890 when the population of non-Western Europeans was much smaller.[65] In effect, this legislation ended the era of the New Immigration. But it did not end this new era of pluralism, which consisted not merely of enforced or cajoled Americanization, but, among the Italians, Jews, Finns, Greeks, and Poles permitted to arrive and stay, of continuing ethnic and religious traditions, adaptations to new circumstances, self-generated and self-defined Americanization, and, when the need was felt, assertion and resistance. To millions of new Americans this was what the hyphen was for.

The immigrant response to Americanization was both positive and qualified. Most Brooklyn immigrants were refugees from political oppression or the collapse of regional economies, glad to be in a freer and more prosperous country. Becoming American was a widely embraced goal. But attempts to make pure, unhyphenated Americans, or anything like them, were doomed to fail, especially when they were linked to contemptuous attitudes toward immigrants and their cultures.

A series of articles in the *Eagle* by Frederick Boyd Stevenson exemplified this contempt. Stevenson insisted that immigrants learn not only to speak in English, but to think in it, and surrender attributes that distinguish them from other Americans. In 1916 he quoted approvingly the German Jew Jacob H. Schiff: "If the Jews in America insisted upon being different from other Americans they would bring upon their posterity a heritage of suffering." In 1924 he asked Joseph A. Guider, the new Brooklyn Borough president, about his attitude toward education. "The Education that teaches One Hundred

Percent Americanism," Guider replied. "One Hundred Percent American-ism!" Stevenson repeated, before turning to a Brooklyn speaker who claimed to be a "Fifty-Fifty American—Fifty Percent of my heart here and Fifty Per-cent of it in the land whence I came." "Why not," Stevenson responded, "put the 100 percent on the other side?"[66]

Although they were featured in the Sunday edition, of which Stevenson was editor, these articles were not representative of the *Eagle*'s coverage of immigration during the rest of the week. More common were descriptions of different sorts of Americanizers, including settlement house workers who appreciated and even learned from immigrant traditions. "Americanization Leaders Plan to Win New Citizens" was the heading of a 1920 article that quoted a Mrs. Schoonhoven, bearer of a fine old Dutch name: "American-ization is not seeking to take away from anyone what he has brought from other shores that is good and beautiful, but is giving him something so fine that he is eager to add it to what he already has."[67] Also differing from Ste-venson was the *Eagle*'s advice columnist, Helen Worth. In the early days of her column, which began in November of 1922, Worth's opinions regarding the presence of hyphenated Americans in Brooklyn were guarded. She did not object when one writer insisted on finding for a mate "a 100 percent American," or when another refused to join a Lonesome Club that admitted "people from all countries and classes."[68] She was skeptical of the prospects of interfaith or interethnic marriages, advising one Jewish correspondent to find a wife within his "church."[69] But as time wore on Worth's attitude toward diversity softened, and by the late 1920s she was firmly on the side of young Protestant women who wanted to marry Catholic or Jewish men over their parents' objections. "Do not let family opposition deter you," she wrote late in 1929. "There are many happy marriages where the parents are of different faiths."[70]

Immigrants, then, faced several, often contradictory attitudes among the natives. And their responses to America included and went beyond the reten-tion of a portion of their European identity. They expressed their interests, and their grievances as well, as in the insistence by Jewish-Americans that Christianity be removed from public schools, or the call by Italian-American IWW members, less than a month before the Palmer raids in Brooklyn, for a longshoremen's strike.[71]

Most immigrants seized the rights of American citizenship along with its obligations in the name of their distinct communities. When a local judge declared that "all aliens are undesirable" and all further immigration must cease—a year before the Emergency Quota Act of 1921—the United Italian Democrats of Brooklyn sent a delegation to the *Eagle* to express their indignation. Rabbi Levinthal of the Brooklyn Jewish Center (a newly built, million-dollar structure on Vaux and Olmsted's Eastern Parkway, itself a statement that Jewish-Americans were a force to be reckoned with) declared that "to shut the gates to aliens would be cutting away from the very principle on which America was founded." Protests were also lodged from Greek, Italian, and Russian small businessmen, and from the president of the New York City Board of Aldermen, a Yiddish-speaking Italian-American Protestant named Fiorello H. La Guardia.[72] Speaking at the Brooklyn Jewish Center four years later, La Guardia, now a congressman, Rabbi Levinthal, Brooklyn-born congressman Emanuel Celler, and others condemned the introduction in Congress of the new Immigration Act. A thousand people attended the meeting; two thousand were turned away.[73]

Protests in Brooklyn and other boroughs and cities did not prevent the enactment of immigration restrictions laws. Nor did they prevent the emergence on the national stage of a new if closely related challenge to Brooklyn's immigrant communities and its much smaller community of native-born African Americans. Once confined to southern states and devoted entirely to the preservation of white supremacy there, the Ku Klux Klan suddenly surfaced in northern states. Stimulated by the increase in Catholic and Jewish immigrants and the first major wave of African American migration from the south to northern cities (and inspired by the 1915 movie, *Birth of a Nation*, that glorified the original Klan) this new KKK reasserted the primacy of white Protestantism in the United States, offering this idea as the purist form of patriotism. By the mid-1920s it claimed a nationwide membership of four or five million men.[74]

A Brooklyn branch appears to have been formed in November of 1922, but it is likely that it existed more on paper than in reality, at least in its early days. Reports of a Klansman addressing a Brooklyn Baptist church in full regalia at the invitation of its pastor that December turned out to be a hoax designed to attract congregants and fill the collection plate.[75] The arrest of eight men in January uncovered a Klan meeting that yielded almost no information to authorities about the Klan's progress in Brooklyn.[76]

Even after the Klan had more time to recruit and organize it had little impact on Brooklyn's non-white and non-Protestant communities. The African American population in Brooklyn had grown to about thirty-two thousand in 1920, and would more than double to sixty-nine thousand during the decade—still a small component of a borough of more than two million souls but large enough to serve as a target of a militantly racist organization.[77] The migration of mostly poor and rural southerners, which accounted for much of the growth of Brooklyn's Black population, reinforced the opinion held by many whites (who found it easier to perceive the poverty of these migrants than the advances of Black Brooklynites of longer standing) that nature and God consigned African Americans to the bottom rungs of society. Racial animosity was stoked in this borough of expanding residential neighborhoods, moreover, by well-publicized incidents of attempted integration.[78] And yet Brooklyn's KKK did little to cultivate this fertile racist ground.

The Klan's primary focus was on Roman Catholics, and more specifically on Catholic parochial schools. Public schools, the Klan argued, should promote Protestantism and white supremacy, and laws should be passed requiring all children to attend them. To advance this idea the Klan formed alliances with a number of Protestant ministers, including in Brooklyn no less a figure than Rev. Newell Dwight Hillis, who lent legitimacy to the Klan and preached against the Catholic school system.[79] But if some Brooklyn preachers gave succor to the KKK, greater numbers, Protestants and Catholics alike, denounced its goals and methods.[80] At the mass meeting to protest the 1924 Immigration Act Monsignor John L. Belford, pastor of Brooklyn's Roman Catholic Church of the Nativity, explained the rise of the KKK and, perhaps unintentionally, its failure in Brooklyn: "The revival of this organization, the Klan, is due to a consciousness of the power of the people against whom they are directing their efforts—the Catholics, the Jews and the negroes." This power, Belford continued, made the men who revived the Klan jealous; hence, their nationwide mobilization of men in robes and hoods to put down groups they despised as enemies of the white Protestant republic.[81]

In Brooklyn, it turned out, the power of Catholics and Jews, if not African Americans, was far too great for the Klan to diminish or defeat. That power came from overwhelming numbers, the rising wealth and organizational strength of Brooklyn's Catholic and Jewish majority, and the refusal of many Protestant ministers to cooperate with the Klan.

It is telling that the KKK flourished for a time well to the east of Brooklyn in Nassau and Suffolk county towns to which many Brooklyn (and Manhattan) Protestants had fled.[82] It gained influence in suburban New Jersey as well. Three years after Monsignor Belford spoke about the Klan at the Jewish Center two hundred hooded and robed Klansmen arrived at the Glenmore Presbyterian Church in Brooklyn in automobiles bearing license plates from New Jersey. The minister surrendered the pulpit to their leader, a man later identified as an ordained Baptist minister from "somewhere in New Jersey." The intruders held their service, got back in their cars, and went home. They may have intended to intimidate, but their visit had little or no impact on Glenmore's Presbyterians.[83]

And so, the KKK did not get much traction in Brooklyn. It little mattered that the Klan had the backing of the latest occupant of the pulpit of
Henry Ward Beecher's church on Brooklyn Heights. The Rev. Hillis' irrel-
evance to the Klan's attempt to restore the Protestantism of white men to
something like its old influence underscores the magnitude of Brooklyn's
transformation.

This is not to say that the long-standing Yankee Protestant hegemony was
replaced by another that was, say, Jewish, or Italian, or (somehow) Jewish *and*
Italian, or by any other ethnic group or alliance. Protestant elites continued
to wield considerable economic power. At the same time, ethnic communities living in Brooklyn during the early decades of the twentieth century were
often able to contest, and even ignore, Protestant cultural interventions, and
did little themselves to shape the values and behaviors of other groups. In
their lived experience (and before the emergence of a formal theory of cultural pluralism) members of each ethnic community found their own place
and tended to their own ways within twentieth-century Brooklyn's urban
and suburban sprawl.[84]

The result was a collection of relatively (but by no means perfectly) homogeneous neighborhoods, sitting side by side, often uneasily, not without
flashes or enduring episodes of interethnic or interracial conflict, but with
no prospect of ruling over or eliminating the other. Two generations earlier,
Irish and German immigrants, and then their children, had introduced a degree of ethnic diversity to Brooklyn, and asserted the need for the city's Yankee rulers to recognize and accommodate to their presence and their ways
of living. More diverse and more numerous, the New Immigrants helped
transform Brooklyn into a place where diversity was not just a countercur-
rent to something larger and more powerful. By the 1920s, the urban mosaic
of ethnic and racial neighborhoods *defined* this borough that was still, in
many ways, a city unto itself. This Brooklyn, perhaps more than Chicago, or
San Francisco, or the immigrant towns of the upper Midwest—or even that
"town across the river," the East River—contributed significantly to a new
understanding of pluralism in American life.

In March 1930, the *Eagle* published, as a Sunday feature, an article by Alice
Rayfiel Seigmeister, titled "Brooklyn's New Citizens." Below that title is a
drawing, extending across the entire page, with a shaded urban skyline dominated by the Brooklyn Bridge. Under it are a dozen images of confident-
looking immigrant types, including an old, bearded Jewish man; a Norwe-
gian seaman in pea jacket and cap, smoking his pipe; a younger, mustachioed
Italian with a slim cigar; and in front of them all a pretty young woman,

her head covered in a shawl but of no definite ethnicity, who stares hope-fully forward. A tour of Brooklyn's ethnic groups, the article is a refutation of the nativism of Frederick Boyd Stevenson. It takes us first to a Spanish, Portuguese, and Cuban settlement along the waterfront from the Brook-lyn Bridge toward Atlantic Avenue, where it borders on "Syrian territory." It then jumps to Bay Ridge and Sunset Park, where Norwegians, Swedes, and "a sprinkling of the Finnish and the Danes" are employed at the sprawling Bush Dock and Shipyard. A much larger leap takes us to Greenpoint where Czechs and Hungarians have joined an existing Polish community. Greeks, Mexicans, and a few other groups are noted while passing on to the much greater concentration of Russian, Hungarian, and Galician Jews in Browns-ville and Williamsburg, and to Italians in South Brooklyn and other places. The Germans and the Irish "are everywhere." "There are other countries, too," Siegmeister explains, but it is growing late. "What's that? The Dutch? Why, of course, there are Dutch. . . . Remember the Cortelyous, the Stuyves-ants and the Remsens?" Yes, the Dutch in this "veritable League of Nations" are remembered. Only one group—the Yankees—is not.[85]

CHAPTER 7

Acceptance, Resistance, Flight

The setting is the living room of a large Victorian-era house in Brooklyn, the home of two aging spinsters, Martha and Abby Brewster, and their middle-aged nephew who believes he is Teddy Roosevelt. The Brewster sisters cling to an old-fashioned gentility and a sense of charitable responsibility that happens to include dispatching lonely old Protestant men to a better world. Their method is a glass of Martha's elderberry wine, the recipe for which includes a teaspoon of arsenic, half a teaspoon of strychnine, and a pinch of cyanide. The men are buried in the cellar (their graves dug by Teddy, who believes he is digging locks for the Panama Canal and interring yellow fever victims), with the Brewster sisters conducting funeral services appropriate to each gentleman's Protestant denomination. The play is *Arsenic and Old Lace,* Joseph Kesselring's Broadway hit comedy of the early 1940s.

The Brewsters are an old Brooklyn family with New England roots extending back to the *Mayflower.* Their home is next door to an Episcopal church, and the play opens with the sisters serving tea to its vicar, the Rev. Dr. Harper, whose daughter Elaine is the love interest of Mortimer Brewster, a newspaper theater critic and another of the sisters' nephews. Rev. Harper is comfortable in the Brewster house, which has hardly changed since Grandfather Brewster built it, except for the electricity the sisters seldom use. But he is troubled by Mortimer's "unfortunate connection with the theatre."

He would be even more troubled if he understood his daughter's preference for plays over prayer meetings and her delight in a romance that promises release from life in the vicarage.

The opening scene is simple enough, despite Teddy's loud bugle-blowing as he charges up San Juan Hill (the staircase). The real farce begins when Mortimer discovers a corpse under the large window seat and learns that this Mr. Hoskins, a Methodist, will soon join eleven other recipients of the sisters' charitable work. The farce accelerates with the arrival of Jonathan, a third nephew who has spent many years in an Indiana prison from which he has recently escaped. Jonathan is accompanied by Dr. Herman Einstein and a lifeless Mr. Spenalzo, the latest of Jonathan's own murder victims. Dr. Einstein's role is to perform plastic surgery on Jonathan's face to help him evade capture by the police. At present, he resembles Boris Karloff (who, in a lovely touch, played Jonathan in the original Broadway production). Jonathan and Dr. Einstein plan to smuggle Mr. Spenalzo into the grave intended for Mr. Hoskins. The sisters discover the plan and refuse to allow it. To Abby, "It's a terrible thing to do—to bury a good Methodist with a foreigner." Martha "will not have our cellar desecrated!"

After a good deal more coming and going Jonathan is arrested, Dr. Einstein flees, Mortimer and Elaine get engaged, and Teddy and his aunts are committed to the Happy Dale Sanitarium. Teddy thinks going there is "bully," and the sisters are happy as well, because "the neighborhood here has changed so." When Mr. Witherspoon, who runs the sanitarium, comes to collect them and the sisters discover that the elderly gentleman is a Protestant with no family, they offer him a glass of elderberry wine. The curtain falls as he raises the glass to his lips.

The Brewster sisters and Teddy belong to a world that no longer exists; their inability to inhabit any other drives the comedy of *Arsenic and Old Lace*. But the sisters' murderous program and the antics of their deluded nephew amount also to the decidedly less comic "race suicide" that the real Theodore Roosevelt often warned against as he observed the "invasion" of Eastern and Southern European immigrants into places like Brooklyn, New York. Neither the spinsters nor Teddy nor Jonathan will leave behind any children. In a plot device borrowed from traditional melodrama Mortimer learns he is the bastard child of a family housekeeper who died in childbirth and is unburdened of the Brewsters' tainted genes, just as he and Elaine escape the stultifying inheritance of Brooklyn's Puritan past. Mortimer and Elaine will go to the theater as often as they like. They exit with a strong hint that they are going to bed together. Race suicide is not on their agenda.[1]

New York audiences no doubt delighted in the Manhattan-born Kesselring's send-up of a once-pretentious "moral suburb" made considerably less imposing—even ridiculous—by the Spenalzos and Einsteins who by then vastly outnumbered the Brewsters and Harpers among its people. Some years before writing *Arsenic and Old Lace* Kesselring lived in an old house much like the one described in his script while teaching at Bethel College in Kansas. A Moravian college in a small Kansas town would have made a good setting for *Arsenic and Old Lace*. But to Kesselring it could only have been set in Brooklyn.

We have uncovered no evidence of spinsters murdering old Protestant men in the real world of early twentieth-century Brooklyn. But we have discovered many responses by Protestants to a Brooklyn that was profoundly different from the city their fathers, mothers, and spinster aunts inhabited only a generation earlier. One of these responses, as we have seen in the settlement houses and some Americanization programs, was an acceptance of Brooklyn's ethnic diversity and a willingness to help smooth immigrants' transition to life in America with some appreciation for their cultural traditions.

That appreciation was by no means universal, but it could be forcefully expressed, even as an imperative of the Protestantism the immigrants threatened to displace. Maude White Hardie, an active Methodist and self-published poet and essayist, wrote of the need to embrace a Brooklyn transformed by immigration since her turn-of-the-century childhood in Stuyvesant Heights. A poem titled "My Country Is the World" concludes: "And all men are my kin / Since every man has been / Blood of my blood; / I glory in the grace / And strength of every trace / Of brotherhood." And a passage in a "Choral Reading" titled "You Are My City, Brooklyn" proclaims: "You have been called the City of Churches, Brooklyn. May you earn the right to bear that title again. Catholic—Protestant—Jew—each and in his own way worshipping and serving the same God." The chorus responds: "It is knowing the Fatherhood of God, / And practicing the Brotherhood of Man, / That makes a city great."[2]

It is impossible to know how many Maude White Hardies resided in Brooklyn during the years of the New Immigration, or how many of her fellow Methodists endorsed her pious and inclusive "Choral Reading." We assume there were more than a few, just as there were some old Brooklynites whose acceptance was based on a very different motive. Fueled mainly from the flow of foreign immigrants across the East River, Brooklyn's population growth generated business opportunities, especially in the development and sale of real estate in the outlying former Kings County towns. In 1879, as the New Immigration was beginning to take shape, there were 409 farms in Kings County; by 1924, the year that immigration was all but shut down, the number had been reduced to 40.[3] As Brooklyn's rural landscape suburbanized, many property sales in Flatbush, Flatlands, New Utrecht, and other places involved older Brooklynites and immigrant speculators, developers, and prospective homeowners. The tenor of these transactions may have been friendly, chilly, or without affect, but clearly, as Jews and other immigrants found their way to the new suburbs, native landowners and real estate brokers profited from dealing with them. In quite different ways the owners of factories and refineries in Greenpoint and Williamsburg benefited from paying low wages to Polish, Hungarian, and Lithuanian workers. Contempt and resentment more than occasionally defined relationships between employers and employees, but the diversity of Brooklyn gave businessmen, most of them still Protestants, good reason to accept and even be grateful for the presence of so many people unlike themselves.

The reverse side of acceptance was a grudging resignation to a force that could not be controlled. Immigrants were arriving in an endless, seemingly unstoppable stream, and Brooklyn would never be the same. Even the full-throated embrace of immigrants by the likes of Maude White Hardie was tinged with nostalgia for a world that validated the mores of a once-dominant Yankee Protestantism. This nostalgia is evident in *Yesterdays on Brooklyn Heights* (1927), not only in James H. Callender's recollections of a "bountiful hospitality and never-failing generosity" among like-minded (and uniformly Protestant and well-to-do) neighbors on the Heights, but also in those of friends and acquaintances who contributed to his book. Mrs. Thomas B. Hewitt, for example, celebrated the "beautiful refinement" of people living in "splendid homes," and recalled hearing the claim of her pastor, the Rev. Charles Cuthbert Hall of the First Presbyterian Church, that "Brooklyn Heights had produced a splendid race of men and women." Callender himself quotes Rev. Hall lauding the Heights for "the simple customs of New England finely blended with the flavor of European influence," and for "the prevalence of broad-minded Christian sentiments." Jessie Stillman remembered post-church promenades across the Heights when "cordiality was never warmer," but emphasized as "the most important fact of all, . . . the existence in our community of so many churches, presided over by men who were real intellectual giants, . . . Richard S. Storrs, Henry Ward Beecher, Charles Cuthbert Hall, Chauncy Brewster, Dr. van Dyke and Mason Clarke. It seems to be an influence which many of us must regard as the most stabilizing of our lives, and I shall never cease to be thankful that I was brought up in the 'City of Churches.'"

The Brooklyn Heights these older residents remembered was a comfortably homogeneous social world. It was also a world that was lost, and the forces of change were not hard to locate. Callender blamed "the influx of alien influences," and Martha W. Olcott the apartment houses that replaced old and elegant single-family homes. An unidentified contributor stated it best: "Houses have gone, homes have gone, friends have gone, and today we of the silvering locks feel at times like pelicans in the wilderness of a new age, of which the delicatessen store and the three-room apartment are signs and symbols."[4]

This same sense of loss was expressed in organizations formed to celebrate and in some ways perpetuate the old way of life, and in frequent retrospective articles on Brooklyn in the *Eagle* and *Brooklyn Life*. The Society of Old Brooklynites and a revived New England Society of the City of Brooklyn, both dating from 1880, survive into the twenty-first century (though with a less nostalgic mission than that of their founders). They were joined by other organizations, such as the Brooklyn branch of the National Society of New England Women, which was founded in 1905. This was part of a larger movement, but its president, Mrs. Stuart Hull Moore, gave the new organization a distinctly local rationale: "Brooklyn has in a measure lost her identity, and is just emerging to a new life, and is in a critical condition. Her position is difficult to define. Her prestige as the City of Churches has waned." That lost identity could and must be reclaimed, she argued, through good works driven by "the spirit and truth and ideals inherited from our New England ancestry to which we proudly point."[5]

This sentiment went beyond the evocation of the good old days of Yankee cultural domination in Brooklyn. It was a battle cry to restore that domination, although by the phrase "good works" Mrs. Moore might have meant a different form of Protestantism, the charitable and social reform initiatives generally subsumed under the term "Social Gospel," rather than the more Calvinist strictures of her Yankee predecessors. Nonetheless, her intent to reestablish the old Yankee presence in Brooklyn was unmistakable.

The same mixture of nostalgia and resistance was expressed at meetings of other organizations, even the seemingly apolitical Society of Old Brooklynites, which in 1924 (with the Ku Klux Klan revival at its height) heard Frederick Boyd Stevenson argue for sturdy maintenance of "the supremacy of the Nordic races."[6] A report on the fiftieth-anniversary dinner of the New England Society lamented that Brooklyn as the "Gibralter of New England" had crumbled away, while "dominance has passed to racial groups hardly of considerable importance in 1880."[7] In these speeches and editorializing the sweetness of nostalgia receded before a sometimes bitter concern for what Brooklyn had become.

Nostalgia among the Dutch was generally less infused with messaging of this sort, perhaps because it more often took the form of festivals celebrating olden times, before New Englanders had largely displaced them, and where the proper costuming of children was more pressing than the remarks of after-dinner speakers. A 1908 celebration of the Dutch settlement of Flatbush (which included events in "the little village of Bruekelen") was a great success, except for the painful wearing of old-fashioned wooden shoes by the women. In the following year the massive two-week Hudson-Fulton Celebration featured two parades on Eastern Parkway honoring Henry Hudson and old New Netherland.[8] The Dutch were active in other historical pageants and formed a Kings County Historical Society in 1911, not to help regain long-lost influence but to preserve old Flatbush farmhouses threatened by suburban development. The list of members was dominated by the most prominent Brooklyn Dutch families—Bergen, Ditmas, Kouwenhoven, Lefferts, Van Brunt, Van Wyck—but was not exclusively Dutch. The Irish industrialist Charles M. Higgins was on it, as were two Jews, Louis L. Levine and Robert W. May.[9]

Nostalgia was a staple of the Brooklyn press during these years. In the *Eagle*, stories about Brooklyn's past took various forms, including childhood reminiscences (the dreary Puritan Sundays of one correspondent were relieved by ringing doorbells, tipping over ash barrels, and breaking windows), descriptions of old Brooklyn institutions, and photographs of old homesteads, downtown buildings, even in one instance two policemen ("How Cops Looked Back in 1869").[10] The year 1930 was particularly rich in Brooklyn nostalgia. Articles on the arrival of the Low and Lefferts families, 101 and 270 years earlier, harbingered a series of "Stories of Old Brooklyn" by Maurice E. McLoughlin.[11] *Brooklyn Life* concentrated most of its reminiscences into the unusually long issue of June 1, 1915, with several articles, including Samuel B. Moore's "Brooklyn—Past and Present," which occupies more than forty richly illustrated pages. "The modern metamorphosis!," Moore began. "Compare the Brooklyn of 1890 with the Brooklyn of 1915. A mere quarter of a century and scarce a vestige is left" of the unique qualities of the old, preconsolidation city. Moore makes scant reference to the arrival of New Immigrants and does not discuss the decline of Yankee influence. This topic was left to Edward Hungerford's, "Across the East River," which dwells briefly on the creation by New Englanders of churches, schools, and a society of remarkably high quality before concluding that Yankee Brooklyn is in its last days: "The New England strain of Americanism in Brooklyn is dying." Despite this tone of regret Hungerford ends on a surprisingly positive note. The immigrants are a significant problem and the Yankees will not solve it; yet the transformation of Brooklyn will be for the good, with "the fusing of her hundreds of thousands of foreign-born into first-rate Americans."[12]

Resistant native white Brooklynites did more than reminisce or complain. Some of those most deeply concerned over the increasing diversity of Brooklyn's population took actions designed to preserve ethnically homogeneous, upper- and middle-class residential enclaves from encroachment by unwanted people. This "circle the wagons" strategy took several forms, including restrictive covenants in residential deeds, defensive practices by real estate agents, the formation of neighborhood associations, and the promotion of residential zoning intended to regulate the construction of apartment houses and other multi-family dwellings. In 1916 the Prospect Park South Association and the Ditmas Park Association petitioned the Commission on Building Districts and Restrictions to be placed in the commission's Zone E, which made the construction of apartment houses economically unfeasible in most instances. The commission approved these petitions and four others as well—all from developing Flatbush neighborhoods—on the grounds that a large majority of property owners supported them.[13] South Midwood was one of the rezoned neighborhoods, and the minutes of the South Midwood Residents' Association include the achievement of an additional and long-sought zoning change preventing the construction of two-family houses on a major street running through this small neighborhood. They include as well a complaint by one of the members that the prospective opening of a beauty parlor violated both the zoning law and the property owner's restrictive covenant.[14]

The neighborhood associations whose records survive did not spend much time on efforts to exclude identified subgroups of Brooklyn's population but focused instead on promoting public amenities such as faster transportation, street paving, lighting, sewerage, school construction, and playgrounds, and on fostering warmer personal relations in what were often new neighborhoods. Their lists of officers, even in neighborhoods where Protestants were dominant, generally included several Irish and German and one or two Jewish or Italian names. Appointed to the executive committee of the Flatbush Taxpayers' Association, Gregory Weinstein was a popular speaker at its annual dinners, causing "some merriment" at the 1909 affair by offering a resolution to rename the new East River bridge after Flatbush rather than Manhattan.[15]

But apart from the attacks on multiple-family dwellings, which were clearly understood as methods for excluding people of the wrong class, race, or ethnicity, a deep social prejudice occasionally broke into the otherwise progressive record. In a typescript incorporated into the 1910 minutes of the Flatbush Taxpayers' Association, president John J. Snyder supported the public school system as "one of the great protections against the demoralizing influence of undesirable emigrants or the shifting to this section of the City, of inhabitants of the congested districts of Manhattan, saturated with ignorance, bigotry [!] and superstitions."[16] Fourteen years later, Lawson H. Brown of the Brooklyn Chamber of Commerce advised the Independent Civic Association of Sheepshead Bay to treat immigrants "in the same friendly way as we do our native born neighbors." Noting an obvious ethnic diversity in his audience, Brown was happy to conclude that this was not a pressing problem in Sheepshead Bay. However: "In other parts of the city it is."[17]

It certainly was in Gates Avenue and other areas in and near Clinton Hill, although in this more central district of Brooklyn the issue was not white ethnicity but race. The Gates Avenue Association dealt with subway service and street traffic, but its deepest concern by far was the possible "colored invasion" from adjacent Bedford (soon to be more commonly known as Bedford-Stuyvesant), where a number of African American families had settled. According to its minutes, the association spent most of its time trying to find ways to prevent Black people from moving into the neighborhood or taking ownership of two nearby churches that were on the market. At least three other associations in the area were consulted, as were real estate agents, who recommended care in placing local properties in the hands of "reliable" dealers. The churches were secured for white congregations through unreported means.[18]

Acting individually or through neighborhood associations, native white property owners largely succeeded in keeping African Americans out of their neighborhoods, but were far less successful in excluding white ethnics. Brooklyn's Jews, Italians, and other New Immigrants greatly outnumbered African Americans, and their accumulation of wealth was achieved in the face of significantly less powerful prejudices than those faced by Black people. Despite zoning restrictions in many neighborhoods, apartment houses were built in large numbers in Brooklyn, generally on commercial avenues or the first residential streets behind them, and blocks of two-family homes (but generally not the three-family "father-son-holy ghost" houses common in New England) dominated in parts of Bedford, Bushwick, and other districts.[19] Eastern and Southern European immigrants moved into these places and into many single-family homes all over the borough, suggesting that individual restrictive covenants were perhaps not as common or as rigidly enforced as many supposed. An *Eagle* article published in 1907 described Flatbush as "the section of ideal homes," where, by law, "houses are detached; and lawns, as well as open spaces about residences, are compulsory." In contrast to other sections of the city, particularly in Manhattan, "where 'race suicide' is encouraged and enforced" by building laws and economic conditions, Flatbush is a fifteen- or twenty-square-mile perpetuation of Brooklyn's long-held suburban ideal.[20] Yet, within a half-dozen years, and increasingly in the years following, that ideal was modified to accommodate apartment houses, two-family homes, and new neighbors who raised the specter of "race suicide" among at least some of the remaining white Anglo-Dutch Protestants. Obviously, not everyone fretted equally about Flatbush's growing diversity. The wagons had been imperfectly circled.

Going beyond these defensive neighborhood-based strategies were attacks by some of Brooklyn's native Protestants on behalf of the old Yankee moral agenda—Sabbath observance; the preservation of Christianity in public schools; temperance (expanded now, as in the nation as a whole, into a campaign for an outright prohibition on drinking); and opposition to the theater (and now movies), gambling, and other amusements. At first glance, the vigor of these attacks seems to contradict claims of diminishing Yankee influence, but a closer look reveals the more challenging circumstances facing a new generation of enforcers. The size of the Yankee army was much reduced, and there were more diverse opinions within the evangelical Protestant community as to how—and whether—to pursue the old agenda. Some now spoke in the less severe tones of the Social Gospel, while a number of Protestant leaders coped with declining church attendance by focusing on sociability, entertainment (including church-sponsored theater!), and a more pleasant church-going experience.[21] Others adhered to older doctrines of salvation and religious feeling, but—especially in response to the horrors of World War I and the unsettling demands of postwar urban modernism—used these doctrines and emotions to cultivate a more inward-looking spirituality. Still others looked beyond their immediate church communities to larger organizations such as the YMCA, the Salvation Army, national tract and Bible societies, and inter-denominational faith organizations, a type of activism that was not always designed to perpetuate the traditional Yankee crusade to impose behavioral strictures on the public at large.

One who did perpetuate that crusade was Canon William Sheafe Chase of Brooklyn's Christ Episcopal Church. Born in Yankee-dominated northern Illinois, Canon Chase was educated at schools in Providence, Rhode Island

BEAUTIFUL WORDS

FIGURE 7.1.   In this 1920 cartoon, "Beautiful Words," Nelson Harding captures an important cultural change in post–World War I Brooklyn (*Brooklyn Daily Eagle*, December 1, 1920).

(including Brown University), and the Theological Seminary in Cambridge, Massachusetts. He was an assistant pastor in Boston before assuming his first pastorate in Woonsocket, Rhode Island.[22] His Yankee credentials, in sum, were as solid as any of the New England clergy who preceded him to Brooklyn. Chase did not lack allies and his was not always the strongest voice, but his visibility and prominence in so many areas reflected the reality that the broader and more unified evangelical base of the nineteenth century was missing from the new Brooklyn.

Protestant moral crusaders such as Chase needed to choose the right field of battle. Consolidation had removed the Brooklyn Common Council, and Chase and his friends often lacked sufficient support within the New York City Board of Aldermen sitting in Manhattan. They had more success outside the city, in Albany, where conservative (mainly Protestant) upstate legislators were dominant, and at times in Washington, when still larger forces aligned with their agenda. The enforcers succeeded on several of these fronts, but especially since they had gone far afield to do so doubts remained about how their reforms would be implemented in Brooklyn, and how long they would remain in effect. The moral crusade, in sum, was not as much a manifestation of local power—akin to the program of Yankee clergy and laymen of the nineteenth century—as it was a rear-guard protest against the loss of that power by a small number of people determined to wield it in the manner of their predecessors.

One battle that remained mostly if not entirely local involved religion in the public schools. Against Jewish objections to Christian daily prayers, Christmas carols, and other such elements of the school day and calendar, the Rev. Newell Dwight Hillis and other Protestant ministers invoked the widely held belief among Brooklyn's Protestants that these practices were appropriate in the public institutions of a republic founded by Christian men and intended to be a Christian nation.[23] Around the turn of the century this dispute was joined to another that evoked substantial Protestant support— the closing of public schools during the celebration of Brooklyn's much-cherished Anniversary Day. The issue arose shortly after the consolidation of the boroughs. New York City's new charter called for the distribution of public school funds according to the number of days schools were open during the year. As Anniversary Day was unique to Brooklyn the loss of one day, or even half a day, would cost its schools a portion of their allocation.[24] This might have been a small matter, but it evolved quickly into an issue of religious privilege.

As in previous years, the celebration excluded Catholics, Jews, and non-evangelical Protestants such as Unitarians and Universalists. Should their children be required to stay home on behalf of a tradition of the evangelical community? In 1902 the school board ordered the Brooklyn schools to remain open on Anniversary Day, but after a barrage of protests from evangelicals reversed itself and ordered them closed. Three years later the state legislature, no doubt after some lobbying, declared the day a legal holiday in Brooklyn.[25] The issue flared up again in 1910 when the schools kept the children in session to take examinations after an agreed-upon noon closing, but was settled the following year when the schools were closed and President William Howard Taft reviewed a parade of one hundred fifty thousand Sunday school children. "Hello, Bill," one little boy called out from within the parade. When the President responded with a smile and a chuckle the emboldened marcher continued, "My name's Bill, too!"[26]

Bookmakers and racetrack gamblers were not likely to greet William Sheafe Chase with a friendly "Hello, Bill." Canon Chase was not active in the preservation of Christianity in the public schools or in the fight for Anniversary Day, but he was a long-standing opponent of racetrack gambling. New

York State laws prohibited betting on horse races as early as the 1870s (even before Brooklyn's three tracks opened), but gamblers, professional and amateur alike, found ways around them. In 1907, however, the attack became more serious, with the introduction of new legislation and hearings that included testimony from Chase that the racetracks were "legalized colleges of gambling."[27] The legislation failed at first, but the active participation of Governor Charles Evans Hughes turned the tide. In June 1908 betting on horse races either at or away from the racetrack became a criminal offense in New York. The focus of the law was not on racing itself or on casual wagering among individuals, who could still bet as long as no paper record was created and no cash changed hands. But this was a small concession and the widespread awareness that large numbers of plainclothes policemen patrolled tracks to enforce the new law constituted a significant deterrent.

New laws in 1910 not only forbade oral betting but held the directors of the clubs that owned the tracks criminally responsible for illegal betting on their premises. That was the deathblow to horseracing in Brooklyn. The Brighton Beach track had closed in 1908; by September 1910 the Gravesend and Sheepshead Bay tracks shut down as well. The restrictive gambling laws were overturned in 1913, but the Brooklyn tracks did not reopen for horseracing. The Sheepshead Bay track hosted automobile racing for a time, but eventually all three tracks were demolished. The land on which they stood was sold to residential real estate developers.[28]

The laws that led to the closing of racetracks were seen as victories for Brooklyn's church leaders and the borough's Puritan traditions. Canon Chase at legislative hearings in Albany, and others closer to home in their churches and church clubs, were clearly part of the attack on gambling. In March 1908 a meeting of the men's clubs of Brooklyn's Eastern District Protestant churches was called in support of Governor Hughes' anti-gambling legislation. A thousand men heard Canon Chase and Reverend Samuel Parkes Cadman give speeches in support of the bill. Two months later a Brooklyn Citizens' Anti-Race Track Gambling Committee arranged for simultaneous Sunday meetings in eighteen Protestant churches, including Plymouth Church (but oddly, not Chase's Christ Church or Cadman's Central Congregational Church).[29] Little wonder, then, that the *Eagle*, which opposed the new laws, grumbled that they "breathe a spirit of intolerance recalling the time when those who whistled on the Sabbath did so at their own peril."[30]

But nearly all contemporary reports on this anti-gambling crusade stressed the pivotal role of Governor Hughes. Hughes was an active Baptist and had lived in Brooklyn during part of his childhood, but he had no connection to Yankee Brooklyn. There is no indication that in framing and pushing through

FIGURE 7.2.   William Sheafe Chase (Historic Images Outlet).

the legislation the governor consulted with or relied on Chase, Cadman, or any other local ministers, nor that the outcome turned on local mass meetings of churches and church clubs. Brooklyn's Protestants may have offered support in various ways, but this was a civic movement, achieved mainly in Albany, a hundred and fifty miles from Brooklyn's borders.

While the three horseracing tracks in Brooklyn lay almost a stone's throw from each other at the southern edge of the borough, baseball was everywhere. And while horseracing was tightly controlled by the wealthy men who owned the tracks (and horses) and was brought to life by a professional cadre of trainers, jockeys, and stable hands, baseball ran the gamut from professional, semiprofessional, and amateur leagues and clubs to pick-up games of young men and boys in open lots and on city streets. Baseball could be played on any day of the week, but it was on Sunday that the largest number of players and fans were free to enjoy a ball game on a sunny summer afternoon. The pious, peaceful, and noncommercial Sabbath was a cornerstone of Brooklyn's Yankee Protestantism. Sunday baseball threatened that Sabbath.

Sabbatarian sentiment had changed since the days when frivolities of any kind were prohibited by custom and by law. Most Brooklyn Protestants no longer saw playing ball on a Sunday afternoon (preferably after a morning spent in church) as a sin, not least because so many of them amused themselves on that day with golf, tennis, yachting, automobile excursions, and other secular pleasures. Sabbatarians focused instead on two other issues—whether a particular game disturbed the prayerful repose of other people, and whether it violated prohibitions against inessential Sunday commercial activity by charging an admission fee.

The first concern focused mostly on amateur baseball and casual pick-up games. Occasional complaints were made about the noise of the games, the profanity of the players, and balls hit into lawns and through windows. A Mrs. Mary Gilbert was sewing by the dining room window of her "handsome house" in Sheepshead Bay on a May afternoon in 1905 when a baseball crashed through the window and hit her under the eye. At the other end of Brooklyn the Rev. P. F. O'Hare of Greenpoint's St. Anthony's Church complained about gambling accompanying a game on a nearby vacant lot, but residents of the neighborhood were more concerned about "unbearable" shouting of players and spectators, which began at nine o'clock in the morning and continued until six o'clock in the evening. A Bath Beach lawyer named Robert O'Byrn was infuriated by a barrage of baseballs and bad language issuing from players within earshot of his house and young daughter. And in Bedford, Police Captain Miles O'Reilly stopped games on Howard Athletic Club's fenced-in field on Saratoga Avenue because balls were hit into the street even after the club built a higher fence and topped that with a very high screen.[31]

The most persistent complaints came from homeowners adjoining Prospect Park parade ground, which, after Sabbath prohibitions of forty-five years, began hosting amateur Sunday baseball in 1912. After some two hundred noisy players showed up on the first Sunday the homeowners formed the Parade Park Association and sought an injunction against the games. They were not mollified by a hastily adopted rule that limited play to the afternoon. The dispute continued until 1914 when the Park Commissioner affirmed the right of amateur clubs to play on Sunday, but mandated they "exercise every care not to annoy more than possible the residents of the houses adjoining the Parade Ground by the careless knocking and throwing of balls into yards and through windows."[32]

To Brooklyn's Sabbatarians a more important problem than profane shouts and errant baseballs was the charging of fees for the privilege of watching baseball games on Sunday. They pointed to Section 265 of the New

York State penal code, enacted in 1787: "All shooting, hunting, fishing, play-ing, horse racing, gaming or other public sports, exercise or shows upon the first day of the week, and all noises disturbing the peace of the day are prohibited."[33] When Brooklyn's one professional team and many semipro-fessional clubs sold tickets on Sunday to fenced and gated fields or advertised games on circulars and in the local papers, they were breaking the law that prohibited "public sports."[34] Stopping their games drew the most attention from the borough's Sunday enforcers.

Subterfuges devised by clubs to make money did not fool anyone who wished not to be fooled. One allowed spectators through the gate free of charge while insisting that each of them purchase a program at an inflated price before being shown to a seat. Fans understood the fifty or seventy-five cents to be the price of admission to the bleachers or grandstand. A second ruse placed a "voluntary" contribution box inside the gate, with an impos-ing guard to "suggest" the spectator drop in fifty cents. Less crude was the declaration that each Sunday game was free to club members and closed to non-members, with a stand outside the gate to enroll new members at weekly dues of fifty or seventy-five cents. Police responses to these tricks varied from stopping games to arresting program sellers, the visiting team's leadoff hitter and the home team's pitcher and catcher (after the first pitch had been delivered), team managers, and even entire teams. Interestingly, many arrests resulted in dismissals by local judges, some of them sympa-thetic to commercialized Sunday baseball.

In January 1907 state assemblyman Leo Mooney introduced a bill to le-galize Sunday amateur baseball. An amateur club manager from Brooklyn, Mooney believed his colleagues would support a bill that explicitly excluded semiprofessional and professional games. He was mistaken, and when an-other bill was introduced in the State Senate the following year opposition speakers representing the Church Federation of Brooklyn, the Kings County Sunday Observance Association, the Kings County Sunday School Associa-tion, the New York State Sabbath Association of Richmond, the League of Episcopal Churches of Brooklyn, and the New York Sabbath Committee, all condemned the bill at a public meeting, most of them objecting to Sunday baseball in any form. One of the speakers was Canon Chase, who argued that the bill was really an attempt to authorize semiprofessional and professional games by making no reference to indirect methods of charging admission. Claiming that he was "all right" with truly amateur games, Chase offered his support for an amended bill with a provision "that no admission is charged directly or indirectly." Apparently, Chase had identified the promoters' real motive, and it is likely his testimony helped kill the bill. Two years later

Chase used the same argument against another bill purporting to authorize only amateur baseball. The bill "is dishonest and deceptive," he wrote, because "the words 'No fee for admission to any such game shall be exacted' directly permit various subterfuges for making money from the game." Passage would end amateur Sunday baseball, he argued, because all the fields would be snapped up by semiprofessionals. Chase once again proposed an amendment to prohibit indirect methods of collecting admission fees. Assemblyman McGrath, the bill's sponsor, replied "that he would accept the amendments if the churches would omit taking contributions on Sunday." But when McGrath made the change the following year the bill did not pass. Apparently, Chase's position on Sunday baseball was less influential than that of even more conservative rural upstate legislators.[35]

Although Chase's testimony highlighted the subterfuges of semiprofessional clubs, the lurking presence in the Sunday baseball controversy was Brooklyn's major league team, the Superbas (not yet called the Dodgers), operated by chief owner and president, Charles H. Ebbets. Longing to make Sunday baseball a reality for his National League club, Ebbets tried the tricks used by the semipros and invented a few of his own. But the police were as active at the Superbas' home field as they were elsewhere in the city and Ebbets was hauled into court on more than one occasion.[36] The few games he managed to get away with fell well short of the Sunday bonanza enjoyed by his league rivals in Cincinnati, Chicago, and St. Louis. Ebbets Field, the grand new home of the Superbas, opened in April 1913, but Sunday laws remained in effect until Ebbets enlisted World War I patriotism to persuade the state legislature to change them.

At the end of June 1917, with American troops in France, Ebbets sold tickets to a Sunday sacred music concert at the stadium, to be followed by a "free" regular season baseball game against the Philadelphia Phillies. The proceeds were earmarked for the Naval Militia of Mercy, the Red Cross, and other war relief organizations. Ten thousand people showed up. Ebbets and team manager Wilbert Robinson were summoned to court and later convicted of conducting a public game on the Sabbath. (As was common in these cases, their sentences were suspended.) But Ebbets was winning in the court of public opinion. When the police shut down Ebbets Field on the following Sunday, the *Eagle*'s story followed the heading "No Sunday Game Tomorrow; Red Cross Loses About $5,000." Ten days later, an article on the second shutdown was headed "Sunday Law Agitators Hurt Every Brooklyn Regiment."[37]

The 1917–18 off-season was pivotal for the legalization of Sunday baseball in Brooklyn. Ebbets and club vice president E. J. McKeever began a

FIGURE 7.3.   Charles Ebbets (Library of Congress Prints & Photographs Division).

public relations campaign that included an appeal to local clergy. "The un-
dersigned," their open letter began, "believing in the sanctity of the Sabbath, have no thought . . . of doing aught to interfere with God's work being
done in this community by you and your brethren." All they sought was
an amendment to the 1787 "blue law" that was now "a 'dead letter' with
respect to every activity against which it is directed except baseball games in
this community at Ebbets Field." Two clergymen responded almost immediately. The Rev. T. J. Lacey of the Church of the Redeemer supported Sunday
major league baseball in Brooklyn, and thought the opposition "senseless, in-
tolerant and antiquated." The other minister, Canon William Sheafe Chase,
denounced Ebbets's attempts to get around the existing law and commercial-
ize the Sabbath.[38]

In March 1918, Canon Chase appeared again in Albany to argue against
a bill legalizing the charging of admission to professional baseball games
played on Sunday. The bill was passed by the Senate in early April.[39] The Assembly approved in the following year and Governor Al Smith signed it into
law. In a concession to upstate legislators the law included a local option,
so the final word on Brooklyn Sunday baseball lay in the hands of the New
York City Board of Aldermen and Mayor John F. Hylan. Chase argued for
rejection by the aldermen, as did representatives from the Baptist Tabernacle

Church of Brooklyn, the Methodist Ministers Association, the Presbyterian Ministers Association, and the Long Island Ministers Association. Nonetheless, the aldermen approved Sunday baseball by a vote of 64 to 0 and Mayor Hylan added his signature. On May 4, 1919, Brooklyn's first indisputably legal professional Sunday baseball game was played at Ebbets Field. Some twenty-two thousand fans bought tickets to watch Brooklyn beat the Boston Braves by a score of 6 to 2.[40]

The playing of that game, with the certainty of many more to come, was a significant loss to Brooklyn's Sabbatarians. But at nearly the same time a more important issue was resolved in a far more favorable manner for Protestant traditionalists. The battle against alcoholic drink had been a centerpiece of the moral reform agenda, in Brooklyn and elsewhere in America, for nearly a century. It took many forms, including temperance societies, publications, lectures, and sermons, as well as the enactment of local licensing and Sunday closing laws. More than a dozen states imitated Maine's 1851 law prohibiting the sale of alcoholic beverages in the entire state and persisted in prohibitory legislation when "Maine laws" were declared unconstitutional in state courts. This broad-based movement, in which the evangelical churches played a prominent role, was fairly effective in reducing the amount of alcohol Americans consumed in their daily lives.[41]

These victories emboldened total abstinence advocates, whose determination grew with increased immigration of groups that threatened not only the goal of reducing or eliminating alcoholic drink in America, but also the dominance of the evangelical Christianity from which the temperance movement had sprung. In 1874 the Women's Christian Temperance Union was founded in Cleveland on total abstinence principles. Unlike earlier societies that made massive efforts to persuade individuals of the evils of drinking, the WCTU focused on the availability of alcoholic drink. Its constitution declared the purpose of the organization to be "the entire prohibition of the manufacture and sale of intoxicating liquors as a beverage."[42] The WCTU grew quickly through state and local chapters and was joined as a national organization in 1895 by the Anti-Saloon League. As the prohibition movement gained momentum it probably did more than any other political issue to pit rural and small-town America against the nation's increasingly diverse cities. But the WCTU (more than the Anti-Saloon League) did continue to raise the issue in cities, where it sought out evangelical allies.

By 1912 several branches of the WCTU were active in Brooklyn, and the long-serving state chairwoman was Brooklyn resident Ella A. Boole.[43] When prohibition arrived in 1919 with the ratification of the 18th Amendment to the US Constitution and the passage of the Volstead Act (formally the National Prohibition Act) a number of Brooklyn's Protestant clergy-men publicly supported the new measures. In May, after the amendment was ratified but before the Volstead Act was passed (both the amendment and the law granting enforcement powers to federal officers were to take effect on January 17, 1920), more than one hundred Protestant clergymen who had formed themselves into a Brooklyn Committee on Loyalty to the Constitution organized a mass meeting at the Brooklyn Academy of Music. An audience of eight hundred heard speeches by seven prominent organiz-ers, including Canon Chase, who blamed the delay in ratifying the amend-ment on foreigners. We will live as "true Americans," Chase promised, after we are done with "poisonous" German beer (to make sure his audience understood the problem lay with allies as well as enemies, Chase added English rum and French wine). Responding to frequent shouts from the audience of "We don't want beer" and "We want prohibition," the meeting adopted resolutions demanding compliance with the 18th Amendment as a civic duty, and described prohibition as keeping faith with "our brave boys in the Army and Navy."[44]

This Protestant mass meeting may have drawn some of its resolve from the well-publicized opposition of the Rev. John L. Belford of the Roman Catholic Church of the Nativity. Rev. Belford ridiculed "the bone dry amend-ment," and noted that the Catholic Church had taken no position on prohi-bition. He had earlier attacked Protestant minister William H. Anderson, who had come from Baltimore to lead the Anti-Saloon League's effort to persuade the New York State legislature to adopt the 18th Amendment.[45] But the battle lines over prohibition in Brooklyn cannot be simply drawn. At-titudes toward prohibition varied within religious denominations as well as between them, and the limits of Protestants' influence over the new Brook-lyn quickly became evident. In the fall of 1919 nine ministers of Protestant churches in Stuyvesant Heights read statements from their pulpits opposing the candidacy of Reuben L. Haskell, who was running for county judge on a "wet" platform. We have no evidence of Protestant clergymen from other districts publicly opposing Haskell; in any case, he won his race by one of the largest majorities ever recorded in Kings County.[46]

Opposition to prohibition laws grew as their unintended consequences became evident. The bootlegging of whiskey and beer provided ample stock for thousands of speakeasies throughout New York City, including Brooklyn; it also fueled the growth of powerful and violent criminal organizations, including one that operated out of Chicago under the firm leadership of a Brooklyn native (born in Vinegar Hill, raised there and in Gowanus) named Al Capone. The Mullan-Gage Act, New York State's initial attempt to align the state with federal prohibition law, was repealed in 1923. Subsequent proposals for replacing it revealed the strength of the "wet" opposition.

Some Brooklyn evangelicals refused to give up—Canon Chase, once again in Albany, was removed from the Assembly floor at one point for lobbying for such a bill—but public sentiment was not on their side, in Brooklyn and in the nation as a whole. Chase's own denomination undermined his efforts to maintain prohibition. In 1927 the National Episcopal Temperance Church Society, meeting in New York, announced that two-thirds of the Episcopal clergy in the United States opposed the Volstead Act and that a majority of the church's temperance society members had voted in favor of repealing the 18th Amendment. John A. Danielson, a lay member of the society, was applauded when he claimed "the growing demand for repeal of Prohibition is a sign of good American citizenship. A baser citizenship would be content to leave an unenforceable law on the statute books and continue to violate it."[47] The 18th Amendment was repealed in 1933. As in the case of Sunday baseball, Canon Chase battled, with fewer and fewer allies, to the end—and lost.

In October 1916 a new moral issue arose in Brooklyn and then quickly, if temporarily, disappeared. Margaret Sanger, a nurse and advocate for sex education and birth control (the latter term was her coinage) opened America's first birth control clinic in the crowded heart of Brownsville.[48] Sanger and her sister, Ethel Byrne, her partner in the venture, advertised the clinic in the press and passed out leaflets (in English, Yiddish, and Italian) on the street. On its first day the clinic received 140 visitors, mostly poor mothers who could not afford to have more children. The clinic performed no medical services and offered only oral advice and instruction to avoid violating Section 1142 of the state penal code, written in imitation of the federal Comstock Law, which outlawed not only the provision of contraceptive devices, recipes, or drugs of any kind, but also the provision of information about them, orally or in writing. Sanger was either unaware of the prohibition against oral advice or was provoking the police to arrest her. If the latter, she put on a good show when, ten days (and 450 visits by Brownsville women) later the police arrived to drag her, protesting "in a towering rage," into a patrol wagon. The show had a sizeable audience of more than a thousand Brownsville residents who gathered outside the clinic after word got around that the police had arrived.[49]

Sanger and her assistant and translator, Fania (Fanny) Mindell, were released from jail the following morning and soon reopened the clinic. On November 15 they were arrested again, this time for "maintaining a public nuisance." Bail was promptly provided, and she left the court threatening

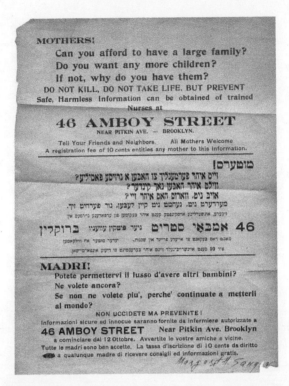

MOTHERS!
Can you afford to have a large family?
Do you want any more children?
If not, why do you have them?
DO NOT KILL, DO NOT TAKE LIFE, BUT PREVENT
Safe, Harmless Information can be obtained of trained
Nurses at

46 AMBOY STREET
NEAR PITKIN AVE. — BROOKLYN.

Tell Your Friends and Neighbors.   All Mothers Welcome
A registration fee of 10 cents entitles any mother to this information.

מוטערס!
וויס איהר פֿערמעגליך צו האבען א גרויסע פֿאמיליע?
וולס איהר האבען נאך קינדער?
אויב ניט, וואַרום האט איהר זיי?
מערדערט ניט, נעהמט נים קיין לעבען, נור פֿערהיט זיך.
זיכערע, אונשעדליכע אינפֿאָרמאַצין קענ מען ערהאלטען פֿון טרײנדסענע נײַרסעס אין

46 אמבאי סטרים נער פיטקין עוועניו **ברוקלין**
זאגט דאס בעקאנט צו אייערע פריינד און שכנות.   יעדער מוטער איז וויללקאמען
פֿאר 10 סענט איטשקריבדזגעלד וינם איהר בערעכטיגט צו רעכט אנגאלמישאן.

MADRI!
Potete permettervi il lusso d'avere altri bambini?
Ne volete ancora?
Se non ne volete piu', perche' continuate a metterli
al mondo?
NON UCCIDETE MA PREVENITE!
Informazioni sicure ed innocue saranno fornite da infermiere autorizzate a
46 AMBOY STREET   Near Pitkin Ave. Brooklyn
a cominciare dal 12 Ottobre. Avvertite le vostre amiche e vicine.
Tutte le madri sono ben accette. La tassa d'iscrizione di 10 cents da diritto
a qualunque madre di ricevere consigli ed informazioni gratis.

FIGURE 7.4. Flyer advertising Margaret Sanger's Brownsville birth control clinic (Collection of Ann Lewis and Mike Sponder).

to open fifty clinics in Brownsville if the police closed her down again.[50] But the clinic was shuttered, this time permanently, and no additional clinics appeared. Sanger stood trial in late January and was convicted of violating Section 1142. Refusing an offer of probation in return for her promise not to violate the state's birth control law again, she served a thirty-day sentence in the city workhouse. Her conviction was upheld on appeal in January 1918, but not without a significant victory for the birth control movement, as the court ruled it was legal for physicians to prescribe birth control measures when they had a medical reason for doing so. This was the first step in the long process of disassembling the state's version of the Comstock Law.[51]

After serving her sentence Margaret Sanger did not return to Brooklyn. Her presence in the borough was brief—about three and a half months from the opening of her clinic to her conviction in the Court of Special Sessions. But in that time (in addition to the help she may have given to 450 women) she garnered a good deal of publicity for a cause that had rarely been in the public eye. The *Eagle*'s coverage was almost always on the paper's front

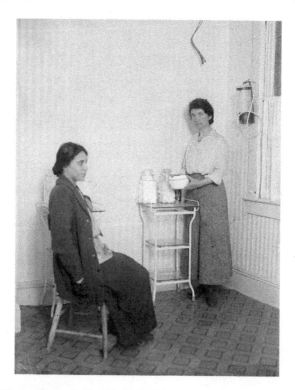

Figure 7.5.   Margaret Sanger (left) and Fania Mindell in the Brownsville clinic (Library of Congress Prints & Photographs Division).

page. Six days after the Brownsville clinic opened the paper published a long interview with Sanger without a word of condemnation, and two days later printed two articles describing the work she was accomplishing with poor women.[52] The *Eagle* did not interview Catholic or Protestant leaders on the issue of a birth control clinic; nor did any priest or minister come forward during the clinic's brief life or the arrests and trials that followed to condemn publicly this clear violation of a law which Catholic and evangelical Protestant clergy nearly unanimously supported. It is likely these leaders felt that Sanger posed little threat to the law, the actions of the police and the courts were sufficient to quell her threat to decency and morality, and it would be best to lie low and not give birth control the fuel of additional publicity.

If that was their strategy it worked for only a few years. In 1921 Margaret Sanger was back in the news with a conference in Manhattan to launch her new organization, the American Birth Control League. The closing session of the conference was scheduled as a public meeting at Manhattan's Town Hall, a large auditorium just opened by the prosuffrage League for Political

Action. This time the church, specifically the Roman Catholic Church, intervened. Archbishop Patrick J. Hayes, who Sanger had invited to the meeting, sent his secretary, Joseph P. Dineen, to coordinate with the police in shutting it down. Sanger managed to sneak into the hall and start her speech but was promptly arrested for disorderly behavior, which she later claimed was part of her plan. Previously covered in the press without much ado, the conference's aborted finale was front-page news, as was the next day's release of Sanger (by an Irish Catholic magistrate) because of insufficient evidence.[53] The American Birth Control League—which was later combined with another Sanger organization to form the Planned Parenthood Federation of America—had received valuable publicity, and it appears that Archbishop Hayes recognized he had made a public relations mistake. The meeting was reconvened five days later in another auditorium and drew a huge crowd. Archbishop Hayes was again invited. This time he sent a representative to attend the meeting.[54]

The Roman Catholic Church was conspicuous in opposing the emerging birth control movement, but on this issue Protestant leaders, including those in Brooklyn, agreed with their Catholic counterparts. That they were opposed to Sanger's movement even as the Catholics did the heavy lifting against her is evident not only from the support Protestant leaders had given to their fellow Protestant Anthony Comstock's earlier crusade against birth control (among other sins), but also from Congressional testimony given some years after the Town Hall raid by Canon Chase.

By then retired from his Brooklyn pastorate and a resident of Washington, D. C., Chase testified in 1932 before a US House of Representatives committee on legislation to legalize the importation and distribution of contraceptives and literature explaining their use. Speaking as superintendent of the International Reform Federation Chase vehemently opposed the bill for "the havoc in manners and morals" it would inflict on the country by promoting illicit sex among the unmarried, promiscuity among the married, and "the bawdy-house business."[55] Chase appeared again two years later before a US Senate subcommittee considering a bill to exempt contraceptives and other "Comstock items" sold or promulgated by doctors, hospitals, medical schools, and pharmacies. To his earlier argument Chase added a judgment, reminiscent of his testimony against the New York State bill purporting to legalize amateur Sunday baseball, that the proposed bill was corrupt. "Very great commercial interests are behind this bill," he claimed, referring especially to those who would prosper from the sale of contraceptives.[56]

Chase was a shrewd reader of legislation and in the secular precincts of legislative committee rooms he spoke the language of politics more frequently than the language of the pulpit. But he left no doubt about his commitment to old evangelical ideals. Best known for his fierce defense of the Puritan American Sabbath, in these hearings he embraced with equal fervor a traditionalist's opposition to the modern birth control movement. That neither he nor his fellow evangelical Protestants spoke publicly against Margaret Sanger in 1916 and 1921—though they may have done so in their individual churches—suggests a caution born of the recognition of limited influence in the larger community. Archbishop Hayes went boldly forward in 1921, and his Protestant allies in the birth control opposition were no doubt glad to recognize him as the stronger force. That the Archbishop got burned in the process may well account for the Protestants' continued reticence. Canon Chase was not known for caution. But when he finally spoke up about birth control, he was distant in time from the Brownsville clinic and the Town Hall raid, and distant in space from Brooklyn.

In his testimony before the Congressional hearings on birth control Canon Chase added comments about the immoral impact of movies. In 1932 he noted that the proposed bill "is, of course, favored by the producers of sex appeal motion pictures and immoral plays and the publishing of indecent literature." In 1934 he focused on the first of the three: "I am deeply concerned about the motion picture, which teaches the young people that free love is a new idea, that the idea of marriage is old fashioned, and that divorce is a natural thing; and that you can't make people good by law."[57] This was a long-standing concern for Chase and a topic on which he was never reticent. Shortly after he assumed his Brooklyn pastorate he joined other local clergy in a protest against theatrical productions on Sunday, and within a few years helped expand its scope to include the increasingly popular medium of motion pictures. In December 1911 he presided over a public meeting sponsored by the Sunday Observance Association of Kings County that included movies as well as vaudeville shows and saloons as Sabbath violators.[58] In subsequent years his opposition extended to the purportedly salacious content of movies and the need to protect public morality through censorship.

A New York Board of Censorship of Motion Pictures was formed as early as 1909, but this name was deceptive. Neither a government agency nor a private-sector organization with censorship authority, the board was composed of a diverse group of progressive social workers, educators, and liberal churchmen assembled at the behest of movie executive William Fox to make recommendations to the mayor of New York City about films that contained immoral content. By 1916 it had become the National Board of Review of Motion Pictures and had shifted from a narrow focus on what might be wrong with individual movies toward promoting films of good quality and recognizing filmmaking as a valuable art form.[59] Responding to lobbying from evangelical Protestants led by Canon Chase and Catholic leaders from across the state, New York legislators passed the Cristman Bill in 1916 to fill the vacuum in film censorship, but the bill was vetoed by Governor Charles S. Whitman.[60]

Early in the following year Frederick Boyd Stevenson called attention to this regulatory vacuum in an *Eagle* article illustrated with a drawing of a dense crowd of men, women, and children waiting to get into a movie theater festooned with a sign reading "Unmoral Muck-Raking Films Shown Here." Superimposed on the crowd is a member of the New York Society for the Suppression of Vice asleep at his desk. Stevenson (himself a member of Brooklyn's Protestant Men's Association and the Flatbush Gardens Civic Association) hoped a new committee of Brooklyn women led by Mrs. Clarence Pennoyer Waterman might waken Brooklyn's slumbering moral enforcers.[61]

The nap continued a while longer. But in February 1921 the latest Stevenson article, "How Brooklyn is Getting into Action for Campaign Against Unclean Movies," reported two large meetings of Protestant church clubs urging motion picture censorship, and printed laudatory letters from Canon

FIGURE 7.6. The New York Society for the Suppression of Vice sleeps while adults and small children line up to see "unmoral muck-raking films" (*Brooklyn Daily Eagle*, January 28, 1917).

Chase and a censorship committee of the Catholic Diocese of Brooklyn. Eight days later, egged on by a speech from Stevenson, a meeting of more than one hundred representatives from Brooklyn churches condemned the National Board of Review as "a farcical camouflage for censorship" and called for passage of a state censorship law.[62]

There appears to have been no Catholic presence at this meeting, but the coalition between Canon Chase and Catholic bishops reappeared in Albany at hearings for another attempt to create a movie censorship board. As it would be six years later in the fight over prohibition, Chase's position was undermined by a group within his own denomination. Charles Lathrop, executive secretary of the Department of Christian Social Services of the Protestant Episcopal Church maintained that voluntary censorship by the movie industry was preferable to state regulation. "Lathrop's opinion stood in stark contrast to the more emotional diatribes presented by Canon Chase," but in the end the procensorship coalition prevailed. The Clayton-Lusk Bill establishing the New York State Censorship Commission was signed into law on May 15, 1921. An attempt to repeal the law in 1922 failed. One of the first witnesses to testify against repeal was William Sheafe Chase.[63]

New York was one of only six states to create movie censorship boards during this period. In 1922 fear of federal regulation led to the creation of the Motion Pictures Producers and Distributors Association (later the Motion Picture Association of America) to represent the industry's interests. The studios induced Postmaster General Will H. Hays to leave the government to head the association. Hays developed a set of criteria for assessing—and self-censoring—the content of movies. Arguing that the process was not sufficiently rigorous, Canon Chase and others lobbied Congress to establish a national movie censorship board.[64] But Martin Quigley, a Catholic movie trade publisher, got there first. Quigley hired a Jesuit priest named Daniel Lord to write a more rigorous censorship code based on Catholic doctrine. This strengthened "Hays Code" was adopted by the association in 1930, heading off Congressional action. The code was strenuously enforced by another Catholic, Joseph Ignatius Breen, who was appointed head of a new Production Code Administration in 1934. Under Breen's twenty-year leadership American movies were censored in ways that even Canon Chase would have approved, even though neither he nor any other Brooklyn Protestant leader had anything to do with the establishment of a system of moral supervision so reminiscent of Brooklyn's old Yankee agenda.[65]

Canon Chase's battles expressed a fundamental discontent with the new Brooklyn, as did the efforts of some homeowners to circle the wagons around native white neighborhoods. But people who were unhappy or just uneasy with what Brooklyn had become had another option, one that was already coming to characterize the twentieth-century American metropolis—flight to the suburbs. Brooklyn, of course, had long been a prominent exemplar of suburban life, from the founding of Brooklyn Heights to the spread of residential neighborhoods into Flatbush, New Utrecht, and the other old Kings County towns. The sobriquet "City of Churches and Homes," fully established by the last decades of the nineteenth century, expressed a dual identity that in many respects merged into one and was the frequent boast of Brooklynites who set themselves apart from the crowded Sodom across the river. A boast about superior morality, it was also about the beauty of sprawling, tree-lined neighborhoods made healthful by ocean and bay breezes. That boast endured during the early decades of Brooklyn's development as a maritime and industrial center, even while thickening Irish and German immigrant neighborhoods offered contrast to upper- and middle-class suburbs inhabited mainly by native Protestants. It endured as well into the years when second generation Irish- and German-Americans moved from the South Brooklyn waterfront and industrial Williamsburg to Bedford, Flatbush, and other suburbs. The boast was much harder to maintain, however, when new bridges and subway tunnels brought masses of Jewish and Italian and Eastern European Catholic immigrants into increasingly crowded neighborhoods that could not be called suburban.

In 1930, under the title "Brooklyn Stands Out Prominently as a Great Center for Homes," the *Eagle* tabulated 244,000 residential buildings in the borough, invoking the long-standing image of endless miles of single-family suburban homes. A closer look, however, evokes a different image. Just under 100,000 of those buildings, according to the *Eagle*, were built to house a single family—an impressive number and the numerically dominant form among Brooklyn's domestic structures. But 80,000 were two-family houses and 65,000 were apartment houses, which means that (assuming roughly equal occupancy rates for each building type) apartment dwellers constituted a majority of the households living in Brooklyn in 1930, outpacing the maximum of 260,000 that lived in one- and two-family homes.[66] As we observed earlier, a number of Brooklyn's apartment buildings were built on or just behind the commercial thoroughfares of suburban neighborhoods and did not compromise the openness of areas covered mainly by individual and duplex houses. But others, especially in the older wards, dominated whole districts of the borough. They did not always add to its beauty. Eight years earlier, Brooklyn was described as "one of the ugliest places in the world" by Frank Alvah Parsons, president of the New York School of Fine and Applied Arts.[67] Parsons was speaking primarily of two downtown eyesores, which hardly seems fair to the borough as a whole. But that it could be spoken at all was a stunning departure from self-congratulatory claims about Brooklyn's beauty.

Brooklyn preserved much suburban space during these years, and even expanded that space into places like Canarsie, Sheepshead Bay, and Marine Park, although many of the homes built there were modest, and beckoned residents some old-stock Brooklynites preferred not to have as neighbors. Brooklyn was still a place to move to. But it was now also a place to move from.

In the early decades of the twentieth century, many middle-class and affluent Protestants concluded that Brooklyn, which by then was teeming with Jews, Italians, and growing numbers of Blacks, had ceased to be an acceptable domestic environment. And so they searched for and found places where they could create new and pleasant neighborhoods filled with people like themselves. This migration out of Brooklyn cannot properly be called "white flight," a term that applies forcefully to the post–World War II decades, when African American, Black West Indian, and Hispanic communities approached a majority of the borough's population. Ironically, during those decades, Jews, Italians, and other white ethnics were a large component of the stream of Brooklynites to more distant suburbs.

FIGURE 7.7. Rowhouses in Sheepshead Bay, East 23rd Street below Avenue W (Eugene L. Armbruster Photograph Collection, 1894–1939, New-York Historical Society).

The transformation of Brooklyn in the early twentieth century affected the borough's most exclusive neighborhoods. We have seen the reactions of some of the oldest residents of Brooklyn Heights to the large apartment buildings, the conversion of fine old brownstones to apartments and boarding houses, and even the corner deli. Some merely complained and hunkered down, but others, according to James H. Callender, moved to Park Avenue in Manhattan, where apartment houses defined the area rather than destroying it.[68] Others moved east to exclusive enclaves on Long Island's North Shore, accessible now by the Long Island Railroad and new automobile parkways that made commutation feasible all the way to Manhattan. A Plymouth Church congregational meeting in 1922 appointed a committee to go over the membership rolls to drop the four or five hundred "who have moved out of Brooklyn and who have not been heard from in a number of years."[69] Emblematic of these losses were merger discussions between the Heights' most iconic churches: Church of the Pilgrims and First Presbyterian; Plymouth Church and Pilgrims. Neither of these mergers was carried out during the 1920s and the problem of fleeing membership remained, a continuing reminder that even this old redoubt of Yankee Protestantism had succumbed to the new Brooklyn.[70]

The most significant migrations were directly eastward to the developing suburban towns of Queens County, and beyond Queens into the mid-island, North Shore, and South Shore towns of Nassau County. The *Eagle* article that tabulated the domestic building stock of Brooklyn boasted that "Brooklyn has more apartment houses than Manhattan, Queens, the Bronx and Richmond [Staten Island] combined. It has more two-family dwellings than the same boroughs together, and ranks second only to Queens in the number of one-family houses."[71] Apart from admitting that Queens had surpassed Brooklyn in single-family homes, the *Eagle* might have acknowledged that many former Brooklynites lived in those homes beyond the borough border.

It is impossible to say which Brooklynites moved to Queens, Nassau, or Suffolk (or the Bronx and Westchester north of Manhattan) during these years, or the degree to which they felt driven by discomforting changes in Brooklyn as opposed to the attractions of more closet space in the larger and generally cheaper homes of more distant suburbs. The US census does not speak of motive but does indicate that while less than one-fifth of Brooklyn's residents in 1930 were native-born to native-born parents, the proportion in Queens was more than one-third. More telling are the advertisements for new homes in Queens and elsewhere. A 1922 *Eagle* article suggested that the critical questions for prospective movers to more distant suburbs involved transportation to Manhattan, healthful high ground, the prospects for increasing property value, and the fourth of a still longer list: "Is the surrounding property restricted so that the community will always remain the same kind and be attractive as at present"?[72] Advertisers almost always stressed this element of their development's appeal. Lynbrook Park in Nassau County, for example, stated in a 1927 full-page ad: "To insure congenial neighbors, it has always been our policy to restrict sales to people of character and refinement."[73] The many advertisements for Jackson Heights in Queens stressed restriction, a 1925 ad listing it as the first of the reasons "Why so Many Brooklyn Families Have Moved to Jackson Heights": "Because they found that they could purchase a new one-family English Garden House in the most carefully restricted residential section of New York City." At the bottom of the ad, in capital letters, was the warning: "SOCIAL AND BUSINESS REFERENCES REQUIRED."[74] "Restrictions" were generally understood to apply primarily to Jews and African Americans, and sometimes also to Catholics, especially those from Italy or Eastern Europe.

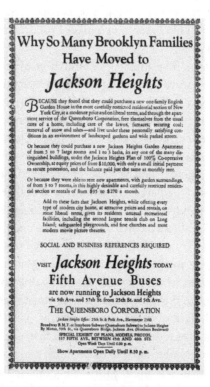

FIGURE 7.8. Advertisement for homes in restricted Jackson Heights, Queens County (*Brooklyn Daily Eagle*, September 1, 1925).

The developers of Queens and Nassau, in other words, were making special efforts to invite white Protestants, from Brooklyn and elsewhere, to their suburban residential projects. Buyers expressed a similar attitude toward the maintenance of their investment. In 1929 a resident of Forest Hills Gardens in Queens chaired a meeting of the Gardens Corporation that discussed a plan "wherein all purchasers of properties in the Gardens must be acceptable to a central committee of property owners, thereby keeping out undesirables and keeping up property values." The chairman of the meeting was Lyman Beecher Stowe, grandson of the author of *Uncle Tom's Cabin*, and grandnephew of Henry Ward Beecher.[75]

Some of the Protestants still living in Brooklyn at the end of the Roaring Twenties could trace their lineage back to New England—perhaps even, like the Brewster sisters of *Arsenic and Old Lace*, to the *Mayflower*. For all their problems, Plymouth Church, the Church of the Pilgrims, and the First Presbyterian Church (late of Cranberry Street) did not fold their tents. But the Pilgrim Fathers no longer resonated so loudly in Brooklyn, even among its remaining Protestants. When Canon William Sheafe Chase left Brooklyn for Washington in 1932 he may have taken with him the last remnants of the old Protestant hegemony. But with him or without him the Brooklyn of 1930 was anything but a Yankee town.

Epilogue

Brooklyn's America

What is an American? Francie Nolan, the heroine of Betty Smith's novel *A Tree Grows in Brooklyn*, encounters this question on the first day at her new school. When the teacher calls the roll, and asks each child her lineage, the answers are alike: "I'm Polish-American. My father was born in Warsaw." "Irish-American. Me fayther and mither were born in County Cork." Only Francie's answer is different, and is offered with pride:

"I'm an American."

"I *know* you're American," said the easily exasperated teacher. "But what's your nationality?"

"American!" insisted Francie even more proudly.

"Will you tell me what your parents are or do I have to send you to the principal?"

"My parents are American. They were born in Brooklyn."

All the children turned around to look at a little girl whose parents had *not* come from the old country. And when Teacher said, "Brooklyn? Hm. I guess that makes you American, all right," Francie was proud and happy. How wonderful was Brooklyn, she thought, when just being born there automatically made you an American![1]

For Francie Nolan, granddaughter of immigrants from Ireland and Austria, the issue was settled. But for her classmates, including the Polish-American and the Irish girl who spoke with the heavy brogue of her parents, the question of nationality was still contested. They, too, had been born in Brooklyn, but did that make them American? What about their parents? We have seen the efforts of groups ranging from "uptown" Jews to Protestant women's clubs to make Brooklyn's twentieth-century immigrants more American, teaching them to read and speak English, understand American civic institutions and norms, and adopt the behavior of native Americans. These efforts were not necessarily hostile, but they often established a standard that left little room for the retention of Old World habits and values.

Frederick Boyd Stevenson went further. He wanted immigrants to *think* in English and rejected the legitimacy of one man's declaration of divided affection for America and his country of origin. Like other old-stock Brooklynites, Stevenson ultimately accepted immigration restriction as the only solution to the problems posed by the New Immigrants, a solution that settled the question Francie Nolan faced on that first day of school. The granddaughter of old immigrants might be acceptable as an American. The New Immigrants were not.

This contest was by no means restricted to Brooklyn. As the number of recently arrived immigrants mounted in America and the tensions generated by World War I and the Russian Revolution increased, it became a national issue of great importance. Theodore Roosevelt, one of the earliest advocates for a robust Americanization program, had no patience with hyphenated Americanism, arguing instead that immigrants must give up all vestiges of prior loyalties, language, and culture and become "Americans pure and simple." Optimistic that this could be done, Roosevelt loudly applauded Israel Zangwill's 1908 play, *The Melting Pot* (it was dedicated to TR), which he understood as a salute to the melting away of alien cultures in response to the day-to-day experience of American life and the remolding of immigrants into an Anglo-Dutch form.[2] He seems not to have considered the possibility of fusing disparate cultures into a new American, only partly in the shape of people like himself.

Roosevelt's friend Madison Grant was skeptical of any such amalgamation of cultures, or of attempts to reshape immigrants into a preexisting American form. Imbued with currently fashionable theories of eugenics and race, Grant (who was descended from original settlers of New Netherland and Massachusetts Bay) published his highly influential *The Passing of the Great Race* in 1916. The book divided the peoples of the world into three enduring and incompatible races, Caucasoids, Negroids, and Mongoloids, with further division of the mostly European Caucasoids into Nordics, Alpines, and Mediterraneans. Superior to the other groups and subgroups, Nordics formed the basic American racial stock, now threatened by the large-scale migrations to the United States of Mediterraneans and Alpines (from Eastern Europe), who were certain to outbreed and even inter-breed with American Nordics, resulting in the latter's "race suicide." Grant's solution was, obviously, neither racial amalgamation nor an intense program of Americanization. Only rigid segregation of the races and, more importantly, the closing off of further immigration would save America.[3] Vice president of the Immigration Restriction League from 1922 until his death in 1937, Grant helped set the ideological context for the Immigration Act of 1924.

Grant was by no means the only racial theorist of this era. In 1920, Lothrop Stoddard published *The Rising Tide of Color against White World Supremacy*, with an introduction by Grant, that was even more dire in its predictions of the coming challenge to Nordic supremacy. Not just America but Western Civilization was threatened by a population explosion among nonwhite races, their migration to parts of the world in which Nordics were dominant, and the impending collapse of colonialism.[4] Like Grant, Stoddard was impressed by eugenics as a mechanism to limit nonwhite populations.

FIGURE 8.1.   Madison Grant (Interfoto/Alamy Stock Photo).

Margaret Sanger may have designed her American Birth Control League as a way of helping poor women. For Stoddard, who was a founder of Sanger's League, and a member of the American Eugenics Society and the Ku Klux Klan, birth control was crucial to the preservation of Nordic dominance.

Many old-stock Americans embraced these ideas before and during the 1920s. Whether one identified as Nordic, Anglo-Dutch, or Anglo-Saxon, the threat of alien invasion could appear real, imminent—indeed, well underway—and transformative of the character of American society. "What does it mean to be a Gentile in New York?" asked *Pearson's Magazine* in 1917. "It means that you are lonesome" in the presence of so many Jews, who are increasing at so rapid a rate that "Gentiles will shortly be on exhibition at the Bronx Zoo, where the children of Israel may regard them with curious eyes." In the city, Jews could not be escaped. "You pay rent to a Jewish landlord, buy your food from a Jewish market man, your medicines from a Jewish druggist, your dry goods from a Jewish merchant." When you have been sick and are discharged from a Jewish hospital where you were treated by Jewish doctors and nurses you might wish to celebrate with a new suit of clothes. You search the city for a Gentile tailor "and when you find one with an Irish name at last you learn later that his true name is Feinheimer." The grim anti-Semitism of this article—the thesis that Jews have taken over the American metropolis—belies its intended humorous tone. *The American Hebrew & Jewish Messenger* reprinted it as a warning to Jews who might not have understood the depth of resentment toward them.[5]

Four years later the *American Hebrew* responded to former Cornell University president Jacob Gould Schurman, who had warned Americans that the much-extolled melting pot was melting very few immigrants. "Either we can never become a homogeneous American people," Schurman declared, "either unassimilated masses of European nationalities must share our domain with us, or we must set limits to the tide of immigration so that a unified national life and consciousness shall remain possible for us." The melting pot does not melt, responded the *American Hebrew*, *"because there is no warmth applied to it."* Attempts to assimilate and Americanize immigrants have not succeeded because they have paid so little heed to the foreigners' own values and feelings. "Patience and love must go into the process. When a famous painter was once asked by a beginner how he mixed his paints, the significant reply was 'With brains, sir.' If we were asked how to make the Melting Pot melt, we should be tempted strongly to say, 'With brains and heart, sir.'"[6]

The American Hebrew accepted the idea of a melting pot, even while it insisted on the legitimacy of foreign cultures, in essence suggesting that assimilation cannot and should not entirely efface those cultures while turning immigrants into true and loyal Americans. Half a dozen years earlier, a brief, two-part article in *The Nation* went well beyond this argument and proved to be far more influential. Horace Kallen's "Democracy Versus the Melting Pot: A Study of American Nationality" was the first of many publications by this young Jewish-American academic that challenged the melting pot itself on behalf of what Kallen called "cultural pluralism."[7] The goal of achieving a unitary American type within a homogeneous culture was not only unrealistic—it was undesirable. Dismissive of the Rooseveltian insistence on an Anglo-Dutch Americanism as mere "cultural primogeniture," Kallen questioned the very idea of homogeneity as the necessary foundation of a democratic society and its civic institutions. As an alternative to the melting pot, he offered the metaphor of the symphony orchestra, with its many instruments of different "timbre and tonality," each essential to the performance of complex symphonic music. Society, too, is complex, Kallen argued, and "each ethnic group is the natural instrument, its spirit and culture are its theme and melody, and the harmony and dissonances and discords of them all make the symphony of civilization."[8]

FIGURE 8.2.   Horace Kallen (Aldino Felicani Sacco-Vanzetti Collection, 1915–77, Boston Public Library).

Kallen assumed the permanent existence of a dominant "Anglo-Saxon" class, which he thought could be persuaded to enact laws embodying the best precepts and practices of American democracy, and usher in a "multiplicity in unity." "Democracy Versus the Melting Pot," however, focused exclusively on groups that had emigrated to the United States from Europe: Irish, Germans, Scandinavians, Poles, and Jews. Published in 1924, Kallen's "Culture and the Ku Klux Klan" contrasted these once derided and exploited immigrants, who had (or would soon) become "more or less stably settled in the United States," to the "steady and cumulative antagonism" still administered to "the Negro." Noting that KKK members were "native, white, and Protestant," Kallen did not mention conflict between ethnic groups and Blacks and implied that cultural pluralism would make racism go away. Kallen's lack of serious and sustained attention to the unique challenges of race in America, according to one eminent critic, was "a fatal elision" in his theory of cultural pluralism.[9]

Kallen's argument stimulated others who were dissatisfied with both "cultural primogeniture" and an Americanization designed to eliminate diversity. In a letter to Kallen, John Dewey urged an "assimilation *to one another—* not to Anglo-Saxonism," and in his own essays wrote of homogenization as a false goal. Randolph Bourne, a friend of Kallen's and a former student of Dewey's, wrote powerfully of a "trans-national America" that gave no primacy to the English culture from which he himself descended, nourishing instead a cosmopolitan mix of cultures, none effacing any other, each contributing to a larger whole characterized by diversity rather than either a homogeneous mass or the imperial rule of a hegemonic group. This, to Bourne, was not merely a goal, but an achievement, for in the era of the New Immigration the United States was already living "that miracle of hope, the peaceful living side by side, with character substantially preserved, of the most heterogeneous peoples under the sun."[10]

It took time for these bold and expansive ideas to become influential beyond the worlds of the academy and urban liberal journalism. In the meantime, during the 1920s at least, the agenda of Madison Grant and Lothrop Stoddard carried significantly more weight among those who wielded disproportionate power in the formulation of public policy. Old-stock Americans celebrated the passage of the immigration restriction acts of 1921 and 1924, which drastically limited the migration to America of Eastern and Southern Europeans. To the defenders of the Nordic race in America the legislation confirmed the supremacy of their ideas and values and, many of them thought, secured a permanent victory over those who spoke of the evils of "cultural primogeniture" and the benefits of "cultural pluralism."

It did neither. Immigration had largely ceased, but the door had been closed too late. Immigrants had already formed their families, built their communities, and set to work toward a better life. Many of them and many more of their children thrived in America, and while that thriving generally involved a significant degree of assimilation it almost never resulted in the abandonment of prior ethnic identities. William Thomas and Florian Znaniecki observed Polish-American communities as something new, enduring, and by their nature different not only from the Nordics that preceded them but also the communities of other hyphenated Americans. In their fine-grained studies, Horace Kallen found confirmation of his predictions of a culturally plural America. During the 1930s the racial theories of Grant and Stoddard lost much of their persuasiveness, a process no doubt hastened by their embrace by Adolf Hitler and other European fascists. As these ideas faded and ethnic communities proved their worth and staying power, the theory of cultural pluralism became more widely accepted, rising to become a fundamental component of the American Creed. The successful fight against Nazism and the realization of the full dimensions of its racist horrors helped confirm the pluralist American ideal, as did the insistence by our first Roman Catholic president that the United States is a nation of immigrants.

Though fundamental to American identity, cultural pluralism—which in the twenty-first century has been supplemented and to some extent supplanted by the concept of multiculturalism—still contends with reassertions of xenophobia and white nationalism, and with considerable resistance from people who do not accept the premise that cultural diversity not only defines America but is one of its greatest strengths. Still, the lady who lifts her lamp beside the golden door knows the value of the wretched refuse of *any* teeming shore. And Brooklynites know that their uniquely vibrant borough, as much as or more than any other place in America, is where huddled masses learned to breathe free.

NOTES

Prologue: America's Brooklyn

1. Nathan S. Jonas, *Through the Years: An Autobiography* (New York: Business Bourse Publishers, 1940), 3.

2. Lionel R. Lindsay, *Gravesend Kid: A Brooklyn Boyhood* (Bloomington: Author-House, 2004), 62–63.

3. William L. Riordon, *Plunkitt of Tammany Hall: A Series of Very Plain Talks on Very Practical Politics* (New York: E. P. Dutton & Co., 1905; 1963), 41.

4. Riordon, *Plunkitt of Tammany Hall*, 42.

5. Clay Lancaster, *Old Brooklyn Heights: New York's First Suburb* (New York: Dover Publications, 1979); Robert Furman, *Brooklyn Heights: The Rise, Fall and Rebirth of America's First Suburb* (Charleston, SC: History Press, 2015); Kenneth T. Jackson, *Crabgrass Frontier: The Suburbanization of the United States* (New York: Oxford University Press, 1985).

Chapter 1. Brooklyn Village

1. On the settlement and early trade and development of Breuckelen, see Henry R. Stiles, *A History of the City of Brooklyn . . .*, vol. 1 (Albany: J. Munsell, 1869); Stephen M. Ostrander, *A History of the City of Brooklyn and Kings County*, vol. 1 (Brooklyn: by subscription, 1894). Later works that allude to these aspects of early Brooklyn include Edwin G. Burrows and Mike Wallace, *Gotham: A History of New York City to 1898* (New York: Oxford University Press, 1999), 35, 36, 46; Russell Shorto, *The Island at the Center of the World: The Epic Story of Dutch Manhattan and the Forgotten Colony that Shaped the World* (New York: Doubleday, 2004), 127; Jaap Jacobs, *The Colony of New Netherland: A Dutch Settlement in Seventeenth-Century America* (Ithaca, NY: Cornell University Press, 2009), 87–88. On the early ferry, see Henry Evelyn Pierrepont, *Sketch of the Fulton Ferry and its Associated Ferries* (Brooklyn: Eagle Job and Book Printing Department, 1879), 13.

2. Jacobs, *Colony of New Netherland*, 159.

3. Daniel Denton, *A Brief Description of New York, Formerly Called New-Netherlands* (London: n.p., 1670), 46.

4. Burrows and Wallace, *Gotham*, 128.

5. On the 1738 census the proportion of slaves in Brooklyn's population was 22 percent, slightly higher than the proportion in Manhattan.

6. Stiles, *History*, 3, 598–600; David Ment, *The Shaping of a City: A Brief History of Brooklyn* (New York: Brooklyn Educational and Cultural Alliance, 1979), 26; Burrows and Wallace, *Gotham*, 390; Ralph Foster Weld, *Brooklyn Village, 1816–1834* (New York: Columbia University Press, 1938), 13; Ostrander, *History*, 2, 24–26.

7. The legal term in New York State for what is elsewhere termed a "township" is "town." But we will use "township" where it seems to convey our meaning more clearly, especially to readers who do not reside in New York.

8. Weld, *Brooklyn Village*, 7–8.

9. The classic analysis of this connection between Protestantism (Calvinism in particular) and the pursuit of material wealth is Max Weber's *The Protestant Ethic and the Spirit of Capitalism*, first published in German in 1905 and in an English translation by Talcott Parsons in 1930 (New York: Scribners). Weber has been challenged, modified, and rebutted many times over more than a century, but his fundamental idea remains relevant in many historical settings. Brooklyn, we claim, is one of them.

10. Guide to the Sands family papers, Brooklyn Historical Society. dlib.nyu.edu/findingaids/html/bhs/arc_096.sands/bioghist.html.

11. Stiles, *History*, 3:381–32; 2:96–97; Ment, *Shaping of a City*, 26–27.

12. Ment, *Shaping of a City*, 26–27.

13. *Census of the State of New York, 1835. . .*

14. Stiles, *History*, 2:98.

15. Stiles, *History*, 1:385; 3:945; James H. Callender, *Yesterdays on Brooklyn Heights* (New York: Dorland Press, 1927), 53; Burrows and Wallace, *Gotham*, 390.

16. Hezekiah Pierrepont spelled his name Pierpont, the Anglicized version of the original Huguenot family name, although, curiously, in his will he instructed his children to revert to the original spelling. Most accounts of his life use Pierrepont, as will we. See Stiles, *History*, 2:147.

17. Historical sources differ as to whether this business was a brewery or a distillery before Pierrepont purchased it. One, Robert Furman, *Brooklyn Heights: The Rise, Fall and Rebirth of America's First Suburb* (Charleston, SC: History Press, 2015), 66, argues that it was a distillery before and after the Revolution, and a brewery while the British occupied the area. Pierrepont distilled Anchor gin in this facility.

18. Stiles, *History*, 2:147–49; Kenneth T. Jackson, *Crabgrass Frontier: The Suburbanization of the United States* (New York: Oxford University Press, 1985), 30–31.

19. Stiles, *History*, 2:151; Callender, *Yesterdays*, 41.

20. A note concerning the word "commuter" seems appropriate here. For some time it has been used to refer to a person who travels daily between suburb and city for work and domestic life. But its original meaning derives from the commutation (substitution, exchange) of a daily fare on a train, ferry, or other form of mass transportation, for a longer-term ticket that is cheaper per individual ride. Hence, it is the fare that is commuted, not the traveler. So, strictly speaking, a person who travels by automobile between work and home is not a commuter, unless he commutes a daily highway or bridge toll for a longer-term charge. And Hezekiah Pierrepont in his rowboat was not one either.

21. The Brooklyn landing of this ferry became the "old landing" in 1795 when a "new landing" was established at the foot of Main Street for a ferry that ran to Catherine Street in New York. Another innovation that deserves mention here was the horse or team boat, introduced around the same time as the steam ferry. It involved the introduction of a treadmill, on which teams of horses walked to turn a vertical shaft attached to a paddle wheel below, usually in the center of a deck connecting two separate hulls. The horse boats were technically successful and offered some competition to the steam ferries for several years. See Stiles, *History*, 3:38–43.

22. Stiles, *History*, 2:149; Pierrepont, *Sketch of the Fulton Ferry*, 27–31.

23. Weld, *Brooklyn Village*, 16–17.

24. *Long-Island Star*, March 20, 1816.

25. *Star*, July 14, 1813.

26. *Star*, November 15, 1815.

27. Stiles, *History*, 2:149; Jackson, *Crabgrass Frontier*, 31.

28. *Star*, December 25, 1823; Jackson, *Crabgrass Frontier*, 31–32; Weld, *Brooklyn Village*, 27.

29. Callender, *Yesterdays*, 83.

30. Stiles, *History*, 2:101–4.

31. *Star*, March 1, 1820. Guy completed two such scenes, which varied mainly in a few of the characters portrayed in the street. Stiles, *History*, 2:88, 101–4, names this painting *Brooklyn Snow Scene*.

32. This was the Catherine Street Ferry. It ran for many years but was never as important as the Fulton Street Ferry.

33. Because of damage to the left side of the painting these two houses are no longer visible. The lithograph reproduced here is a better representation of Guy's original composition than the painting in its current state.

34. Callender, *Yesterdays*, 68–69.

35. *Star*, September 5, 1822; September 12, 1822.

36. *Star*, September 1, 1823.

37. Burrows and Wallace, *Gotham*, 450.

38. Elizabeth Leavitt Howe, *My Early and Later Days: Their Story for My Children and Grandchildren* (n. p., 1898), 19. Fisher Howe Papers, New-York Historical Society.

39. Howe, *My Early and Later Days*, 32.

40. Clay Lancaster, *Old Brooklyn Heights: New York's First Suburb* . . . (New York: Dover Publications, Inc., 1979), 20, 67, 69; Furman, *Brooklyn Heights*, 22–23.

41. *Star*, June 28, 1820, June 5, 1823.

42. *Star*, July 7, 1825.

43. Weld, *Brooklyn Village*, 200–203; Stiles, *History*, 3:886–91.

44. *Star*, July 8, 1824; June 7, 1827.

45. Weld, *Brooklyn Village*, 32; Stiles, *History*, 3:896–97.

46. Weld, *Brooklyn Village*, 62.

47. Weld, *Brooklyn Village*, 63–66; Stiles, *History*, 3:652–55; Eugene Armbruster, *The Olympian Settlement in Early Brooklyn, New York* (New York: n. p., 1929), 7–8; Anon., *St. Ann's Church, (Brooklyn, New York)* . . . (Brooklyn: F. G. Fish, 1845).

48. Weld, *Brooklyn Village*, 70–71. Being independent of the Episcopal Church, the Methodist organizations of the United States are called churches, not chapels, as they are in England, where they remain within the formal structure of the Church of England. On Judge Garrison's role in Brooklyn's Methodist Church, see Stiles, *History*, 3:700–701.

49. These events are described in a pamphlet, Reverend David B. Cousin and Reverend Valerie E. Cousin, *Welcome to Bridge Street*, reproduced on the Bridge Street Church's website, at www.Bridgestreetbrooklyn.org/wp-content/uploads/2015/11/About-Bridge-Street.pdf. See Stiles, *History*, 3:702, 707, and Weld, *Brooklyn Village*, 71, for accounts that make no mention of fees charged to Black members of the Sands Street church.

50. Weld, *Brooklyn Village*, 60.

51. Stiles, *History*, 3:636–37.

52. Stiles, *History*, 3:702, 741–42.

53. Howe, *My Early and Later Days*, 19–21, 24–32.

54. Weld, *Brooklyn Village*, 78–79. See also Weld, *A Tower on the Heights: The Story of the First Presbyterian Church in Brooklyn* (New York: Columbia University Press, 1946).

55. Weld, *Brooklyn Village*, 79.

56. *Star*, May 3, 1815; September 27, 1815.

57. *Star*, April 10, 1816. For a detailed recollection of the founding of this society, see *The Brooklyn Eagle*, May 15, 1854.

58. *Star*, July 3, 1816.

59. Weld, *Brooklyn Village*, 94.

60. *Star*, April 10, 1823; May 22, 1823; May 29, 1823; March 16, 1826; May 11, 1826.

61. Weld, *Brooklyn Village*, 111.

62. Weld, *Brooklyn Village*, 122, 126, 129; *Star*, July 9, 1829.

63. Weld, *Brooklyn Village*, 98–99, 194–97, 216, 218–19, 237–40, 252–53.

64. Weld, *Brooklyn Village*, 263.

65. *Star*, April 1, 1830.

Chapter 2. The City of Brooklyn

1. *Long-Island Star*, April 24, 1834. There was also a dinner that evening at Duflon's Military Garden, with tickets priced at $1.50. The following week's paper reported a large turnout for the procession and church ceremony but disappointing attendance at the dinner. *Star*, May 1, 1834.

2. *Star*, May 1, 1834.

3. *Census of the State of New York, 1825* (Albany, 1826).

4. *Star*, December 8, 1825.

5. *Star*, December 29, 1830, December 14, 1831, December 21, 1831.

6. *Star*, January 4, 1832.

7. [Henry Evelyn Pierrepont], *Historical Sketch of the Fulton Ferry, and its Associated Ferries* (Brooklyn: Eagle Job and Book Printing Department, 1879), 12–15. In New York, as in all the states, the awarding of a city charter does not extinguish the power of the state legislature to regulate the policies of that city, or even to revoke the city's charter.

8. Henry R. Stiles, *A History of the City of Brooklyn* . . . (Brooklyn: n.p., 1870), 3:518.

9. *Star*, April 3, 1833, April 24, 1833.

10. *Star*, October 16, 1833.

11. *Star*, May 8, 1833, October 16, 1833, December 18, 1833, January 2, 1834, January 9, 1834, January 16, 1834, January 23, 1834, April 10, 1834.

12. *Star*, April 10, 1834.

13. This is mostly correct, and we have used the term "tidal strait" ourselves. The only qualification to be made here is that the Harlem River empties into the East River, mingling with the salt water of the Sound and Bay at Hell's Gate. But the Harlem River (as a branch of the Hudson River) is itself a brackish tidal estuary, so it offers only a limited volume of fresh water to the East River, and the flow there is,

in sum, far more tidal than riverine. It is quite reasonable to describe the East River as an "arm of the sea."

14. *Star*, May 14, 1835.

15. *Star*, May 15, 1845.

16. *Star*, January 5, 1837.

17. *Census of the State of New York, for 1835* (Albany, 1836); *Compendium of the Enumeration of the Inhabitants and Statistics of the United States* . . . (Washington, 1841), 18, 22; *Census of the State of New York, for 1845* (Albany, 1846).

18. *Brooklyn Daily Eagle*, September 2, 1845.

19. *Star*, May 26, 1845. In this issue the *Star* announced the opening of a branch office on Atlantic Street for the accommodation of its South Brooklyn customers. The Atlantic Street terminus of the Brooklyn and Jamaica Rail Road Company (soon merged into the Long Island Railroad) was an important impetus for the opening of the South Ferry. The Long Island Railroad, once built to an eastern terminus at Greenport, Long Island, provided a rail and ferry link between New York and Boston. It would take several years for this link to be superseded by an inland, all-rail system.

20. Joseph Alexiou, *Gowanus: Brooklyn's Curious Canal* (New York: New York University Press, 2015), 91–106; Stiles, *History*, 3:558, 575–80. On the details of James S. T. Stranahan's New England background, see *Eagle*, September 3, 1898.

21. *Star*, September 22, 1842.

22. Clay Lancaster, *Old Brooklyn Heights: New York's First Suburb* (New York: Dover Publications, 1979), 68.

23. Mrs. E. R. Steele, "Brooklyn," *The Ladies' Companion: A Monthly Magazine; Devoted to Literature and the Fine Arts*, November 1841, 18.

24. *Star*, November 14, 1842.

25. *Eagle*, July 21, 1845.

26. *Star*, May 10, 1838. Five years later, as the depression began to lift, the *Star's* appraisal was much the same: "In the convulsions which have racked our gigantic neighbor, . . . Brooklyn has been the gainer." *Star*, May 13, 1843.

27. One of the latter was John R. Pitkin's proposal for a large new community to be known as East New York on land he had acquired in the Town of New Lots at the eastern end of Kings County. He publicized his project during the early months of the depression, but it attracted little interest and was not heard from again. *Star*, August 21, 1837. We will return to Pitkin's proposal and the later development of East New York in chapter 4.

28. Clay Lancaster, *Old Brooklyn Heights*, 32–32; Stiles, *History*, 2:253; *Star*, August 7, 1837, August 11, 1846; *Eagle*, August 17, 1849.

29. *Census of . . . New York, for 1835; Census of . . . New York, for 1845; The Seventh Census of the United States: 1850* . . . (Washington, 1853).

30. *Eagle*, November 5, 1849. A similar observation was made as early as 1840 in J. T. Bailey, *An Historical Sketch of the City of Brooklyn and the Surrounding Neighborhood, Including the Village of Williamsburgh* . . . (Brooklyn: J. T. Bailey, 1840), 25.

31. Quoted in *Star*, June 30, 1853.

32. Stiles, *History*, 2, 300.

33. *Population of the United States in 1860*. . . (Washington, 1864). In 1800 New York City and Philadelphia each had populations of approximately sixty thousand. In 1860 a Brooklyn neighborhood named Williamsburg numbered sixty-five thousand.

34. The parts of Gowanus that lay along the meandering Gowanus Creek, and the marshes and mill ponds that bordered it on the east, remained rural despite Daniel Richards' efforts during the late 1840s to canalize the creek and provide Brooklyn with the extensive inland commercial waterway that was in fact achieved by others a dozen or so years later. See Alexiou, *Gowanus*, 108–19. Alexiou writes of Richards as a forgotten man: "Not even an obituary exists for this elusive innovator, so he likely died in relative obscurity sometime around 1875. . . . Most details of his personal life are lost" (122).

35. Alexiou, *Gowanus*, 128–30, 134–35.

36. Jon C. Teaford, *The Unheralded Triumph: City Government in America, 1870–1900* (Baltimore: Johns Hopkins University Press, 1984). Teaford's post–Civil War analysis is relevant to Brooklyn in the immediate pre–Civil War period.

37. The free roaming of pigs in Brooklyn's streets was a common complaint, and a frequently visited subject over many years in the local press. Referring in 1845 to a new effort to clear the streets of pigs as "an important reform," the *Eagle* observed: "During the last week the porkers, as if anticipating a curtailing of their ancient privileges, and snuffing danger in the breeze, have mustered in unusual force, and extended the field of their operations. Not content with perambulating the streets and sidewalks—poking a stray vegetable out of the gutter here and there and reposing listlessly in styes of their own creation—they have penetrated through gateways and fences, examining the collections of yards and open lots, and running riot in unguarded areas." Conceding that the pigs had been relied upon for years to clear garbage from the streets, the *Eagle* concluded: "If it should be found necessary, in the end, to restore these valuable scavengers to the exercise of their duties and the enjoyment of their privileges, we shall at least have the satisfaction of knowing that it couldn't be helped." *Eagle*, October 20, 1845.

38. Nearly the entire issue of the *Star*, April 29, 1859, is devoted to the celebration of the new water supply system. See *Star*, November 20, 1855, for a typical warning of fraud in one of the early initiatives for building this system.

39. *Eagle*, June 30, 1854; Stiles, *History*, 3:571–72.

40. Stiles, *History*, 2:49–50.

41. *Star*, August 10, 1844. Dozens of editorials in this vein, as well as letters from readers, could be cited here.

42. *Eagle*, March 23, 1846. On the origin of the Fort Greene (Washington Park) proposal, see Stiles, *History*, 3:616–17.

43. *Star*, May 4, 1847.

44. *Star*, July 27, 1847, December 4, 1847, January 5, 1848; *Eagle*, January 5, 1848.

45. *Star*, January 4, 1848, January 5, 1848; *Eagle*, January 4, 1848, January 5, 1848.

46. *Star*, January 14, 1848; *Eagle*, January 14, 1848.

47. *Star*, January 24, 1848, March 1, 1848, March 27, 1848, April 11, 1848. Spooner would never see that park on Prospect Hill. Three weeks after he wrote that April editorial, he retired from the *Star*, and six months after that, he was dead at age sixty-five. The *Star*'s new editor, Alden's son Edwin B. Spooner, described what he claimed was the largest funeral ever held in Brooklyn for a private citizen, noting that among the pallbearers for this Whig newspaperman was John Greenwood, whose contributions to the Democratic party included suggesting the name for the *Brooklyn Eagle*. Some articles on Greenwood in the *Star*, in addition to Greenwood's gesture

at Spooner's funeral, attest to the mutual respect of these two devoted Brooklynites. *Star,* November 25, 1848, November 28, 1848. On Greenwood's role in naming the *Eagle,* see Raymond A. Schroth, *The Eagle and Brooklyn: A Community Newspaper, 1841–1955* (Westport, CT: Greenwood Press, 1974), 28.

48. Stiles, *History,* 3:622–30; Thomas J. Campanella, *Brooklyn: The Once and Future City* (Princeton: Princeton University Press, 2019), 75–78; *Star,* August 13, 1838, May 28, 1845, *Eagle,* April 13, 1848 (which suggest that at an early date tickets were required for visitors in carriages and on horseback); *Eagle,* September 20, 1844. Green-Wood was for some time a popular subject in parlor magazines, some of which dwelt on the fact that this had been the site of the Battle of Brooklyn during the American Revolution. See, for example, "Greenwood Cemetery," *The New World; a Weekly Family Journal of Popular Literature, Science, Art and News,* May 11, 1844, 593–94; "Greenwood Cemetery," *The Ladies' Repository; a Monthly Periodical Devoted to Literature, Art and Religion,* August 1854, 344–47; "Greenwood Cemetery," *Hours at Home: A Popular Monthly of Instruction and Recreation,* August 1868, 359–64.

49. *Ladies' Repository,* 344. It was, at first, a Protestant god. According to a recent article on Green-Wood in the journal *Irish America,* the first Catholic burials did not occur for some years, as "it was generally considered a Christian burial place for white Anglo-Saxon Protestants of the better classes." Michael Burke, "The Irish of Green-Wood Cemetery," *Irish America* (February/March 2013).

50. *The Brooklyn and Kings County Record: A Budget of General Information; with a Map of the City, an Almanac, and an Appendix, Containing the New City Charter* (Brooklyn: William H. Smith, 1855), 13; *Population of the United States in 1860.*

51. In Barron v. Baltimore Chief Justice John Marshall wrote of the Bill of Rights: "These amendments demanded security against the apprehended encroachment of the general government—not against those of local governments." The Supreme Court did not apply the First Amendment to states and localities until well into the twentieth century.

52. *Eagle,* February 18, 1845, February 2, 1848, June 12, 1851.

53. *Brooklyn and Kings County Record,* 104–41. There were a small number of Roman Catholic organizations as well. We turn to these in the next chapter.

54. *Eagle,* November 26, 1856. Elizabeth Howe was "1st Directress" of this organization.

55. Stuart M. Blumin, ed., *New York by Gas-Light: And Other Urban Sketches by George G. Foster* (Berkeley: University of California Press, 1990), 154. On the "third tier" and New York prostitution more generally, see Timothy J. Gilfoyle, *City of Eros: New York City, Prostitution, and the Commercialization of Sex* (New York: Norton, 1992).

56. *Eagle,* May 5, 1857. Interestingly, this piece was published at a time when support for the theater in Brooklyn was beginning to grow.

57. These themes of suburban retreat and renewal were commonplace in the Brooklyn press. E.g., "If the business doers of New York will make Brooklyn the place of their homes and their churches—if after the stir and fever of business they will come to their residences to sleep, and calm their minds, and renew them for exertion, by the tranquil and contemplative observance of the Sabbath, we shall be content." *Star,* September 21, 1853.

58. James H. Callender, *Yesterdays on Brooklyn Heights* (New York: Dorland Press, 1927), 187.

59. *Star*, January 9, 1837, November 9, 1841, November 17, 1841.

60. *Star*, November 16, 1842.

61. *Eagle*, November 22, 1853.

62. *Eagle*, April 4, 1857.

63. *Star*, February 4, 1839, February 11, 1839, June 10, 1839. These concerts were performed at the First Dutch Reformed Church and the First and Second Presbyterian churches. Maurice Edwards, in *How Music Grew in Brooklyn: A Biography of the Brooklyn Philharmonic Orchestra* (Lanham, MD: Scarecrow Press, 2006), reports three concerts by a Sacred Music Society at St. Ann's Episcopal Church in 1829.

64. Edwards, *How Music Grew in Brooklyn*, 3–5; Callender, *Yesterdays*, 198; *Eagle*, November 28, 1848, May 20, 1858; *Star*, November 20, 1841, November 22, 1841, December 1, 1841, for a sampling from a brief period of late autumn concerts in Brooklyn.

65. Stiles, *History*, 3:911.

66. *Star*, February 10, 1851, March 27, 1851.

67. Stiles, *History*, 3:912; *Star*, August 21, 1852.

68. *Star*, December 1, 1841.

69. *Star*, October 6, 1855.

70. Quoted in *Eagle*, November 5, 1858.

71. Stiles, *History*, 3:913.

72. Robert Furman, *Brooklyn Heights: The Rise, Fall and Rebirth of America's First Suburb* (Charleston, SC: History Press, 2015), 107–71; *Star*, October 13, 1859, January 16, 1861; *Eagle*, January 16, 1861.

73. *Star*, January 16, 1861; *Eagle*, January 16, 1861.

74. Horatio Gray, *Memoirs of Benjamin C. Cutler, D.D.: Late Rector of St. Ann's Church, Brooklyn, N. Y.* (New York: Anson D. F. Randolph, 1865), 400–401.

75. *Eagle*, January 23, 1861.

76. *Eagle*, December 14, 1861. The *Eagle* refers here to the ongoing controversy over theater at the academy, not to the specific plays, which were announced the following week. See *Eagle*, December 20, 1861; *Star*, December 20, 1861.

77. *Star*, January 11, 1862. The *Star*'s article includes the letter, written by John Greenwood on behalf of the academy board, urging the rejected impresario to propose more "sterling" plays.

78. *Star*, August 3, 1852, August 9, 1852, August 13, 1852, October 6, 1852, February 14, 1853, July 3, 1854, February 12, 1855; *Eagle*, February 26, 1855. German beer gardens were generally ignored by the enforcers of the Sunday closing laws, partly because beer was not yet thought to be a dangerously intoxicating beverage. And because the gardens were understood to be vital institutions within the German immigrant community, there was little political will to interfere with their Sunday operations. We return to this subject in the next chapter.

79. *Star*, October 20, 1854. Whitman had already submitted a more plainly written appeal to the Brooklyn Common Council to allow the horse cars to run on Sunday. *Star*, July 6, 1854.

80. *Eagle*, February 7, 1856.

81. *Star*, March 13, 1857.

82. *Eagle*, March 14, 1857.

83. *Eagle*, March 14, 1857.

84. *Eagle*, April 8, 1857; *Star*, April 9, 1857, May 13, 1857.

85. *Eagle*, May 18, 1857.

86. *Star*, February 25, 1858.

87. *Star*, February 25, 1861; *Eagle*, December 13, 1861.

88. *Star*, June 19, 1837, May 25, 1841. Some later historical sketches refer to parades beginning in 1829, and newspaper accounts of celebrations of the 1850s seem to date the anniversary from this first parade rather than to the founding of the Sunday School Union Society itself. We were unable to find any mention of a celebration in the *Star* in 1829. This might only mean that the celebration began as a small affair, not worthy of editorial notice, and only gradually grew into the very large event we are about to describe.

89. *Star*, May 22, 1850.

90. *Eagle*, May 21, 1856.

91. *Star*, May 13, 1841. Cutler's Episcopal Church later withdrew to hold its own anniversary celebration. Eventually, Brooklyn's Anniversary Day (later Brooklyn Day, then Brooklyn-Queens Day) became a purely secular public school holiday, and in 2005 was expanded to the entire city. Countless New York City parents today, no doubt including many in Brooklyn, wonder why they have their children underfoot for a holiday so close to the end of the school year.

92. *Star*, March 3, 1856.

93. For numerous examples of ridiculing combat between rival political papers in every American region during this era, see Glenn C. Altschuler and Stuart M. Blumin, *Rude Republic: Americans and Their Politics in the Nineteenth* Century (Princeton: Princeton University Press, 2000).

94. *Eagle*, September 13, 1844.

95. *Eagle*, January 16, 1861.

96. Stiles, *History*, 3:785–87.

97. David McCullough, *The Great Bridge: The Epic Story of the Building of the Brooklyn Bridge* (New York: Simon & Schuster, 1972), 520, 535.

98. *Eagle*, November 21, 1881.

99. Debby Applegate, *The Most Famous Man in America: The Biography of Henry Ward Beecher* (New York: Doubleday, 2006), esp. 193–95; Stiles, *History*, 3:787–78. Stiles describes Storrs' theological conservatism in a rather odd way: "As a theologian he is a Calvinist (though not a fatalist) and a Puritan throughout" (787). No one would describe Beecher as "a Puritan throughout."

100. Applegate, *The Most Famous Man in America*, 372.

101. The Old School doctrines of New England Calvinism conformed to five principles established by the Synod of Dort (Dordrecht) of 1618–19, which are nicely recalled by the very Dutch acronym TULIP: Total depravity, Unconditional election, Limited atonement, Irresistible grace, and the Perseverance of saints. What these odd phrases conveyed was the idea that only a limited number of people were predestined to go to heaven through the gift of God's saving grace. Attempts at salvation by anyone not endowed with this grace are futile, as would be any attempts by the elect (those saved through grace) to avoid salvation. This set of doctrines was difficult to maintain in the real world, and modifications appeared over time, most notably in the early nineteenth-century "New Haven Theology" attributed mainly to Nathaniel William Taylor of the Yale Divinity School. Taylor argued that people

had a "power to the contrary," which really meant an ability to affect their own salvation, and which meant also accepting responsibility for their own sins, a profoundly non-predestinarian doctrine that can be traced back to the theologian Jacobus Arminius, whose heresies gave rise to the Synod of Dort in the first place. Taylor's ideas helped justify the new wave of revivalism known as the Second Great Awakening and were serious enough to cause a formal schism in the Presbyterian Church and less formal divisions among Congregationalists. After some hesitation, Lyman Beecher embraced this New School of thought and maintained that in doing so he remained a true Calvinist and no Arminian.

102. Applegate, *The Most Famous Man in America*, 171, 214–15, 462.

103. *Star*, December 20, 1844.

104. *Star*, December 20, 1844; Stiles, *History*, 3:856–57. Bushnell's lecture provoked an angry response from one Yankee Brooklynite, who pointed out that most of Brooklyn's Episcopalians, clergy and laity alike, were New Englanders. *Star*, January 3, 1845.

105. *Eagle*, December 23, 1853.

106. *Eagle*, December 7, 1852. Greenwood's last gesture shocked the editor of the New York *Advertiser*, who reminded his readers that the president of an Irish benevolent association in Brooklyn, at a dinner of the New England Society of New York eight years earlier, toasted Plymouth Rock as "the Blarney Stone of New England." That this good-natured toast was greeted with laughter by the audience hardly seemed to matter. Ethnic tensions were real, and the dinners of these societies did not do a great deal to overcome them. See *Eagle*, December 27, 1844, December 11, 1852.

107. Callender, *Yesterdays*, 117–18. Callender does not date this story, but it occurs just after a specific reference to the Heights in the 1850s.

108. *Star*, February 13, 1851. See *Eagle*, April 29, 1850, for a sterner rebuke.

109. *Star*, July 17, 1834, July 3, 1834.

110. *Star*, September 4, 1833.

111. *Star*, September 4, 1837.

112. *Star*, September 12, 1839.

Chapter 3. On the Waterfront

1. Walt Whitman, "Crossing Brooklyn Ferry," *Leaves of Grass* (Boston: Thayer and Eldridge, 1860–61), 380–81.

2. Herman Melville, *Moby-Dick: or, the Whale* (New York: Penguin Books, [1851] 2003), 3–4.

3. *Brooklyn Evening Star*, January 19, 1857. The earlier ice bridge was reported on January 20, 1852.

4. Debby Applegate, *The Most Famous Man in America: The Biography of Henry Ward Beecher* (New York: Doubleday, 2006), 289.

5. E.g., *Star*, March 2, 1834, May 12, 1845, May 20, 1852, April 8, 1856, January 22, 1857, February 8, 1859, February 24, 1859. The *Brooklyn Daily Eagle* of May 5, 1853, includes an amusing letter describing a large sign placed outside a Montague Street retail store urging shoppers "Don't Go To New York." The signmaker's imprint was that of Messrs. Oliver & Brothers, New York.

6. *Star*, April 20, 1846, April 22, 1846, April 24, 1846.

7. *Star*, January 8, 1859.

8. *Star*, May 20, 1852, January 12, 1854, February 7, 1854.

9. *The Brooklyn and Kings County Record: A Budget of General Information; with a Map of the City, and Almanac, and an Appendix, Containing the New City Charter* (Brooklyn: William H. Smith, 1855), contains a list of only sixteen industrial firms (74–83). This is the same publication that lists 142 churches (see chapter 2). *The New York State Register for 1842...* (New York: J. Disturnell, 1842) (as reported in the *Star*, May 13, 1842) was certainly more accurate in listing forty firms. Note that this was not a local publication and had no stake in privileging the religious and suburban character of mid-nineteenth-century Brooklyn.

10. *Census of the State of New York for 1855...* (Albany, 1857).

11. Edward G. Burrows and Mike Wallace, *Gotham: A History of New York City to 1898* (New York: Oxford University Press, 1999), 660–61; Craig Steven Wilder, *A Covenant with Color: Race and Social Power in Brooklyn* (New York: Columbia University Press, 2000), 56–58.

12. US Bureau of the Census, *Statistics of the United States . . . in 1860* (Washington, 1866), xviii.

13. Ralph Foster Weld, *Brooklyn Village, 1816–1834* (New York: Columbia University Press, 1938), 81.

14. *Star*, August 1, 1822, October 9, 1823.

15. *Star*, July 8, 1824, March 23, 1826, March 29, 1827, February 19, 1829, May 26, 1829.

16. *Star*, May 29, 1828.

17. *Star*, September 8, 1836.

18. Not yet a national holiday, Thanksgiving was proclaimed each year as a day of prayer by the governor of New York. The date varied but was always late in the year. Johnson's sermon was delivered on December 10, 1835.

19. *The Christian Witness*, published in Boston, defended Johnson's sermon, while Philadelphia's *Episcopal Recorder* attacked it. See *Star*, February 4, 1836, February 8, 1836.

20. *Star*, December 21, 1835.

21. *Star*, June 19, 1834, October 3, 1832, April 2, 1835.

22. *Star*, February 15, 1836.

23. *Star*, August 27, 1835.

24. Burrows and Wallace, *Gotham*, 544–45. Contrary to Burrows and Wallace, the *Eagle* claimed that the Native American Democrats did enjoy a brief success in Brooklyn before merging with the Whig Party: *Eagle*, November 2, 1849.

25. *The Statistical History of the United States from Colonial Times to the Present* (Stamford, CT: Fairfield Publishing, 1965), 57. The only tabulations of Brooklyn's immigrants before the US census of 1860 are on various state censuses, and before 1855 these report only "Aliens not naturalized," which obviously undercounts the total immigrant population by unknown amounts. For what it's worth, the number of "Aliens not naturalized" in Brooklyn rose from 782 (7.2 percent of the total population) in 1825 to 12,196 (20.5 percent) in 1845. See *Census of the State of New York, 1825* (Albany, 1826); *Census of the State of New York, for 1845* (Albany, 1846).

26. *Census . . . for 1855*. A small number of immigrants born in Great Britain were children of Irish couples who had fled first to England, Scotland, or Wales before migrating again to the United States.

27. *Statistics of the United States . . . in 1860*.

28. *Eagle*, November 2, 1849. This long article looks back at the forming of the Native American Democrats fourteen years earlier and lists its founding members.

29. *Star*, December 1, 1846, December 12, 1846, December 22, 1846.

30. *Star*, February 6, 1847, February 17, 1847, February 19, 1847, February 26, 1847, February 27, 1847, March 1, 1847. Several public meetings held in June of that and the following year focused on Irish liberation rather than famine relief and appear to have consisted entirely of Irish participants: *Star*, June 21, 1847, June 22, 1847, June 27, 1848. The brief movement for Irish famine relief was over by this time in Brooklyn.

31. *Star*, February 8, 1847.

32. *Star*, January 10, 1848.

33. *Brooklyn and Kings County Record.*

34. For reports on new Catholic churches, see, e.g., *Star*, February 4, 1856, September 3, 1859, June 19, 1860; *Eagle*, December 10, 1852, September 9, 1861. In this last piece the *Eagle* includes the new St. Ann's Roman Catholic Church under the City of Churches umbrella.

35. *Star*, May 18, 1855.

36. *Star*, July 24, 1855.

37. *Star*, May 15, 1854, May 22, 1854, May 29, 1854; *Eagle*, May 29, 1854.

38. *Star*, June 5, 1854; *Eagle*, June 5, 1854.

39. *Star*, June 8, 1854, June 9, 1854, June 13, 1854.

40. *Star*, June 13, 1854, June 19, 1854.

41. *Eagle*, July 10, 1854.

42. *Eagle*, November 10, 1854, November 11, 1854, November 16, 1854, November 18, 1854.

43. *Eagle*, June 18, 1853. See also *Star*, March 25, 1854.

44. *Star*, October 9, 1854. A Brooklyn police report for September of 1853 lists 694 cases of drunkenness and disorderly conduct and another 726 cases of assault and battery out of 2,057 recorded crimes. Seventy-six arrests were made that month for fighting in the streets. *Star*, October 20, 1853.

45. *Star*, January 9, 1841, March 6, 1844, August 28, 1841. See also February 13, 1837, June 21, 1838, May 18, 1840, June 8, 1848, August 26, 1852, September 7, 1852, December 2, 1852, March 7, 1853, April 25, 1853, May 15, 1854, October 3, 1854, September 19, 1855, May 9, 1859.

46. *Eagle*, esp. October 18, 1903. For correspondents' claims that Irish Catholic firemen *were* fomenting violence, see *Star*, June 9, 1854; *Eagle*, December 15, 1856. In response to the latter, "Constitution" replied that "religion has nothing to do with the Fire Department," and that the Irish Catholic companies "perform three quarters of the hard labor that is done at fires." *Eagle*, December 16, 1856. There is no mention of ethnic or sectarian conflict between Brooklyn's fire companies or their runners in a massive survey of firefighting in nineteenth-century New York and Brooklyn: J. Frank Kernan, *Reminiscences of the Old Fire Laddies and Volunteer Fire Departments of New York and Brooklyn* . . . (New York: M. Crane, 1885). See esp. 651, where runners are described as "the bane of the Volunteer Department of Brooklyn for many years."

47. *Star*, June 13, 1854, June 15, 1854.

48. *Eagle*, May 14, 1848.

49. *Eagle*, August 16, 1847, September 26, 1849; Francis Morrone, *Fort Greene [and] Clinton Hill: Neighborhood & Architectural History Guide* (Brooklyn: Brooklyn Historical Society, 2010), 5–6.

50. *Eagle*, March 28, 1856.

51. T. O. Mabbett, ed., Jacob E. Spannuth, comp., *Doings of Gotham: Poe's Contributions to The Columbia Spy* (Pottsville, PA: Jacob E. Spannuth, Publisher, 1929), 59–60.

52. *Star*, March 19, 1855.

53. *Eagle*, January 28, 1894.

54. *Star*, July 6, 1841, July 5, 1860.

55. *Eagle*, January 28, 1894; *Hearnes' Brooklyn City Directory, for 1850–51 . . .* (Brooklyn: Henry R. & William J. Hearne, 1850).

56. *Star*, December 20, 1844.

57. It also misses the vast number of Irish girls and young women who worked and lived in middle- and upper-class homes as domestic servants—the "girls at service" ogled and insulted by young men on the streets of Brooklyn Heights. These serving women accounted for a good deal of the spread of the Irish population away from the waterfront and through the suburban districts of Brooklyn.

58. *Eagle*, January 3, 1855, January 5, 1855, January 6, 1855, January 8, 1855, April 17, 1855. For evidence that Irish policemen were re-appointed when the Democrats resumed control of the Common Council, see *Eagle*, January 10, 1857, January 20, 1857. In the latter article the *Eagle* noted that two years earlier, in the wards controlled by Know Nothing aldermen, "every man who had a Celtic or Teutonic name, though his ancestors had lived here for generations, was ruthlessly guillotined."

59. *Eagle*, May 31, 1848.

60. *Eagle*, September 21, 1857.

61. *Eagle*, September 21, 1857.

62. *Hearnes' Brooklyn Directory . . . for 1851–52 . . .* (Brooklyn: Henry R. & William J. Hearne, 1851); *Reynolds' Williamsburgh Directory . . . for 1851–52* (Williamsburgh: Samuel & T. F. Reynolds, 1851); *Reynolds' City Directory . . . for 1852* (Williamsburgh: Samuel & T. F. Reynolds, 1852).

63. *Eagle*, April 24, 1857.

64. *Star*, January 14, 1847; *Eagle*, May 31, 1855.

65. *Eagle*, August 14, 1852.

66. *Star*, September 21, 1853.

67. *Eagle*, April 20, 1855, June 1, 1857.

68. *Eagle*, August 17, 1857.

69. *Eagle*, August 17, 1857.

70. Wilder, *A Covenant with Color*, 37; *Census for 1820* (Washington, 1821), 21; *Compendium of the Enumeration of the Inhabitants and Statistics of the United States . . .* (Washington: Thomas Allen, 1841), 21; *Statistics of the United States . . . in 1860*, 335.

71. Wilder, in *A Covenant with Color*, is forceful in claiming this connection between Brooklyn's Southern business and white attitudes toward the local African American population (45–58).

72. Henry R. Stiles, *A History of the City of Brooklyn* (Brooklyn: np, 1870), 3: 702, 707.

73. *Brooklyn and Kings County Record.*

74. *Star*, January 15, 1824, October 4, 1827, April 29, 1830, May 26, 1830, June 2, 1830, April 3, 1833.

75. *Star*, December 11, 1841.

76. Judith Wellman, *Brooklyn's Promised Land: The Free Black Community of Weeks-ville, New York* (New York: New York University Press, 2014), 13–14.

77. *Star*, March 9, 1852.

78. *Star*, February 12, 1859.

79. Wellman, *Brooklyn's Promised Land*, 47, 52.

80. Applegate, *The Most Famous Man in America*, 284.

81. *Eagle*, March 29, 1860.

82. *Eagle*, April 16, 1861, April 22, 1861. See also: *Star*, April 16, 1861; Raymond A Schroth, S. J., *The Eagle and Brooklyn: A Community Newspaper, 1841–1955* (Westport, CT: Greenwood Press, 1974), 59–69.

83. *Eagle*, February 22, 1864. On Marianne Fitch Stranahan and her leadership, see L. P. Brockett, M. D., and Mrs. Mary C. Vaughan, *Woman's Work in the Civil War: A Record of Heroism, Patriotism and Patience* (Philadelphia: Seigler, McCurdy & Co., 1867), 65–68.

84. *Eagle*, February 23, 1864.

85. *Eagle*, February 23, 1864.

86. *Eagle*, March 7, 1864, March 8, 1864.

87. *Star*, August 6, 1862.

88. *Eagle*, August 5, 1862. See also August 8, 1862, and August 10, 1862, for the *Eagle*'s coverage of court proceedings generated by the assault on the factories. A serious question that arose at these proceedings was whether the mostly Irish police had acted quickly and effectively enough to stop the assault.

89. *Eagle*, February 18, 1863.

90. For the most detailed descriptions of these events, see Iver Bernstein, *The New York City Draft Riots: Their Significance for American Society and Politics in the Age of the Civil War* (New York: Oxford University Press, 1990); Barnet Schecter, *The Devil's Own Work: The Civil War Draft Riots and the Fight to Reconstruct America* (New York: Walker & Co., 2007). For an excellent, briefer description, see Burrows and Wallace, *Gotham*, 887–99.

91. *Eagle*, June 14, 1863.

92. *Eagle*, July 15, 1863.

93. *Eagle*, July 16, 1863.

94. *Eagle*, July 16, 1863.

Chapter 4. Toward a New Brooklyn

1. The story of the building of the Brooklyn Bridge is compellingly told in David McCullough, *The Great Bridge: The Epic Story of the Building of the Brooklyn Bridge* (New York: Simon and Schuster, 1972). McCullough recounts the story of the meeting between Kingsley and Murphy and declares: "Possibly the story is true" (113). The story is repeated in William R. Everdell and Malcolm MacKay, *Rowboats to Rapid Transit: A History of Brooklyn Heights* (Brooklyn: Brooklyn Heights Association, 1973), 24, and in Francis Morrone, *Fort Greene [and] Clinton Hill: Neighborhood & Architectural History Guide* (Brooklyn: Brooklyn Historical Society, 2010), 32.

2. McCullough, *Great Bridge*, 519.

3. McCullough, *Great Bridge*, 519–20.

4. *Brooklyn Daily Eagle*, May 24, 1883, May 25, 1883. The *Eagle*'s version of William Kingsley's campaign for the bridge, which describes meetings with James Stranahan, *Eagle* editor Thomas Kinsella, and other influential Brooklynites as well as Henry Murphy, makes no mention of a meeting with Murphy on December 21, 1866. But immediately following the statement that Kingsley's urgings finally succeeded in turning "speculation" into "practical effort," it notes that Murphy, who was then a powerful member of the New York State Senate, introduced and pushed through the bill that authorized the building of the bridge. The story of the December evening by Henry Murphy's fireplace is not disproved by the *Eagle*'s report. It is neither confirmed nor disproved by the account of Kingsley's approach to Murphy in Edwin G. Burrows and Mike Wallace, *Gotham: A History of New York City to 1898* (New York: Oxford University Press, 1999), 934–35.

5. *Eagle*, December 10, 1888; McCullough, *Great Bridge*, 545.

6. Julian Ralph, "The City of Brooklyn," *Harper's New Monthly Magazine*," 86 (April 1893), 652.

7. For a good compendium of the relevant census data, see Blake McKelvey, *American Urbanization: A Comparative History* (Glenview, IL: Scott, Foresman and Company, 1973), 73. Brooklyn's population increased by 105 percent between 1880 and 1900, while Manhattan's increased by 59 percent. The equivalent figures for Philadelphia, Boston, and Baltimore are 53 percent, 55 percent, and 53 percent, respectively. A small amount of the growth in two or three of these cities, including Brooklyn, is attributable to the annexation of new territory rather than to population increase within their 1880 boundaries.

8. There was also a severe economic depression during five years or so of the mid-1870s, but whether Brooklyn's growth slowed or accelerated during these years is difficult to determine. Recall that the depression of 1837–43 had increased migration from New York City to Brooklyn. Between 1880 and 1900 there were no wars and a brief if severe economic downturn during the mid-1890s.

9. Ralph, "City of Brooklyn," 652.

10. Ralph, "City of Brooklyn," 652.

11. *Eagle*, March 25, 1868.

12. The steam dummy was a locomotive consisting of a steam engine encased within a small rail car designed to give it the appearance of a streetcar. Its job was to haul one or two streetcars over city rail lines, replacing the horses that had moved these cars since the rails had been put down on the city's streets. The hope that disguising the engine in this way would be less offensive to people's eyes and ears and less frightening to the horses that remained on the streets was not always realized. But the people who rode the new steam cars did appreciate their speed, which was generally two to three times that of the horse cars. The opinion of the horses has not been recorded.

13. *Long-Island Star*, August 21, 1837.

14. *Eagle*, September 29, 1879, July 24, 1886, March 25, 1894.

15. *Eagle*, January 17, 1868.

16. *Eagle*, July 27, 1878, February 7, 1879, July 9, 1880, June 13, 1885, July 24, 1886; *The Statistics of the Population of the United States . . .* (Washington: Government Printing Office, 1872), 211; *The Eleventh Census: 1890. Part I.—Population* (Washington: Government Printing Office, 1892), 470; *Census Reports: Volume I: Twelfth Census*

of the United States, Taken in the Year 1900. . . (Washington: United States Census Office, 1901), 279.

17. Marc Linder and Laurence S. Zacharias, *Of Cabbages and Kings County: Agriculture and the Formation of Modern Brooklyn* (Iowa City: University of Iowa Press, 1999), 202–44.

18. Linder and Zacharias, *Of Cabbages and Kings County*, 131–33.

19. Linder and Zacharias, *Of Cabbages and Kings County*, 240–42; Adina Back and Francis Morrone, *The Flatbush Neighborhood History Guide* (Brooklyn: Brooklyn Historical Society, 2008), 30–43; *Eagle*, October 5, 1869, October 7, 1869, September 16, 1883, October 12, 1897.

20. *Eagle*, November 21, 1867.

21. *Eagle*, September 29, 1883, September 21, 1884.

22. Linder and Zacharias, *Of Cabbages and Kings County*, 229.

23. *Eagle*, June 29, 1890, April 19, 1896, October 12, 1897.

24. *Eagle*, December 29, 1895.

25. *Eagle*, October 12, 1897.

26. "To Coney Island," *Scribner's Monthly*, 20 (July 1880); John F. Kasson, *Amusing the Million: Coney Island at the Turn of the Century* (New York: McGraw-Hill, 1978); Oliver Pilat and Jo Ranson, *Sodom by the Sea: An Affectionate History of Coney Island* (Garden City, NY: Garden City Publishing Co., Inc., 1943).

27. Kasson, *Amusing the Million*, 29.

28. Kasson, *Amusing the Million*, 30–33.

29. For a typical complaint, see "Wicked Coney Island," *Eagle*, August 14, 1897.

30. *Eagle*, August 31, 1868.

31. *Eagle*, May 31, 1881.

32. For an evocative history of McKane's rule in Coney Island and the role of Brooklyn's political leaders in bringing him down, see Pilat and Ranson, *Sodom by the Sea*, 25–49.

33. *Eagle*, April 24, 1895.

34. *Eagle*, August 10, 1897.

35. Kasson, *Amusing the Million*, 34–50.

36. *Eagle*, September 29, 1879; June 29, 1890.

37. Henry R. Stiles, *A History of the City of Brooklyn* . . . (Brooklyn: n. p., 1870), 2:483, 491; 3:578ff; Joseph Alexiou, *Gowanus: Brooklyn's Curious Canal* (New York: New York University Press, 2015).

38. *Eagle*, October 17, 1886.

39. *Eagle*, March 27, 1887.

40. *Eagle*, October 17, 1887.

41. Eleanora W. Schoenebaum, "Emerging Neighborhoods: The Development of Brooklyn's Fringe Areas, 1850–1930" (PhD diss., Columbia University, 1976), 30.

42. Ralph, "City of Brooklyn," 652.

43. *Eagle*, August 15, 1871.

44. *Census of the State of New York for 1875*. . . (Albany, 1877), 234–44; *Twelfth Census*, 279. Before Bedford began its rapid post–Civil War development it was occupied mainly by Irish immigrants who sought cheap housing beyond the city's built-up areas. Some working-class immigrants remained as Bedford increasingly became a middle-class suburb, although there was a pronounced shift in the local immigrant

population from Irish to Germans. Historical overlays of this sort are common as cities expand. See Schoenebaum, "Emerging Neighborhoods," 43–44.

45. *Eagle*, January 19, 1890.

46. *Eagle*, April 19, 1896. Lucas J. Rubin, *Brooklyn's Sportsmen's Row: Politics, Society and the Sporting Life on Northern Eighth Avenue* (Charleston, SC: History Press, 2012).

47. *Eagle*, March 23, 1890.

48. Jennie N. Child Manuscript, "Early Memories of Brooklyn, 1890s–1900s," Brooklyn Historical Society archive. See also Francis Morrone, *Park Slope: Neighborhood & Architectural History Guide* (Brooklyn: Brooklyn Historical Society, 2012).

49. Morrone, *Fort Greene [and] Clinton Hill*, 30–31.

50. Morrone, *Fort Greene [and] Clinton Hill*, see the photograph on 31. The west side of Washington Park faced a hospital, a jail, and very few homes, and on the north side, along Myrtle Avenue, there was a small collection of workers' homes. These were no longer the shanties we described earlier, but they were not commonly considered part of the Fort Greene neighborhood.

51. *Eagle*, February 10, 1878, February 17, 1878. The *Eagle*'s survey was neither scientific nor complete, and it should be noted that it included twice as many residents of Brooklyn Heights as of Clinton Hill. Two notable omissions from the "golden guild" were Fort Greene's William C. Kingsley and Abner C. Keeney, both of whom were extremely wealthy. Both were also powerful voices in Brooklyn's Democratic Party, and both were highly influential in the offices of the *Eagle* (Kingsley was a part owner of the paper). If they had asked not to be included in these articles they certainly would not have been. On Charles Pratt and Clinton Hill see Morrone, *Fort Greene [and] Clinton Hill*, 65–71. John B. Manbeck, consulting ed., *The Neighborhoods of Brooklyn* (New Haven: Yale University Press, 1998), 59, notes the slightly later arrival in Clinton Hill of Pfizers (Charles, and also Charles Eberhart) of the Pfizer drug company, Bristols (probably William McLaren) of Bristol-Myers (but Edward Robinson Squibb lived in Brooklyn Heights), Underwoods (John Thomas) of the typewriter manufacturing company, and Liebmanns (Joseph, Henry, or Charles, sons of Samuel), who brewed Rheingold Beer.

52. *Eagle*, May 7, 1891.

53. *Eagle*, February 17, 1878.

54. *Eagle*, August 29, 1878.

55. *Eagle*, September 17, 1893. An *Eagle* article in 1885 was somewhat less sanguine about Brooklyn' tenements, which were increasing rapidly in number and in quality "getting down to that of the New York slums." But even this piece noted improvements in some buildings, the problem then becoming that the very poor were forced out by rising rents. *Eagle*, May 9, 1885. The 1878 commissioners' report suggests that about one-fifth of Brooklyn's population lived in dwellings of three or more families. Edward Richards, ed., *A Historical and Descriptive Review of the City of Brooklyn* . . . (New York: Historical Publishing Company, 1883), 64, claims that it was one-fourth, but that New York's tenement population was two-thirds of that city's total.

56. Jacob A. Riis, *How the Other Half Lives: Studies among the Tenements of New York* (New York: Charles Scribner's Sons, 1890); Stephen Crane, *Maggie: A Girl of the Streets* (New York: D. Appleton, 1896).

57. Stiles, *History*, 3:618–22. To follow evolving editorial opinion regarding Prospect Park, its cost, and other issues, see *Eagle,* December 6, 1858, September 30, 1859,

January 28, 1860, May 29, 1860, January 25, 1864, July 22, 1864, February 5, 1866, March 19, 1866, June 20, 1867, February 3, 1868, June 6, 1868, February 19, 1870, February 21, 1870, March 10, 1870, June 24, 1871, March 11, 1872, October 8, 1872. For a discussion of the planning of the park, see Thomas J. Campanella, *Brooklyn: The Once and Future City* (Princeton: Princeton University Press, 2019), 79–94.

58. For an excellent analysis of Olmsted's writings about the moral and behavioral benefits of city parks, see Laura Wood Roper, *FLO: A Biography of Frederick Law Olmsted* (Baltimore: Johns Hopkins University Press, 1973).

59. *Eagle*, January 29, 1868, April 17, 1875, November 18, 1876. As early as 1868 Olmsted wrote that the land through which these parkways ran was destined for suburban development. See Linder and Zacharias, *Of Cabbages and Kings County*, 137. James Stranahan thought the same of the land around the park. See Elizabeth Macdonald, *Pleasure Drives and Promenades: The History of Frederick Law Olmsted's Brooklyn Parkways* (Chicago: Center for American Places at Columbia College, 2012), 63–64, and Campanella, *Brooklyn*, 94–105. On the effects of Eastern Parkway on Weeksville and Carrsville as independent communities see Macdonald, *Pleasure Drives and Promenades*, 183, and Judith Wellman, *Brooklyn's Promised Land: The Free Black Community of Weeksville, New York* (New York: New York University Press, 2014), 211–25.

60. For a comprehensive list of antebellum Brooklyn's cultural institutions, see Melissa Meriam Bullard, *Brooklyn's Renaissance: Commerce, Culture and Community in the Nineteenth-Century Atlantic World* (New York: Palgrave Macmillan, 2017), 17–18.

61. Ralph, "City of Brooklyn," 654.

62. *Eagle*, December 12, 1888.

63. *Eagle*, April 20, 1872.

64. *Eagle*, November 29, 1865.

65. *Eagle*, April 20, 1872.

66. *Eagle*, April 15, 1877, December 8, 1888.

67. *Eagle*, April 20, 1872, December 16, 1876, March 27, 1881, February 9, 1882, May 14, 1882, December 18, 1883, February 17, 1885, February 22, 1886, January 9, 1889, January 29, 1889, March 9, 1890, April 6, 1990, December 28, 1890, January 19, 1891.

68. *Eagle*, December 24, 1893.

69. *Eagle*, April 15, 1877, March 17, 1884.

70. *Eagle*, December 28, 1890.

71. *Eagle*, January 18, 1891.

72. *Eagle*, February 19, 1889. On privacy and the Brooklyn clubs, see Bullard, *Brooklyn's Renaissance*, 336ff.

73. *Eagle*, January 17, 1889. See also Robert Furman, *Brooklyn Heights: The Rise, Fall, and Rebirth of America's First Suburb* (Charleston, SC: History Press, 2015), 226.

74. *Eagle*, November 21, 1897. In his insider's reminiscence of life on the Heights James H. Callender notes, "It was not until after the Civil War that Society, with a big S, began to lift its head." James H. Callender, *Yesterdays on Brooklyn Heights* (New York: Dorland Press, 1927), 244.

75. *Brooklyn Life: A Journal of Society Literature Drama and the Clubs*, vol. 1, no. 1 (March 8, 1890).

76. Journeay and Burnham was originally on Atlantic Street. Its movement to Fulton (actually Flatbush Avenue near Fulton) was important to the solidification

of Brooklyn's downtown on and near the upper part of Fulton Street, beyond the approaches to the bridge.

77. *Eagle*, April 4, 1857.

78. *Eagle*, August 5, 1894.

79. *Eagle*, October 24, 1867, June 18, 1873, September 1, 1878; Stiles, *History*, 3:914–17.

80. *Eagle*, May 27, 1877.

81. *Eagle*, May 28, 1869.

82. *Eagle*, September 4, 1871.

83. Debby Applegate, *The Most Famous Man in America: The Biography of Henry Ward Beecher* (New York: Doubleday, 2006), recounts these themes. Beecher's "Amusements" lecture and its aftermath are discussed on 215–18. On Beecher's endorsement of Pears' Soap see Burton Bledstein, *The Culture of Professionalism: The Middle Class and the Development of Higher Education in America* (New York: Norton, 1976), 52.

84. At least two other Brooklyn clergymen, though, did join Beecher in endorsing commercial products. The Rev. W. W. Hicks promoted Drake's Plantation Bitters, while some years later the Rev. Thomas DeWitt Talmage endorsed Dr. Tucker's No. 59, both products falsely promising to cure many ailments—in common parlance, "snake oil." See *Eagle*, May 23, 1866, December 22, 1895.

85. *Brooklyn Evening Star*, July 26, 1855, June 18, 1858, October 8, 1858; *Eagle*, September 1, 1858, September 2, 1858, September 4, 1858, September 7, 1858.

86. *Eagle*, July 21, 1858, August 18, 1858; *Star*, September 11, 1858.

87. *Eagle*, June 2, 1890.

88. *Eagle*, June 30, 1890.

89. Remarkably, an editorial protesting the exclusion of non-evangelical groups from the 1885 celebration referred to Rev. Evan Johnson's controversial sermon, "Toleration," fifty years after he delivered it to his Brooklyn parishioners on Thanksgiving Day in 1835. *Eagle*, May 3, 1885.

90. *Eagle*, May 28, 1897.

91. On one occasion the *Eagle* suggested that Anniversary Day might best be celebrated privately rather than with a public parade, but this was offered on behalf of exhausted children rather than the preservation of other people's access to the city's streets. *Eagle*, May 29, 1873. In nearly every other year the paper expressed enthusiasm for the parade.

92. *Eagle*, December 16, 1871.

93. *Eagle*, July 11, 1868, June 11, 1869, June 12, 1869.

94. *Eagle*, July 2, 1872.

95. *Eagle*, July 3, 1880.

96. *Eagle*, January 27, 1869.

97. *Eagle*, September 4, 1875.

98. *Illustrated Annual New York & Brooklyn Churches: 1874* (New York: Nelson & Phillips, 1874), 39–61; *Census of the State of New York for 1875. . .* (Albany, 1877), 19.

99. *Census . . . for 1875*, 275.

100. *Eagle*, March 17, 1869.

101. *Eagle*, October 24, 1881.

102. In 1892 *Brooklyn Life* wrote of the sale of an old Methodist Church in Dutchtown, "it having been found that 'the population of the neighborhood had become

so largely composed of foreigners,' it was impossible to maintain it." *Brooklyn Life*, July 30, 1892.

103. *Eagle*, May 12, 1882, May 22, 1882. Four years later the *Eagle* pointed out several church buildings in the older wards that were themselves converted to businesses: a bookbindery, a chair factory, a carpet store, even a theater. *Eagle*, April 4, 1886

104. *Eagle*, August 4, 1889.

105. *Eagle*, December 11, 1888, August 4, 1889.

106. *Eagle*, May 23, 1883.

107. *Eagle*, April 4, 1886.

108. *Eagle*, November 2, 1875, November 5, 1875, November 10, 1875, November 16, 1875, November 20, 1875. In this last article the *Eagle* offered the opinion that Moody and Sankey did have these effects: "They have given the philosophical a new study, and the devout a new inspiration, and the resulting effect of their campaign on the church economies of the City of Churches will, we think, be vast and vital."

109. *New York Times*, April 13, 1902.

110. *Eagle*, April 13, 1902.

111. *Eagle*, July 2, 1882.

112. *Eagle*, August 25, 1878.

113. For a good retrospective look at Comstock's career, including an interview with Comstock himself, see *Eagle*, January 18, 1914. This long article is titled "Anthony Comstock Won Fame in Brooklyn."

114. *Eagle*, August 21, 1884.

115. *Eagle*, July 2, 1882.

Chapter 5. Newcomers

1. Julian Ralph, "The City of Brooklyn," *Harper's New Monthly Magazine* 86 (April 1893), 664–66.

2. *1900 Census: Volume VIII. Manufactures, Part 2. States and Territories* (Washington: United States Census Office, 1902), 592, 628–35.

3. Brooklyn was overtaken by Chicago, America's quintessential boomtown, early in the 1880s.

4. *1900 Census: Volume VIII. Manufactures, Part 2*, 629; *1900 Census: Volume I. Population, Part 1* (Washington: United States Census Office, 1902), 631; U. S. Bureau of the Census, *Statistics of the United States, . . . in 1860* (Washington, 1866), xviii.

5. The phrase was coined by W. W. Rostow in *The Stages of Economic Growth: A Non-Communist Manifesto* (Cambridge, Eng.: Cambridge University Press, 1961).

6. *The Statistical History of the United States from Colonial Times to the Present* (Stamford, CT: Fairfield Publishers, [1965]), 56–57. Jewish immigrants made up an indeterminate but surely significant portion of the German total during the last two decades of this era. They formed an even larger portion of the migrants from Eastern Europe, then and in the decades to come. The United States Immigration Service did not record immigrants' religious affiliations or identities, so we can only estimate the number of Jewish immigrants to this country.

7. *1900 Census: Volume I. Population, Part 1*, 631, 669. The native-born with native-born parents amounted to 27 percent of Brooklyn's population in 1900.

8. The Diocese of Brooklyn's "Chronological List of Brooklyn Parishes, 1822–2008" is available at http://dioceseofbrooklyn.org.

9. Eleanora W. Schoenebaum, "Emerging Neighborhoods: The Development of Brooklyn's Fringe Areas, 1850–1930" (PhD diss., Columbia University, 1976), 84.

10. Department of the Interior, Census Office, *Statistics of the Population of the United States at the Tenth Census* . . . (Washington: Government Printing Office, 1882), 865.

11. Raymond A. Schroth, S. J., *The Eagle and Brooklyn: A Community Newspaper, 1841–1955* (Westport, CT: Greenwood Press, 1974), 65, 70–72; *Brooklyn Daily Eagle*, February 11, 1884, February 12, 1884.

12. Harold Coffin Syrett, *The City of Brooklyn, 1865–1898: A Political History* (New York: Columbia University Press, 1944), 66–69, 88–89; *Eagle*, December 1, 1899.

13. Henry R. Stiles, *A History of the City of Brooklyn* . . . (Brooklyn: n. p., 1869), 2:492–94; *Eagle*, February 12, 1873. Kalbfleisch was the second of Brooklyn's seven foreign-born mayors (out of twenty-four men who served before the consolidation with New York City in 1898), the first having been Jonathan Trotter, who was elected Brooklyn's second mayor in 1835. But as an English immigrant Trotter fell within the Anglo-Protestant tradition. Two other Englishmen and two Germans besides Frederick Schroeder, served as Brooklyn mayors. Jeremiah Johnson, who was elected mayor in 1837, was an Anglo-Dutch New Yorker.

14. That chronicle forms an important part of Steven H. Jaffe and Rebecca Amato, *Envisioning Brooklyn: Family, Philanthropy, and the Growth of an American City* (Brooklyn: Brooklyn Historical Society, [2016]), 82–149.

15. William I. Thomas and Florian Znaniecki, *The Polish Peasant in Europe and America; Monograph of an Immigrant Group* (Chicago: University of Chicago Press, 1920), 5:x–xi.

16. *Eagle*, March 18, 1870.

17. *Eagle*, February 27, 1874.

18. *Eagle*, March 17, 1874.

19. *Eagle*, March 17, 1876, March 19, 1878, March 17, 1879.

20. *Eagle*, March 17, 1884, March 7, 1885, March 17, 1888.

21. *Eagle*, March 17, 1894.

22. This issue is discussed, especially in relation to the appeal of Irish nationalism to immigrants of differing circumstances, in Timothy Meagher, *The Columbia Guide to Irish American History* (New York: Columbia University Press, 2005), 198–213. Meagher examines standard works such as Thomas N. Brown, *Irish-American Nationalism, 1870–1890* (Philadelphia: Lippincott, 1966), and Kerby Miller, *Emigrants and Exiles: Ireland and the Irish Exodus to North America* (New York: Oxford University Press, 2013) and finds no resolution there of the issue of working-class participation.

23. *Eagle*, January 25, 1880, May 30, 1882.

24. *Eagle*, May 20, 1876.

25. The American Protective Association, founded in 1887 in Clinton, Iowa, was an anti-Catholic organization active mainly in the Midwest. It appears to have had little presence in Brooklyn.

26. *Eagle*, July 2, 1882. Father Malone's death in 1899 was front-page news in the *Eagle*, which also printed a very long obituary and an appreciation of this Catholic priest by Richard Storrs and other Protestant ministers. *Eagle*, December 29, 1899.

27. Jaffe and Amato, *Envisioning Brooklyn*, 16–43. Shortly before Father Fransioli died he was feted at the Academy of Music on the golden anniversary of his ordination. Attending the banquet were Seth Low, J. S. T. Stranahan, and other leading Brooklyn Protestants. *Eagle*, October 18, 1890.

28. *Eagle*, February 15, 1871.

29. The most detailed description of *Pfingsmontag* in Brooklyn is in the *Eagle*, May 21, 1874.

30. *Eagle*, January 16, 1881.

31. The notable exception was Austria, which was excluded largely because of the continuing presence of the ruling Hapsburgs. This was the "Little German" rather than the "Big German" unification plan that would have included Hapsburgs (whose empire included many non-German-speaking peoples) and Hohenzollerns in the same polity, and this only five years after Prussia defeated Austria in a brief but decisive war.

32. *Eagle*, April 4, 1876

33. *Eagle*, May 2, 1876.

34. *Eagle*, May 13, 1876.

35. *Eagle*, May 6, 1881.

36. *Eagle*, March 21, 1890.

37. *Eagle*, September 27, 1891.

38. Samuel P. Abelow, *History of Brooklyn Jewry* (Brooklyn: Scheba Publishing Company, 1937), 6–8, 14–15; *Brooklyn Evening Star*, March 18, 1856, June 14, 1860, January 10, 1862, August 30, 1862; *Eagle*, June 13, 1886, September 27, 1891. Some of these reports and recollections treat Baith Israel as the first formally organized Jewish congregation in Kings County, and Beth Elohim as the second.

39. *Eagle*, September 30, 1875, September 8, 1877.

40. *Eagle*, June 13, 1886, September 27, 1891, *The American Hebrew and Jewish Messenger*, August 20, 1897.

41. Abelow, *History of Brooklyn Jewry*, 310–27; *Eagle*, March 10, 1876, January 8, 1878, November 29, 1882, March 4, 1885, February 14, 1887, April 4, 1892, July 23, 1897; *American Hebrew*, October 27, 1883, February 18, 1887, April 18, 1890, May 13, 1892.

42. *Eagle*, April 26, 1883, December 29, 1892; *American Hebrew*, November 10, 1882, November 24, 1882, June 29, 1883, May 6, 1892.

43. *Eagle*, May 27, 1884, September 27, 1891.

44. *Eagle*, June 13, 1886. For examples of the *Eagle*'s philo-Semitism, see January 22, 1870, December 30, 1870, March 3, 1876, August 7, 1876, March 4, 1885, February 13, 1886, December 29, 1992.

45. *Eagle*, April 25, 1895.

46. *American Hebrew*, May 6, 1892.

47. *Eagle*, February 24, 1905. This is a reprint from the *Christian Union*, which published a version of the sermon from Beecher's extensive notes. Beecher, we should note, was also criticized for encouraging religious diversity. An 1879 cartoon in *Puck*, America's foremost humor magazine, titled "The Religious Vanity Fair," depicted a self-satisfied Beecher, sitting on a couch, while a Catholic bishop, a Jewish mohel ("The Original Jacob"), a Mormon, a Baptist, an Episcopalian, and a Methodist hawk their wares. Cited in Jon Butler, *God in Gotham: The Miracle of Religion in Modern Manhattan* (Cambridge, MA: Harvard University Press, 2020), 28.

48. *American Hebrew*, April 1, 1887.

49. *Eagle*, September 27, 1891.

50. *American Hebrew*, April 14, 1899.

51. *Eagle*, January 31, 1896.

52. The *Herald* interview was reprinted in the *Eagle.*, July 22, 1879. Corbin's anti-Semitism went beyond his hotel management. He was also the founder of the remarkably named American Society for the Suppression of the Jews. See Thomas J. Campanella, *Brooklyn: The Once and Future City* (Princeton: Princeton University Press, 2019), 109.

53. *Eagle*, July 23, 1879.

54. *The Statistics of the Population of the United States . . .* (Washington: Government Printing Office, 1872), 386.

55. *Eagle*, September 1, 1876.

56. *1900 Census: Volume I. Population, Part 1*, 631.

57. *Eagle*, June 18, 1881.

58. *Eagle*, March 16, 1882.

59. *Eagle*, September 22, 1883.

60. *Eagle*, December 14, 1891.

61. *Eagle*, May 30, 1886.

62. *Eagle*, August 17, 1892, May 28, 1893.

63. *Eagle*, January 2, 1863, January 3, 1863, January 31, 1863, June 10, 1863, June 2, 1865, April 27, 1875, December 12, 1886, May 16, 1889, July 13, 1890, April 11, 1891.

64. *Eagle*, October 23, 1865.

65. *Eagle*, November 14, 1865.

66. *Eagle*, May 16, 1863, January 30, 1866. See also Theodore Hamm, ed., *Frederick Douglass in Brooklyn* (Brooklyn: Akashic Books, 2017), 19–31; Hamm, "Frederick Douglass at BAM," *BAMblog* (January 11, 2017). Hamm points out that Douglass delivered several speeches in Brooklyn, including two more at the Brooklyn Academy of Music.

67. Phyllis F. Field, *The Politics of Race in New York: The Struggle for Black Suffrage in the Civil War Era* (Ithaca, NY: Cornell University Press, 1982), 187–219; *Eagle*, October 28, 1869.

68. *Eagle*, June 2, 1875, June 16, 1875, September 7, 1875, September 13, 1875, September 27, 1875, December 24, 1881, January 8, 1882, March 24, 1882, March 26, 1882, June 11, 1883, December 1, 1883.

69. *Eagle*, March 3, 1869. These episodes are reviewed in Judith Wellman, *Brooklyn's Promised Land: The Free Black Community of Weeksville, New York* (New York: New York University Press, 2014), 148–53.

70. *Eagle*, June 6, 1880.

71. *Eagle*, July 11, 1882.

72. *Eagle*, December 12, 1883.

73. Wellman, *Brooklyn's Promised Land*, 154–61. The key meeting of the board of education is reported in detail in *Eagle*, March 8, 1893.

74. *Population of the United States*, 1872 [1870 US census], 211, 439.

75. *Tenth Census*, 670; *Eagle*, January 8, 1882.

76. *1900 Census . . . Population*, 631. The more precise proportion was 1.6 percent, almost exactly what it was in 1860.

77. *Eagle*, February 3, 1878, January 14, 1883.

78. Craig Steven Wilder, *A Covenant with Color: Race and Social Power in Brooklyn* (New York: Columbia University Press, 2000), 138, 142.

79. Syrett, *City of Brooklyn*, 70–86.

80. *Eagle*, March 8, 1891, March 14, 1892.

81. *Eagle*, January 14, 1883.

82. *Eagle*, December 18, 1892.

83. *Eagle*, April 23, 1893.

84. *Eagle*, August 28, 1865, December 23, 1892.

85. *Eagle*, October 18, 1870; Wellman, *Brooklyn's Promised Land*, 3, 176.

86. *Eagle*, August 6, 1868; Wellman, *Brooklyn's Promised Land*, 100, 125–26. The claim that the society operated in nine southern states is from the *Eagle*. Wellman describes schools in six states and the District of Columbia.

87. *Eagle*, February 23, 1866.

88. *Eagle*, April 6, 1868, March 17, 1871; Wellman, *Brooklyn's Promised Land*, 127.

89. Wilder, *A Covenant with Color*, 140–41.

90. *Eagle*, May 23, 1891.

91. *Eagle*, August 2, 1884. See also the *Eagle* reports on August 2 of each year up to 1877.

92. An interesting aspect of this conflict was the way it reflected differences in Brooklyn's social and economic—and beer drinking—geography. An agent for one of the companies, the F. & M. Schaeffer Brewing Company, explained to a reporter why he wasn't concerned about the boycott: "Most of our beer . . . is sold on the principal streets of the Western District. The bulk of the trade unions of the city are in the Eastern District [mainly Williamsburg, Greenpoint, and Bushwick], and over there the consumption of beer is almost entirely confined to that manufactured in the Eastern District breweries." *Eagle*, March 21, 1881.

93. *Eagle*, March 26, 1873, October 14, 1874, March 21, 1881, March 15, 1891.

94. *Eagle*, May 5, 1882.

95. *Eagle*, April 22–May 11, 1886, May 17, 1886.

96. *Eagle*, January 14–February 14, 1895.

97. *Eagle*, September 5, 1887, September 1, 1888, September 4, 1888, September 8, 1891, September 5, 1892, September 2, 1893. These and articles describing other years' parades capture the character of the event.

98. *Eagle*, March 14, 1886. The *Eagle*'s article puts quotation marks around these statements by Mrs. Barnard, but whether these are her words or the reporter's may be questioned.

99. Butler, *God in Gotham*, 22–3.

100. *Brooklyn Life*, June 1, 1915; Gertrude Lefferts Vanderbilt, *The Social History of Flatbush, and Manners and Customs of the Dutch Settlers of Kings County* (New York: D. Appleton & Co., 1881), 9; Ralph Foster Weld, *Brooklyn Is America* (New York: Columbia University Press, 1950), 9.

101. *Eagle*, November 15, 1885; *New York Times*, November 15, 1885.

Chapter 6. Transformation

1. Harold Coffin Syrett, *The City of Brooklyn, 1865–1898: A Political History* (New York: Columbia University Press, 1944), 270.

2. Syrett, *The City of Brooklyn*, 272. For Syrett's complete discussion of consolidation, see 245–73. See also Edwin G. Burrows and Mike Wallace, *Gotham: A History of New York City to 1898* (New York: Oxford University Press, 1999), 1,219–36. The

most complete analysis is David C. Hammack, *Power and Society: Greater New York at the Turn of the Century* (New York: Russell Sage Foundation, 1982), 185–229.

3. Hammack, *Power and Society*, 209–10.

4. Burrows and Wallace, *Gotham*, 1,227.

5. Hammack, *Power and Society*, 211.

6. Hammack, *Power and Society*, 211

7. *The Statistical History of the United States from Colonial Times to the Present* (Stamford, CT: Fairfield Publishers, [1965]), 56–57.

8. Department of Commerce, Bureau of the Census, *Thirteenth Census of the United States Taken in the Year 1910: Volume III: Population: 1910* (Washington: Government Printing Office, 1913), 189. The East Side (soon to be more widely known as the Lower East Side) has no formal boundaries, and informal understandings of its limits have shifted over time. In the early twentieth century it was generally known as the area on the East River bounded on the north by 14th Street, on the south (roughly) by Canal Street, and the west by the Bowery and Fourth Avenue; Manhattan wards 7, 10, 11, 13, and 17.

9. Manhattan's East Side, however defined, lost about half of its population during these years. See, for example, Kenneth T Jackson, *Crabgrass Frontier: The Suburbanization of the United States* (New York: Oxford University Press, 1985), 185.

10. Department of Commerce, Bureaus of the Census, *Fifteenth Census of the United States: 1930: Population*, vol. 3, part 2 (Washington: Government Printing Office, 1932), 279. The American-born children of the New Immigrants outnumbered their parents (and foreign-born siblings) in 1930, as most of the latter arrived in the United States before World War I and the postwar immigration restriction laws of 1921 and 1924, giving them plenty of time to expand their families in this country. The four immigrant grandparents of one of this book's authors, for example, raised eleven children, nine of whom were born in the United States.

11. Department of Commerce, *Fifteenth Census of the United States* 300–303, 382.

12. This estimate of the Jewish proportion of Brooklyn's Eastern European population reflects local patterns of settlement and should not be extrapolated to the nation as a whole. Large numbers of Polish Catholics, for example, settled more thickly in other places such as Chicago. The Jewish proportion of Chicago's Eastern European population was undoubtedly significantly lower than Brooklyn's and the nation's was surely lower as well. Our estimate of 85 percent for Brooklyn is perhaps too conservative, given the likelihood that some Jewish immigrants in the borough did report Russian, Polish, or some other language besides Yiddish as their mother tongue.

13. For a comprehensive history, see Deborah Dash Moore, gen. ed., *City of Promises: A History of the Jews of New York*, 3 vols. (New York: New York University Press, 2012).

14. *American Hebrew and Jewish Messenger*, October 14, 1910; *Brooklyn Daily Eagle*, March 26, 1916. See also Alter F. Landesman, *Brownsville: The Birth, Development and Passing of a Jewish Community in New York* (New York: Bloch Publishing Company, 1969), 96.

15. *Eagle*, November 18, 1900.

16. *Eagle*, April 6, 1904; *American Hebrew*, September 15, 1905. It may seem strange that East Side landlords raised rents just as the Williamsburg Bridge made it easier

for their tenants to move away. But even apart from new laws that made tenement operation more expensive, we should note that these were peak years of Eastern and Southern European immigration into the United States, and the pressure on East Side real estate was greater than the release of pressure from outmigration to Brooklyn and other places. Several years later the East Side began to lose population.

17. *Eagle*, October 16, 1908.

18. See, for example, the article on "The Brooklyn Jewish Community," *Eagle*, May 24, 1907, where this outward spread of Brooklyn's Jews is featured.

19. *Jewish Daily Bulletin*, March 14, 1928. This interesting study by the Bureau of Jewish Social Research includes an estimated Jewish population of 787,000 in Brooklyn in 1925, which accords well with our estimate of 750,000–850,000 in 1930.

20. Michael Gold, *Jews without Money* (New York: Horace Liveright, 1930; Avon Books, 1965), 152–59.

21. Gold's portrayals were prefigured by nonfictional reports of Jewish immigrants who were reluctant to leave the East Side even in the face of crippling rent increases. See, for example, *Eagle*, April 6, 1904.

22. *Eagle*, March 26, 1916.

23. *American Hebrew*, October 14, 1910, September 18, 1914.

24. An incisive and richly detailed telling of this and other aspects of the Jewish migration to America is Irving Howe, *World of Our Fathers: The Journey of the East European Jews to America and the Life They Found and Made There* (New York: Harcourt Brace Jovanovich, 1976). Another important source is Moses Rischin, *The Promised City: New York's Jews, 1870–1914* (Cambridge, MA: Harvard University Press, 1962).

25. Gerald Sorin, "Mutual Contempt, Mutual Benefit: The Strained Encounter between German and Eastern European Jews in America, 1880–1920," *American Jewish History* 81 (Autumn, 1993): 34–59.

26. Landesman, *Brownsville*, 173–84. The Hebrew Educational Society of Brooklyn was modeled on an existing Educational Alliance on Manhattan's East Side. Landesman was for a time the executive director of the HES.

27. Daniel Soyer, "Brownstones and Brownsville: Elite Philanthropists and Immigrant Constituents at the Hebrew Educational Society of Brooklyn, 1899–1929," *American Jewish History* 88 (June 2000): 181–207. The report in 1916 of the retiring president of the HES lists the organization's goals. The first two on the list are "to Americanize the immigrant," and "to keep alive in the community Jewish ideals and Jewish thought." *American Hebrew*, January 21, 1916.

28. For examples of this ongoing protest, see *Eagle*, February 3, 1906, December 23, 1906, February 1, 1907, December 2, 1907, December 20, 1910, January 14, 1914, October 4, 1915.

29. Alfred Kazin, *A Walker in the City* (New York: Grove Press, 1951), 11–12. A similar memoir of growing up in Brownsville, which emphasizes the impact of an ethnically homogeneous neighborhood, is William Poster, "From the American Scene: 'Twas a Dark Night in Brownsville," *Commentary* (May 1950): "To a child," Poster writes, "Brownsville was a kind of grimy Eretz Yisrael without Arabs. Living in a world all Jewish, where no alien group imposed its standards, he was secure in his own nature." Until about age twelve, Poster writes, "a Brownsville child scarcely saw any members of other ethnic groups except for teachers and policemen, and never really felt that the Jews were anything but an overpowering majority of the human

race. . . . What social shame he did feel was simply for his own lack of shame when, outside the boundaries of Brownsville, he ran up against those for whom a nervous consciousness of the opinions of the world had become a badge of superiority. . . . The amazing thing, then, was not that Brownsville produced some criminals, freaks, and barbarians, but that so many did manage somehow to obey the laws, attend school, and go on to become proper or even distinguished citizens."

30. *Eagle*, September 14, 1902.

31. Department of Commerce, Bureau of the Census, *Fourteenth Census of the United States . . . Volume III: Population: 1920* (Washington: Government Printing Office, 1922), 710; *Fifteenth Census*, 3:301, 303.

32. *Eagle*, September 14, 1902. By 1908 these nine or ten Italian settlements had expanded to fifteen: *Eagle*, August 16, 1908. See also Marianna Randazzo, *Italians of Brooklyn* (Charleston, SC: Arcadia Publishing, 2018); Raymond Guarini, *New York City's Italian Neighborhoods* (Chicago: Arcadia Publishing, 2019).

33. *Eagle*, November 12, 1905.

34. *Eagle*, April 12, 1904.

35. *Eagle*, December 8, 1904. Six months after this settlement house opened, as reported in the Italian-American press, the treasurer complained that the American benefactors were doing all the work and asked for more Italians to participate: *Il Progresso*, June 8, 1905.

36. *Il Progresso*, June 29, 1905, October 7, 1905, January 20, 1910, January 9, 1900.

37. *Eagle*, May 9, 1902.

38. *Eagle*, August 15, 1899.

39. Interestingly, most of the Italian immigrants who celebrated Italian national holidays in Brooklyn were from areas of Italy (Sicily, Calabria, Naples, and others) that most vigorously resisted unification. Parochial identities did remain alive, as we have just seen, but removal from the inter-regional squabbles of the new Italy, and no doubt the failure of native Americans to recognize regional differences among the Italians in their midst—Italians were Italians, not Sicilians or Neapolitans—helped build a broader Italian identity within the Italian-American community. To this day, descendants of Sicilian immigrants fiercely defend the reputation of the Genoese sailor, Christopher Columbus.

40. *Il Progresso*, October 13, 1900, October 12, 1910, September 20, 1905, August 21, 1900, July 4, 1905.

41. *Eagle*, November 5, 1918.

42. *Eagle*, November 3, 1901, May 9, 1902, April 22, 1906, May 14, 1911, February 20, 1916.

43. *Eagle*, July 18, 1902, October 6, 1903, November 27, 1908; *Il Progresso*, March 7, 1900.

44. *Eagle*, May 20, 1900.

45. *Il Progresso*, July 11, 1905; Paul Moses, *An Unlikely Union: The Love-Hate Story of New York's Irish and Italians* (New York: New York University Press, 2015).

46. *Eagle*, July 27, 1902, September 29, 1904, October 8, 1904, January 1, 1905, February 20, 1907, March 11, 1907, September 1, 1907, November 17, 1907, July 27, 1908, May 9, 1910, August 30, 1911.

47. *Il Progresso*, June 22, 1905, July 11, 1905, September 29, 1905, October 14, 1905, October 15, 1905, December 10, 1905, July 14, 1910.

48. The *Eagle* printed cartoon images of Italian criminals doing the work of the Black Hand, and, on at least two occasions, police photographs of Black Hand suspects: March 21, 1909, September 7, 1911, March 10, 1907, May 24, 1907.

49. *Eagle*, October 23, 1904, February 3, 1916,

50. "Chronological List of Brooklyn Parishes, 1822–2008," https://dioceseof-brooklyn.org.

51. *Fifteenth Census*, 3:300–303. One national group that did not increase significantly in size during this period was the Chinese. There were just over one thousand Chinese immigrants in Brooklyn in 1930, about two hundred fewer than in 1900. The Chinese Exclusion Act had been in force for nearly half a century, and the only surprise is that the number of Chinese-born residents in 1930 was not even smaller. Second-generation Chinese, who were not identified on the census, contributed to the size of this ethnic community, but the overall growth of the latter could not have been significant.

52. *Eagle*, January 30, 1910, February 6, 1910, February 27, 1910, March 27, 1910, October 20, 1913, March 12, 1916, July 5, 1918.

53. *Eagle*, November 26, 1917, December 11, 1917, May 30, 1918, May 10, 1918, July 8, 1918, September 26, 1918.

54. *Eagle*, November 16, 1918, November 30, 1918, March 30, 1919, April 28, 1919, May 7, 1919, July 14, 1919.

55. *Eagle*, August 27, 1914.

56. *Eagle*, October 24, 1915.

57. *Eagle*, April 3, 1916.

58. *Eagle*, December 13, 1917.

59. *Eagle*, January 20, 1919.

60. *Eagle*, February 12, 1919.

61. *Eagle*, April 20, 1919.

62. *Eagle*, October 29, 1919.

63. *Eagle*, November 9, 1919.

64. *Eagle*, November 14, 1919.

65. For a general history of US immigration policy, including the 1921 and 1924 acts, see Aristide R. Zolberg, *A Nation by Design: Immigration Policy in the Fashioning of America* (Cambridge, MA: Harvard University Press, 2006). Another study of the twentieth-century laws is Katherine Benton-Cohen, *Inventing the Immigration Problem: The Dillingham Commission and its Legacy* (Cambridge, MA; Harvard University Press, 2018).

66. *Eagle*, May 28, 1916, March 1, 1925.

67. *Eagle*, December 9, 1920.

68. *Eagle*, March 4, 1923, April 5, 1923.

69. *Eagle*, October 5, 1923.

70. *Eagle*, February 6, 1929, August 19, 1929. Interracial marriage, however, remained unacceptable, as in the case of a white woman who wished to marry a Chinese man. *Eagle*, August 3, 1927.

71. *Eagle*, October 12, 1919, December 17, 1925, May 7, 1929.

72. *Eagle*, March 31, 1920.

73. *Eagle*, March 3, 1924.

74. Linda Gordon, *The Second Coming of the KKK: The Ku Klux Klan of the 1920s and the American Political Tradition* (New York: Liveright Publishing Corporation, 2017).

An older but still valuable study is Kenneth T. Jackson, *The Ku Klux Klan in the City, 1915–1930* (New York: Oxford University Press, 1967).

75. *Eagle*, December 18, 1922.

76. *Eagle*, January 26, 1922, January 29, 1922, February 2, 1923.

77. *Fourteenth Census*, 2:1,353; *Fifteenth Census*, 3:279.

78. *Eagle*, July 27, 1915, March 30, 1918, April 23, 1921, May 7, 1924.

79. *Eagle*, December 4, 1922, May 4, 1923, May 31, 1923. Hillis had earlier been drawn to the eugenics movement, but this energetic and outspoken clergyman also spoke out passionately for the rights of African Americans and was an important advocate for city planning in Brooklyn. See Thomas J. Campanella, *Brooklyn: The Once and Future City* (Princeton: Princeton University Press, 2019), 220–37.

80. *Eagle*, December 11, 1922, December 16, 1922.

81. *Eagle*, March 3, 1924.

82. *Eagle*, September 24, 1923, November 18, 1923, November 19, 1923.

83. *Eagle*, June 27, 1927.

84. Horace Meyer Kallen, *Cultural Pluralism and the American Idea: An Essay in Social Philosophy* (Philadelphia: University of Pennsylvania Press, 1956); Kallen, "Democracy versus the Melting Pot," *The Nation* (February 18, 25, 1915); Randolph Bourne, "Trans-National America," in *Randolph Bourne, Selected Writings, 1911–1918*, ed. Olaf Hansen (New York: Urizen Books, 1977). We return to the concept of cultural pluralism in the epilogue.

85. *Eagle*, March 9, 1930.

Chapter 7. Acceptance, Resistance, Flight

1. Joseph Kesselring, *Arsenic and Old Lace* (New York: Dramatists Play Service, 1941). In the play's film version, which was subject to a strict code regarding all things sexual, Mortimer and Elaine are married. We are grateful to our friend Ralph Janis for bringing to our attention the Brooklyn setting of this classic American comedy.

2. Maude White Hardie papers, 1909–47, Brooklyn Historical Society archive.

3. Marc Linder and Lawrence S. Zacharias, *Of Cabbages and Kings County: Agriculture and the Formation of Modern Brooklyn* (Iowa City: University of Iowa Press, 1999), 301.

4. James H. Callender, *Yesterdays on Brooklyn Heights* (New York: Dorland Press, 1927), 43, 101–2, 106–7, 131–32.

5. *Brooklyn Daily Eagle*, May 4, 1906.

6. *Eagle*, April 9, 1924.

7. *Eagle*, March 2, 1930.

8. *Eagle*, April 30, 1908, September 5, 1909.

9. *Eagle*, February 14, 1911, September 1, 1912, August 19, 1914, May 9, 1915.

10. *Eagle*, April 12, 1900, June 12, 1904, April 15, 1909, March 22, 1912, February 5, 1922, April 2, 1922, April 6, 1922, November 26, 1922, October 28, 1927, January 13, 1929, November 11, 1929. This is a sampling of a larger array of such items.

11. *Eagle*, March 31, 1930, April 3, 1930, May 8, 1930, May 12, 1930, June 10, 1930, December 26, 1930, December 31, 1930.

12. *Brooklyn Life*, June 1, 1915, 35–77, 81–86.

13. *Eagle*, May 20, 1916, May 29, 1916. Zone E did not prohibit apartment house construction, but by mandating that a residential structure be surrounded by an open area of a certain ratio to the size of the structure, the commission ensured that apartment houses would generally require lots too large for profitable rental operations.

14. Brooklyn neighborhood associations and civic organizations publications, Brooklyn Historical Society archive.

15. Flatbush Taxpayers' Association records, 1896–1914, Brooklyn Historical Society archive.

16. Flatbush Taxpayers' Association records.

17. Independent Civic Association of Sheepshead Bay, Inc. records, 1922–75, Brooklyn Historical Society archive.

18. Gates Avenue Association records, 1922–44, Brooklyn Historical Society archive.

19. *Eagle*, January 16, 1927.

20. *Eagle*, April 21, 1907.

21. These strategies met with mixed success. Helen Worth, the *Eagle*'s advice columnist, addressed on several occasions the decline of churches and church-related social clubs, noting at one point the latter were "languishing, perhaps because of lack of interest among the young people." *Eagle*, February 28, 1923.

22. *Eagle*, February 1, 1932.

23. *Eagle*, November 29, 1907.

24. *Eagle*, May 4, 1899.

25. *Eagle*, May 24, 1902, May 26, 1902, May 29, 1902, June 6, 1905.

26. *Eagle*, June 11, 1910, June 14, 1910, June 8, 1911.

27. Steven A. Reiss, *The Sport of Kings and the Kings of Crime: Horse Racing, Politics, and Organized Crime in New York, 1865–1913* (Syracuse: Syracuse University Press, 2011), 303.

28. Thomas J. Campanella, *Brooklyn: The Once and Future City* (Princeton: Princeton University Press, 2019), 120–23; Reiss, *Sport of Kings*, 302–35. These two excellent accounts differ on a small number of minor details.

29. *Eagle*, March 23, 1908, May 17, 1908.

30. *Eagle*, August 2, 1910.

31. *Eagle*, July 15, 1901, May 20, 1905, June 11, 1905, April 29, 1906, May 27, 1906, April 20, 1909.

32. *Eagle*, May 27, 1912, May 29, 1912, June 1, 1912, June 3, 1912, May 25, 1914.

33. *Eagle*, June 16, 1905.

34. *Eagle*, June 25, 1905.

35. *Eagle*, January 16, 1907, January 9, 1908, February 13, 1908, May 3, 1910, May 9, 1910, February 10, 1911, February 16, 1911. See also Charles DeMotte, *Bat, Ball and Bible: Baseball and Sunday Observance in New York* (Washington, DC: Potomac Books, 2013), esp. 108–9.

36. *Eagle*, April 16, 1904, April 14, 1906, June 19, 1906, June 30, 1917, July 2, 1917.

37. *Eagle*, July 7, 1917, July 17, 1917.

38. *Eagle*, October 24, 1917, November 23, 1917, November 24, 1917.

39. *Eagle*, March 20, 1918, March 26, 1918, April 5, 1918.

40. *Eagle*, April 6, 1919, April 19, 1919, April 22, 1919, April 29, 1919, May 2, 1919, May 4, 1919. May 5, 1919. The establishment of major league Sunday baseball in New

York City may have had an indirect effect on the building of Yankee Stadium. The Yankees had been subletting the Polo Grounds from the Giants for their home games, an arrangement that limited the Giants to only thirteen Sunday home games for the 1920 season, while Brooklyn scheduled nineteen, the difference in revenue amounting to more than the proceeds of the Yankee sublease for the entire year. The *Eagle* speculated in February that the Giants would not renew the sublease for that reason, forcing the Yankees to find a new home. *Eagle*, February 14, 1920. After some hesitation the sublease was renewed, but, for whatever reasons, the relationship between the Giants and Yankees did not last. Construction of Yankee Stadium began in 1922.

41. W. J. Rorabaugh, *The Alcoholic Republic: An American Tradition* (New York: Oxford University Press, 1979).

42. *Constitution, By-Laws, and Order of Business of the Women's Christian Temperance Union: 1876* (Toronto: n.p., 1876).

43. *Eagle*, January 13, 1912.

44. *Eagle*, May 24, 1919.

45. *Eagle*, February 11, 1919.

46. *Eagle*, November 3, 1919, January 11, 1920.

47. *Eagle*, April 26, 1926, October 27, 1927.

48. For full accounts, old and new, of Margaret Sanger's career, see David M. Kennedy, *Birth Control in America: The Career of Margaret Sanger* (New Haven: Yale University Press, 1970); Ellen Chesler, *Woman of Valor: Margaret Sanger and the Birth Control Movement in America* (New York: Simon & Schuster, 1992); R. Marie Griffith, *Moral Combat: How Sex Divided American Christians and Fractured American Politics* (New York: Basic Books, 2017).

49. *Eagle*, October 22, 1916, October 24, 1916, October 26, 1916.

50. *Eagle*, November 15, 1916, November 16, 1915.

51. *Eagle*, January 29, 1917, January 30, 1917, February 2, 1917, February 5, 1917, January 8, 1918; "One Hundreth Anniversary of the Brownsville Clinic—A Media Opportunity," Margaret Sanger Papers Project, https://sangerpapers.wordpress.com.

52. *Eagle*, October 22, 1916, October 24, 1916.

53. *Eagle*, November 13, 1921, November 14, 1921, November 15, 1921. The *Eagle* was one of many newspapers to cover the Town Hall meeting and its aftermath.

54. "Looking Back at the Town Hall Raid," Sanger Papers Project.

55. *Birth Control: Hearings Before the Committee on Ways and Means, House of Representatives, Seventy-Second Congress, First Session, on H. R. 11082* (Washington: Government Printing Office, 1932), 88–97.

56. *Birth Control: Hearings Before a Subcommittee of the Committee on the Judiciary, United States Senate, Seventy-Third Congress, Second Session, on S. 1842...* (Washington: Government Printing Office, 1934), 126–30.

57. *Birth Control: Hearings ... on H. R. 11082*, p. 89; *Birth Control: Hearings ... S. 1842*, 130.

58. *Eagle*, December 20, 1911.

59. National Board of Review of Motion Pictures records, 1907–71, New York Public Library archives.

60. Nancy J. Rosenbloom, "From Regulation to Censorship: Film and Political Culture in New York in the Early Twentieth Century," *Journal of the Gilded Age and Progressive Era* 3, no. 4 (October 2004), 374, 386.

61. *Eagle*, January 28, 1917. On Stevenson's memberships, see the obituary in the *New York Times*, August 5, 1938.

62. *Eagle*, February 13, 1921, February 22, 1921.

63. Rosenbloom, "From Regulation to Censorship," 396–400.

64. *Eagle*, January 13, 1927.

65. On the Catholic role in the creation of a movie censorship system, see Frank Walsh, *Sin and Censorship: The Catholic Church and the Motion Picture Industry* (New Haven: Yale University Press, 1996).

66. *Eagle*, June 10, 1930.

67. *Eagle*, January 1, 1922.

68. Callender, *Yesterdays on Brooklyn Heights*, 20, 221

69. *Eagle*, December 9, 1922.

70. *Eagle*, January 31, 1929, February 7, 1929, March 7, 1929, March 8, 1929. Plymouth Church and Church of the Pilgrims would merge in 1934.

71. *Eagle*, June 10, 1930.

72. *Eagle*, April 30, 1922.

73. *Eagle*, April 3, 1927.

74. *Eagle*, September 1, 1925.

75. *Eagle*, October 24, 1929.

Epilogue: Brooklyn's America

1. Betty Smith, *A Tree Grows in Brooklyn* (New York: HarperPerennial, [1943] 1992), 148–49. Both of our fathers had similar real-world experiences. Stuart's father was asked on his first day of school to stand and announce his name to the class. When he said "Paysha" the teacher insisted that he state his American name. Greatly flustered, the little immigrant boy could think only of the name his father Herschel had adopted when he set up his tailoring shop. "Harry," he announced. And so Harry he became in the American schoolroom that day, and Harry he remained for the next eighty years. When Glenn's father arrived in the United States from Russia (by way of China), an immigration official asked him his name. "Grisha," he said. "That's not an American name," the official declared. The seven-year-old boy managed, in broken English, to indicate that his Hebrew name was Tzvi Hersh. "Let's give him Harry," the official said to his colleague. "We have already given out a lot of Harrys," the other man said. "Let's call him Herb." And so it was.

2. Mike Wallace, *Greater Gotham: A History of New York City from 1898 to 1919* (New York: Oxford University Press, 2017), 914–16.

3. Madison Grant, *The Passing of the Great Race: The Racial Basis of European History* (New York: Charles Scribner's Sons, 1916).

4. Lothrop Stoddard, *The Rising Tide of Color against White World-Supremacy* (New York: Charles Scribner's Sons, 1920).

5. *The American Hebrew & Jewish Messenger*, January 19, 1917. The *Brooklyn Daily Eagle* turned the stereotyping of New Immigrants in a different direction: "We have no colony of Calabrians among whom the indifference to human life is so great as it is among the mountaineers of Kentucky; we have no such drunkenness among any of our imported populations as we have among the makers of moonshine whisky and among the New Englanders who pass laws to prohibit liquor and refuse to abide

by them; and if it is charged that the Jews are over fond of money and will cheat, when was the Yankee ineffective as a money getter, and how long is it since our drugs and our food products ceased to be adulterated?" *Eagle*, May 25, 1903.

6. *Eagle*, February 11, 1921.

7. Kallen, the son of a rabbi, was born in what is now Poland, and was brought to the United States when he was five. Educated at Harvard, he was reputedly denied an appointment there because he did not speak discretely; dismissed from the Princeton faculty in 1905 because he was an atheist; and forced to resign from the University of Wisconsin faculty in 1918 because he defended the rights of pacifists during U. S. participation in World War I. Kallen became a founder of the far more tolerant New School for Social Research in New York City in 1919 and served on its faculty for the remainder of his career. *New York Times*, February 17, 1974.

8. Horace M. Kallen, "Democracy Versus the Melting Pot: A Study of American Nationality," *The Nation* 100 (February 18, 25, 1915): 190–94, 267–70. See also Sidney Ratner, "Horace M. Kallen and Cultural Pluralism," *Modern Judaism* 4, no. 2 (May 1984): 185–200; Wallace, *Greater Gotham*, 920–22.

9. Horace M. Kallen, "Culture and the Ku Klux Klan," in Kallen, *Culture and Democracy in the United States: Studies in the Group Psychology of the American Peoples* (New York: Boni and Liveright, 1924); John Higham, *Send These to Me: Jews and Other Immigrants in Urban America* (New York: Atheneum, 1975). See also Werner Sollors, "A Critique of Pure Pluralism," in *Reconstructing American Literary History*, ed. Sacvan Berkovitch (Cambridge, MA: Harvard University Press, 1986).

10. Hansen Lasch, *The Radical Will: Selected Writing of Randolph Bourne* (New York: Urizen Books, 1977); Ratner, "Horace M. Kallen and Cultural Pluralism," 187–88; Wallace, *Greater Gotham*, 922–24.

Index

Abbott, Lyman, 149, 167
abolitionism, 87–88
Abraham, Abraham, 179
Abyssinian Benevolent Daughters of Esther Association, 157
"Across the East River" (Hungerford), 202
Adams, Thomas, Jr., 108
Adler, Felix, 139
African Americans, 204, 247n71, 263n79
  Black churches, 157
  Civil War and, 91–92, 248n88
  early residents, 16, 84–85, 152
  fraternal organizations and, 157–58
  job discrimination, 156
  Ku Klux Klan, 193–94
  Methodism and, 21
  suffrage, 153
  See also Carrsville; Weeksville
African Civilization Society, 157–58, 258n86
African slaves, 8, 84
African Wesleyan Methodist Episcopal Church, 21
African Woolman Society, 85–86
Albany, 27, 29–30. See also legislation, New York State
Alden, John, 22
American ("Know Nothing") Party, 72–73, 75, 80, 247n58
American and Foreign Anti-Slavery Society, 38, 87
American Birth Control League, 218–19, 231
American Defense Society, 188
American Eugenics Society, 231
American Hebrew and Jewish Messenger, 149, 231
Americanization, 188–89, 191–92, 196, 199, 203, 229–33, 266n1
American Protective Association, 255n25
American Society for the Suppression of the Jews, 257n52
Ancient Order of Hibernians, 141–42, 255n22
Anderson, Samuel, 86

Anderson, William H., 215
anti-Catholicism. See nativism and anti-Catholicism
Anti-Saloon League, 214–15
anti-Semitism, 148–50, 178–79, 185, 231, 257n52
anti-slavery movement. See abolitionism
Anti-Vaccination League, 139
Applegate, Debby, 54
architects and builders. See Davis, Alexander Jackson; Eidlitz, Leopold; Pollard, Calvin
Arsenic and Old Lace (Kesselring), 197–99, 263n1
assimilation
  eugenics and race, 230
  foreign culture and, 6, 231, 233–34
  Germans and, 188
  Italian stereotype, 183
  Jews and, 179
  numbers of foreign born, 137
  response to, 189, 191–92, 229, 260n27
  second generation, 142
  story of, 140, 260n29
Association for the Suppression of Vice, 23
Astral Oil, 109, 135
Athenaeum, 44–45
Atlantic Avenue, 109, 170, 196
Atlantic Basin, 5, 31, 33, 66, 71, 74, 76, 89, 93–94
Atlantic Dock Company, 31
Atlantic Street, 30–31, 66, 72–73, 77, 107, 252n76

Baptist church, 3, 22, 25, 151
Baptist Tabernacle Church, 213
Barnard, Mrs., 162–63, 258n98
Baron de Hirsch Fund, 178
Barron v. Baltimore (1833), 241n51
baseball, 124, 209–14, 264n40
Bath Beach, 174, 210
Bay Ridge, 2, 95, 102–3, 107, 138, 169, 182, 186, 196

269